Helping People
Through
Difficult Ti

D0377821

FIRST AID
for Emotional Hurts

Edward E. Moody Jr., Ph.D.

REVISED AND EXPANDED EDITION

randall house

Printed in the United States of America

ISBN 13: 9780892655649

To my dear wife Lynne, who is always prepared
to aid those who are hurting.

Table of Contents

Introduction

We must prepare ourselves to administer emotional first aid to one another. After Job lamented the great tragedy and pain he had experienced (Job 3), his friend Eliphaz reported an observation. In the past Job had instructed, strengthened, upheld, and made firm those who had stumbled and were feeble (Job 4:3-4). Then Eliphaz said, "But now it has come to you, and you are impatient; it touches you, and you are dismayed" (Job 4:5). All of us know those who have emotional needs, and we are called to help them. Yet we must remember, we too will have periods of life where trouble comes to us and touches us. I may help you today, but you may help me tomorrow. The goal of this book (and all of the First Aid resources) is to equip ourselves to strengthen one another in the most difficult situations that come to us throughout our lives.

Much has happened since the first edition of this book was released nearly ten years ago. On occasion the original book was given to those who were depressed, anxious, or recently bereaved, which was not the purpose of that book. One bereaved person told me, "That was information I was not ready for yet." That led me to write a series of booklets that could be given directly to those who struggle with depression, grief, addictions, and many other difficulties. I have updated this book and more clearly delineated tools and techniques you may use with those you try to help. I have also tried to describe the ways you might use the booklets with those you encounter.

This book is written for a wide audience. Many people will have opportunity to help a family member, classmate, or co-worker in America. However, I realize that many will use this book in other countries that may have limited access to mental health professionals. I have attempted to provide the reader, wherever they may be, with tools to help in various situations or settings. It is my prayer that God will use these resources to help people through the most difficult times in their lives and that His name is glorified.

Eddie Moody

Chapter 1

THE CALL

*"Come to Me, all who labor and are heavy
laden, and I will give you rest."*

Jesus, Matthew 11:28

A few years ago, I was about to walk into a grocery store when I received a call. I stopped and looked down at my cell phone, "Why would Nicholas Tan be calling me on a Saturday afternoon?" I answered the phone and Nicholas, a teenager at our church said, "Are you in town?" I sensed something was wrong. "Yes," I responded, "Is everything okay?" He said his father, Jeng Yoong, had become ill. The family had been enjoying dinner at a restaurant in town when Jeng Yoong went into cardiac arrest. A bystander observed Jeng Yoong at the moment of the sudden arrest. She rushed across the room and began to perform CPR. She helped Jeng Yoong survive until he arrived at a local hospital and was eventually transferred to a major hospital where he underwent surgery. Jeng Yoong's survival began with a woman who knew what to do to help him and responded immediately to meet his need.

Every year, 350,000 people in the United States go into cardiac arrest outside of a hospital and 90 percent of them die. Jeng Yoong was one of the few who survived because someone knew how to perform first aid and took the time to help him.[1]

Much effort has gone into equipping people to administer physical first aid. However, the purpose of this book is to propose a different type of aid, first aid for emotional hurts. We often overlook the importance of emotional aid. At the moment that Jeng Yoong began to experience physical problems, his wife and two children experienced great emotional stress. Fortunately, there were people there to help with those needs as well. When I arrived at the restaurant that day, I was met by a patron who stayed with Jeng Yoong's children as the first responders worked on their dad. Then I noticed two people from our church. Another patron had taken the phone of Jeng Yoong's wife, Michelle, and began calling her friends so they could come and help. As I drove away from the restaurant to take Jeng Yoong's children to the hospital, two more people pulled alongside and clasped their hands together and mouthed "praying" as encouragement. Their aid made these emotional hurts a bit more bearable.

Often, we concentrate on helping people with their physical needs but emotional needs are important also. It has been estimated that as many as 1 in 4 Americans will experience a mental health problem or abuse substances at some point in their lifetime. In 2014, nearly 44 million Americans aged 12 and older experienced a mental health problem, and for almost 10 million adults, this was a serious mental illness that met standard psychiatric diagnostic criteria—very debilitating conditions. In 2013, 17 million adults said they were misusing or dependent on alcohol, and 24 million people over the age of 12 said they had used illicit drugs during the prior month.[2]

Emotional Concerns Reported by College Students in Past Year	
Concern	*Percentage*
Depression & difficulty functioning	30
Feeling overwhelmed	85
Exhausted (not from physical activity)	80
Feeling very sad	60
Feeling very lonely	57
Overwhelming anxiety	50
Feeling hopeless	45

One Thing Can Lead to Another	
Hurt	*Can Lead To*
Anger and bitterness	Depression and divorce
Poor self-image	Eating disorders and depression
Unaddressed fear	Anxiety
Unaddressed trauma	Anxiety, depression, panic attacks
Rejection and disappointment	Depression

We are very likely to encounter someone with an emotional need. Consider the table above,[3] and the table indicating the concerns of college students.[4] We all know people who experience significant losses, suffer from depression, and struggle with anxiety, an addiction, or some type of mental illness. In fact, anxiety and depression are far more prevalent than many physical problems like sudden cardiac arrest. It is estimated that every year, 40 million adults in the United States, age 18 and older, or 18 percent of the population, struggle with some type of anxiety disorder. Depression is believed to affect more than 15 million American adults, or about 6.7 percent of the U. S. population every year over the age of 18.[5] Unfortunately, many do not get the aid they need. Every year on average, 44,193 people take their lives in the United States (an average of 121 a day).[6]

There are even more common emotional hurts like the death of a loved one, the breakup of a significant relationship, disappointment over failing to get a promotion, or failing to get into the school to which one applied. Left unaddressed, these hurts develop into major problems. Though we have pastors, professional counselors, psychologists, and other helping professionals who can help with these problems, there are many who never reach these professionals, like the victim of sudden cardiac arrest who does not survive long enough to benefit from a cardiologist.

Therefore, we would do well to learn emotional first aid techniques. You may be wondering if you can really help someone struggling emotionally. Research dating back to the 1960s indicates that you can. In one landmark study, nonprofessionals were found to be as effective at helping people as professionals.[7]

Today, there is a growing body of research on Psychological First Aid that is used to help people in the aftermath of traumatic events. Guy Winch has discussed how the

> *He heals the brokenhearted and binds up their wounds.*
> Psalm 147:3

application of emotional first aid is very beneficial to our everyday lives. Practicing emotional first aid can enhance and save lives. We need to learn these techniques because when people are in distress, they tend to seek those who are closest to them to help.

> *" . . . Love the Lord your God with all your heart and with all your soul and with all your strength and with all your mind, and your neighbor as yourself."*
> Luke 10:27

The Calling

We are called to love God and love people. So, aren't Christians called upon to administer emotional first aid? The words of Jesus (Matthew 25:31-46) seem to indicate that emotional first aid is not optional for the believer. But what does administering emotional first aid look like? Certainly, Jesus ministered to the emotional hurts of others. Jesus fulfilled the prophecies that indicated He would be a Wonderful Counselor (Isaiah 9:6) possessing wisdom and knowledge (Isaiah 11:2). The gospels describe Jesus' compassion for the harassed and helpless (Matthew 9:36).

> *When he saw the crowds, he had compassion for them, because they were harassed and helpless, like sheep without a shepherd.*
> Matthew 9:36

Jesus administered aid to those who were grieving and trapped in sin. There are examples of the aid He administered to a widow who lost a son (Luke 7:13) and harlots and tax collectors entangled in sin (Matthew 9:11). Jesus invited everyone who hurt to come to Him for aid (Matthew 10:28). How does one get aid from Jesus since He does not have a private practice in the suburbs or an office at the local clinic?

Jesus told His followers how to get this aid in John 14 as He began to prepare them for His departure. He promised He would not abandon them, but He would send a "Helper, to be with you forever, even the Spirit of truth" (John 14:16b-17a). Jesus said this "Helper, the Holy Spirit . . . will teach you" (John 14:26). Jesus acknowledged we would not be able to see the Holy Spirit. Jesus indicated that it was advantageous for Him to depart so the Holy Spirit would come to us (John

> But the Helper, the Holy Spirit, whom the Father will send in my name, he will teach you all things and bring to your remembrance all that I have said to you.
>
> John 14:26

16:7). Jesus' words indicate that the Holy Spirit can help people with whatever problems they face. In particular, Jesus promised that the Holy Spirit would convict us of sin (John 16:8-9) and guide us into all truth (John 16:13). But the Holy Spirit does not have an office in the suburbs or at the local clinic either. How does the Holy Spirit meet these needs?

> Therefore, we are ambassadors for Christ, God making his appeal through us. We implore you on behalf of Christ, be reconciled to God.
>
> 2 Corinthians 5:20

This is where we who are Christians come in. The Christian is called to administer emotional first aid. Paul wrote that every Christian is an ambassador for Christ. God works through the Holy Spirit residing within believers to help people become reconciled to God. Christians are the hands and feet of Christ today. When a Christian comes alongside a hurting person to aid them, Jesus is there (Matthew 18:20). The Christian represents Christ to those who are in need. Even though Christians are called to "do good to everyone" and to "bear one another's burdens" (Galatians 6:2, 10), it often seems like there are not enough responders to provide aid to those in need.

> Bear one another's burdens, and so fulfill the law of Christ. So then, as we have opportunity, let us do good to everyone, and especially to those who are of the household of faith.
>
> Galatians 6:2, 10

13

All of us are very busy these days with places to go and things to do. This is not a new problem. Long ago Jesus told a story about this kind of situation (Luke 10:25-37). There was a man who made a journey through a country that was known for its danger. Most dared not make the journey, and people said those who did went through the area at their own risk. As most people probably predicted, the man was accosted, assaulted, and robbed. In the end, he was lying on the side of the road bleeding. His assailants left him to die. Maybe he was about to give up hope of surviving when he heard someone traveling on the road. Perhaps he moaned or cried out to draw their attention to his plight. It was to no avail. The traveler, though a very religious person, passed by on the other side of the road and sped away. The bleeding man's heart must have sunk. Soon, he heard the shuffling of another traveler approaching. His spirits lifted. He cried out for help yet again. Although he had much in common with the wounded man, the traveler also passed by on the other side of the road and continued his journey. There seemed to be little hope for the hurting man, and he could probably feel his life slipping away. Then he heard the sound of a third traveler. The man who had been assaulted might have lacked the energy to lift his head, but the traveler rushed to his side. The wounded man got a glimpse of the traveler and realized he was quite different in many ways. However, what was really noticeable was the difference in attitude between this man and the others who had passed him by. This traveler was willing to risk his life and expend great energy and fortune to aid a stranger. The survivor was very fortunate to have the Good Samaritan come to his aid.

You have probably heard that Bible story many times. As you hear it, with whom do you identify? Are you one of those who pass by on the other side of the road and continue with your journey, or do you stop and help? Perhaps you can even relate to the wounded traveler.

As Jesus told this story, He wanted us to emulate the Good Samaritan. Most who encountered the wounded traveler continued with their business. They saw the needy man, but refused to respond to him. Perhaps, they did not know what to do or see any way in which they could respond so they passed by.

> *Now by chance a priest was going down that road, and when he saw him he passed by on the other side. So likewise a Levite, when he came to the place and saw him, passed by on the other side.*
>
> Luke 10:31-32

Barriers to Responding

What if we do not respond? Too often it seems like the hurting people at our workplaces, schools, families, and even our churches are passed by. This has always been the case. Most passed by the wounded traveler: there was only one Good Samaritan. But that does not mean that it is okay to pass by. When we pass by, it hurts our Lord. The gospel of Matthew records a moment when Jesus looked at those struggling with all kinds of afflictions at Capernaum. He had compassion for them and lamented, "The harvest is plentiful, but the laborers are few" (Matthew 9:35-38).

> *And Jesus went throughout all the cities and villages, teaching in their synagogues and proclaiming the gospel of the kingdom and healing every disease and every affliction... Then he said to his disciples, "The harvest is plentiful, but the laborers are few; therefore pray earnestly to the Lord of the harvest to send out laborers into his harvest."*
>
> Matthew 9:35-38

What Made Jesus Angry?

> *And he looked around at them with anger, grieved at their hardness of heart, and said to the man, "Stretch out your hand." He stretched it out, and his hand was restored.*
>
> Mark 3:5

When we fail to respond, Jesus grieves. In another passage (Mark 3:5), we see an event where there was a man who had an injured hand. Those around Jesus and the man lacked empathy for him. Jesus was grieved and angered by their lack of concern for him. The Lord views our failure to respond to those in need of aid as dereliction of duty, like a soldier who leaves his post. We are called to consider and encourage one another. The writer of Hebrews warned us not to neglect each other (Hebrews 10:24-25). Further, Paul told us we have an obligation to bear with the failings of the weak (Romans 15:1), and to build them up (Romans 15:2). Paul indicated that he was indignant when someone fell. So, it is not okay for us to pass by the one in need. You might say when we became believers we signed up to be a helper, a first responder to the spiritual and emotional needs of others.

The majority of the people passed by the wounded traveler. Unfortunately, this neglect continues today when the wounded are ignored at work, schools, in neighborhoods, in families, and even churches. Therefore, we must be aware of the barriers that impede our ability to respond and know how to deal with them.

> *By this we know love, that he laid down his life for us, and we ought to lay down our lives for the brothers. But if anyone has the world's goods and sees his brother in need, yet closes his heart against him, how does God's love abide in him? Little children, let us not love in word or talk but in deed and in truth.*
>
> 1 John 3:16-18

Will Someone Else Deal With It?

Too frequently, we may avoid a friend or co-worker in need because we think someone else will deal with it. You have probably heard of the account of the murder of Kitty Genovese in Queens, New York in 1964. It was reported that many of her neighbors heard something or saw glimpses of the attack upon her, but they did not come to her aid. This is often described as the "bystander effect." Interestingly, people are less likely to respond and help an individual in need when other people are present but not helping. More people being present decreases the likelihood that someone will come to their aid.

This may happen with emotional needs because we think, "We have people to take care of that kind of thing—pastors, psychologists, professional counselors, and health care practitioners." It will help us to think about emotional problems the way we think of many physical problems. We have cardiologists, but we still administer proper first aid when an individual goes into cardiac arrest. We know the ill person will never make it to the hospital to benefit from the treatment of those professionals unless we respond. If we answer our calling to "Love your neighbor as yourself" and respond, others will follow and needless suffering can be averted. The best way to defeat the bystander effect is to respond. When one person responds, another tends to follow and pretty soon the needs of the person have been met.

> *Look carefully then how you walk, not as unwise but as wise, making the best use of the time, because the days are evil.*
> Ephesians 5:15-16

Time

It is also very possible that the people who passed by the wounded traveler were simply too busy to stop. We all have very active lives. The travelers on the Jericho Road were no different. It would have sidetracked their plans to stop and help the wounded man. Besides, they were not friends with the man nor related to him. Would God really expect them to take time to help a total stranger? Time is the most valuable investment we can make in others.

Helping people does take time, so it is important that we invest it wisely. I used to work as a staff psychologist for the North Carolina Department of Juvenile Justice. Some of the youngest youth at the facility required most of my time. I began to use a technique called pair counseling with them in which they learned new ways of developing relationships and solving problems. This technique was very time consuming. However, as I looked at my time, I realized I was spending less time on them than before the intervention. Before pair counseling, I spent a lot of time with these youth on suicide watch or in isolation after they had committed an assault or some other major infraction. Further, they spent more time at the facility because they had trouble maintaining the behavior necessary to be released.[8] I saved time (and a lot of trouble) by investing time with them early in their stay at the facility.

Some people, because of their circumstances or life challenges, will require more of your time. You can invest in them and use that time prosocially (like taking the time to listen to someone who is hurt or disappointed). Should the disappointment lead to depression, you might find yourself taking time to take them on a walk to fight depression. However, should the depression develop into suicidal ideation, you might spend that time remedially (like trying to get them involuntarily committed because they are a danger to themselves). Sometimes, a time investment can go a long way in changing the trajectory of a person's life. The Lord asks us to "make the best use of our time and you just might prevent a lot of unnecessary trouble" (my paraphrase of Ephesians 5:16).

For God gave us a spirit not of fear
but of power and love and self-control.
2 Timothy 1:7

Fear

Perhaps the travelers passed by the wounded traveler because of fear. It was said that only a fool would travel alone the road from Jerusalem to Jericho. Yet all of the people in Jesus' story seem to have been traveling alone. Perhaps those who passed by were afraid they too would become a victim if they stopped to help. They would have been putting their lives at risk. This barrier is cited often today. It is a legitimate concern. For example, there is fear in helping a victim of domestic violence. One may wonder, "What if the abuser comes after me?" It can be frightening to help someone who is hearing voices or someone addicted to a substance. Whatever situation we are in, we often wonder, "If I respond, could I get hurt?" The answer is, yes. In some cases, the one you are trying to help may even hurt you. One of my first jobs was as a clinical therapist in an alternative school. I worked with troubled youth, and one in particular who had experienced severe abuse. One day we had a field trip and this young man attacked another youth. I quickly restrained him from behind.

18

He leaned down and bit me. I immediately thought, "Well, hurt people hurt people." I still find that to be true. Sometimes the people you are trying to help turn on you and hurt you. They may not bite you (physically), but they may disparage you or hurt you in any number of ways. Does that mean we shouldn't try to help them? Not at all! We have a long list of those who have been harmed trying to help people by spreading the gospel. We should try to help them, and it is worth it. Getting hurt helping people is like a running back getting bruised on a tackle or a baseball player getting scratched trying to steal second. We will get a few bumps and bruises, but the football player sees the first down marker moved in the direction of the end zone, and sometimes the baseball player gets into scoring position. We may get hurt, but we also help the person get a little closer to where they need to be.

> *For though by this time you ought to be teachers,*
> *you need someone to teach you again the basic principles*
> *of the oracles of God. You need milk, not solid food.*
> Hebrews 5:12

Helpless

It is not always a lack of concern, time, or fear that keeps us from responding. Sometimes we do not respond because we feel inadequate, even helpless. When faced with people having problems, who hasn't wondered, "But I don't know what to say or do"?

Perhaps those individuals who passed by the wounded traveler on the road to Jericho felt helpless at the sight of him. Were they physicians? Where would they start even if they wanted to help him? Perhaps they whispered prayers for him as they rushed by. It is even possible they did not know how to help him or could not imagine what they could do to help. We might feel that same sense of helplessness when we encounter people with serious problems. We sincerely want to help them, but we do not know what to say or do or even where to start. This is just like a person who observes someone go into cardiac arrest, but they cannot help because they do not know CPR.

One day there was an accident near the church where I pastor. A driver was traveling at a high rate of speed, ran off the road, overcorrected, and the car flipped over several times. Immediately the car began to burn. A passerby pulled over, stepped out of his car and used his fire extinguisher to extinguish the flames. Tragedy averted. Had this man not prepared by having that fire extinguisher in his car, there would have been a different outcome. Sometime in the past he prepared for the day when he would encounter an accident. When he saw the accident, he was ready and responded.

We listen to the news and we know people get killed in accidents, children tragically drown, some people struggle with depression, veterans have experienced trauma, and others are entangled with substances and sexual sins. Rather than bemoan these situations, we would do well to prepare ourselves to help people with them. If you are a Christian, you simply need to know the basics of Scripture and how to apply them. God expects us to be ready to aid the wounded traveler when we come across him. The goal of this book is to prepare you so the Lord will never need to say to us "you ought to be teachers" or "you ought to be ready to help the depressed or traumatized." Let us get ready so we are less tempted to pass by.

> *For it is God who works in you, both to will and to work for his good pleasure.*
> Philippians 2:13

Be Ready

Sometimes we need to be reminded of how God has already prepared us to help in the crises we encounter. He knows what we will encounter tomorrow, so He is preparing us for it today. A few years ago, I checked my email and the subject line read, "Help!" The email was from a recent graduate of the university where I am a professor. The former student was working as a school counselor. There had been a shooting at her school and the school was locked down. She knew she would be dealing with traumatized students and faculty as soon as the lockdown was lifted. She asked, "What do I do?" I quickly wrote back to her and reminded her of various tools and techniques she had learned in her different classes, "You remember in Crisis Counseling when you learned . . . and how in assessment we discussed . . . ?" Later she wrote back and indicated that as her day went along, the training she had received "kicked in."

I have felt the same way and I bet you have too. I have encountered various people in need, and wondered, "What do I do?" Sometimes, I even say to myself, "God knew I would be here in this situation" and begin to think about various teachings from the Bible and how those apply to the particular event.

> *I myself am satisfied about you, my brothers,*
> *that you yourselves are full of goodness, filled with*
> *all knowledge and able to instruct one another.*
> Romans 15:14

Sometimes, it is good to remind ourselves that Paul noted he was satisfied. We are up to the task of helping others because the Christian is full of goodness and knowledge. Because of that, Christians are able to instruct one another (Romans 15:14). In a different circumstance, Jesus told His disciples that the Holy Spirit would teach them what to say when they were called before councils (Luke 12:12). Similarly, the Holy Spirit will help you know what to say or do as you seek His guidance and prepare to help those around you. So be ready!

> *Which of these three, do you think, proved to be a neighbor to the*
> *man who fell among the robbers?" He said, "The one who showed*
> *him mercy." And Jesus said to him, "You go, and do likewise."*
> Luke 10:36-37

Go and Do Likewise

Fortunately, the story of the wounded traveler on the road from Jerusalem to Jericho did not end with those who passed by. The Good Samaritan did stop and help the wounded traveler. After telling the story, Jesus told those people listening to him to "go and do likewise" or to go and be like the Samaritan. But what does God want us to do?

> *But a Samaritan, as he journeyed, came to where he was, and when he saw him, he had compassion.*
>
> Luke 10:33

Emotional First Aid

God wants us to go to people who are wounded rather than pass them by. The Good Samaritan met the specific needs of the wounded traveler when he "came to" him and "had compassion" (Luke 10:33) for him. When we go to a person, rather than avoiding them, we begin to get a sense of their struggle, which helps reduce that persons feeling of isolation. We do not know what the Good Samaritan may have said to the wounded traveler, but we do know that he performed specific tasks. He "bound up wounds," poured medicine upon the man, put the man on his animal, and "took care of him" (Luke 10:34). This is like providing for basic needs as done with psychological first aid, like giving bottled water to someone after they have received bad news or offering to clean the house of a family who is preparing for visitors after the death of their loved one. This is what the person did who stayed with Jeng Yoong's children that day in the restaurant, and the other bystander as she called Michelle's friends to get help. These are simple yet very helpful tasks. Note, as well as helping the wounded traveler, the Good Samaritan found further help for the wounded man by taking him to an inn where he paid for the services he received (Luke 10:35-36). An example for us would be paying for a young couple in a struggling marriage to receive marriage counseling. The acts the Good Samaritan performed are similar to the expectations Jesus de-

> *He went to him and bound up his wounds, pouring on oil and wine. Then he set him on his own animal and brought him to an inn and took care of him. And the next day he took out two denarii and gave them to the innkeeper, saying, 'Take care of him, and whatever more you spend, I will repay you when I come back.'*
>
> Luke 10:34-35

scribed of His followers. In Jesus' example, His followers gave food and drink. They also welcomed, clothed, visited, and "came to" (Matthew 25:35-36) those in need (Matthew 25:40). We will examine this closer later.

The Aid Gap

Emotional First Aid could assist in closing the mental health treatment gap. There is a major aid gap. For example, in the United States it is estimated that in 2013, 28 million people needed treatment for a substance abuse problem, and less than 1 in 10 received any treatment.[9]

The problem is even worse outside of the United States. For example, the World Health Organization has estimated that the gap between the number of people with emotional disorders and the number who actually receive evidence-based care—is as high as 70 percent to 80 percent in many developing countries.[10]

Vikram Patel has pointed out that in developing countries, the treatment for emotional problems has focused almost entirely on hospital or clinic based approaches where there are often few mental health professionals available. He indicated that if we are to help those in developing countries, we will need to equip more non-mental health professionals to address mental health concerns.[11] Wherever we may be, we need to know how to appropriately respond to these needs.

> *For I was hungry and you gave me food, I was thirsty and you gave me drink, I was a stranger and you welcomed me, I was naked and you clothed me, I was sick and you visited me, I was in prison and you came to me. And the King will answer them, "Truly, I say to you, as you did it to one of the least of these my brothers, you did it to me."*
>
> Matthew 25:35-36, 40

Respond

In discussing giving CPR to someone who has gone into cardiac arrest, the Mayo Clinic Staff writes, "It's far better to do something than to do nothing."[12] Think of emotional first aid similarly.

Both the Good Samaritan and those commended by God in the final judgment "came to" or responded to those who were in need. The first step to providing emotional first aid is to simply respond by coming to the person. We often worry about saying the right thing to someone in need. Responding is not about saying the right thing—it is about doing the right thing like we see in both Luke 10 and Matthew 25. When we are on track spiritually, it is actually harder for us to walk by the wounded traveler to avoid the one in need.

You might say we were made to respond. Have you ever attended the visitation or delivered a dish of food after a death and wanted to do more? That is because helping is part of your spiritual DNA since we are called to "Bear one another's burdens" (Galatians 6:2). Helping people is something spiritually healthy believers instinctively desire to do. Consider a sample of helpers found in the Old Testament Scriptures.

Burden Bearing in the Old Testament

Responder	**Person Helped**
Noah	Saved family by building ark (Genesis 9)
Job	Helped others by providing guidance (Job 29:12-16, 21-25; 31:18, 32)
Abraham	Rescued Lot and the Kings of Sodom (Genesis 14)
Rebecca	Helped Abraham's servant by watering camels (Genesis 24)
Joseph	Provided counsel to the butler, cupbearer (Genesis 40), Egypt (Genesis 41:55), comforted his brothers (Genesis 45:5; 50:21)
Moses	Helped Jethro's daughters (Exodus 2:17) and provided counsel to Israel (Exodus 18)
Jethro	Counseled Moses (Exodus 18)
Rahab	Helped the Israelite spies (Joshua 2)
Ruth	Stayed with Naomi after the death of her husband and sons (Ruth 1)
David	Played the harp for Saul (1 Samuel 16), provided for Mephibosheth (2 Samuel 9)

Nathan	Confronted and counseled David (2 Samuel 12)
Solomon	Provided counsel and guidance to Israel (1 Kings 3) and the Queen of Sheba (1 Kings 10)
Elijah	Helped the widow with her needs and after the death of her son (1 Kings 17)
Elisha	Provided support for Elijah (1 Kings 19:19-21)
Jonah	Reluctantly counseled (preached to) Nineveh (Jonah)
Hosea	Bought Gomer out of slavery (Hosea)
Daniel	Provided counsel to Nebuchadnezzar (Daniel 4)

There were times when each of these individuals put their interests aside to respond to the needs of another. For example, Noah spent a significant amount of time building an ark that saved his family. Abraham put his life at risk to rescue Lot. Rebecca put her needs aside one day to help an elderly man with his camels. Each of these people (many of whom are referred

> These all died in faith, not having received the things promised, but having seen them and greeted them from afar, and having acknowledged that they were strangers and exiles on the earth.
> Hebrews 11:13

to as heroes of the faith in Hebrews 11) took the time to respond to someone in need. That is what the Good Samaritan did. He went to the person in need (responded) and he felt compassion. This is the first and most important step in helping, but it is a difficult step.

A few weeks after my friend Jeng Yoong experienced cardiac arrest, I visited with the manager of the restaurant. She was clearly impacted by what had happened, as were the people who tried to help Jeng Yoong and his family. The manager told me the company paid for all the patrons' meals that night, an indication of the stress they had experienced. These people came to the restaurant to spend a relaxing evening with family or friends. By chance they came across people in need and they responded to help. This is the same attitude of the Good Samaritan who "by chance" (Luke 10:31) came across the wounded traveler. Consider the number of times you have gone somewhere for one reason, but unexpectedly encountered someone in need. Our lives are often altered "by chance." I observed with the restaurant manager that though this event was initially stressful, it was clearly rewarding for those who responded.

Consider the guilt the priest and Levite may have felt for failing to help the wounded traveler. They probably knew they should have helped, but they failed to respond. In the case of Jeng Yoong, there was no guilt for failing to help on the part of the patrons or manager. Instead, there was a sense of fulfillment on the part of those who helped, knowing they had done what they could to aid someone in need.

> *Even as the Son of Man came not to be served but to serve, and to give his life as a ransom for many.*
> Matthew 20:28

Serve

You too know this feeling. On occasion, you may have planned to watch a movie or catch a game, but instead after learning of a friend in need, you responded and attempted to meet the need. Why did this feel so rewarding? You served. Responding is the mindset of Christ (Philippians 2:4-5). It requires us to focus on the interests of others, and serve as the One who came to serve did for us. However, we often need to remind ourselves to stay in Christ's mindset. Even Christians can see self-interest get in the way of serving others.

> *Let each of you look not only to his own interests, but also to the interests of others.*
> Philippians 2:4

When I invite people to church, a frequent question I receive is "What programs does your church offer?" Sometimes I sense they are choosing a church like one might choose a restaurant. I understand from where they are coming. We want to grow personally and we want what is best for our family. However, the response points to a myth that is pervasive in our culture, and has impacted the church which is: "It's all about me."

> *But as for you, teach what accords with sound doctrine.*
> Titus 2:1
>
> *And let our people learn to devote themselves to good works,*
> *so as to help cases of urgent need, and not be unfruitful.*
> Titus 3:14

Self-centeredness is contrary to Scripture, and is the enemy of responding to the needs of others. Interestingly, when looking at people who have experienced tragedy, those who are willing to try to help other people actually cope better with loss. One researcher described it this way, "Paradoxical as it may seem, giving help is the best way of being helped."[13] So, helping is helpful to the helper, and self-absorption is self-defeating. We would be healthier emotionally if we "church-shopped" for a place to serve rather than a place to be served. Paul described the service gifts that should be utilized in the church in 1 Corinthians 12 and pointed out that if one member suffers, we all suffer together. This may not sound very appealing, but Paul indicated that this was to our benefit.

Serving Gifts

4 Now there are varieties of gifts, but the same Spirit; 5 and there are varieties of service, but the same Lord7 To each is given the manifestation of the Spirit for the common good.

11 All these are empowered by one and the same Spirit, who apportions to each one individually as he wills.

26 If one member suffers, all suffer together; if one member is honored, all rejoice together.

1 Corinthians 12

Paul discussed helping those who were weaker in the church and described the weak as "indispensable" (1 Corinthians 12:22). In other words, we impoverish ourselves when we walk past the needy person. Not only do we fail to help them, we miss out on the

> *Train yourself for godliness.*
> 1 Timothy 4:7b

27

contribution they would have provided to our own lives. Therefore, we are called to labor in love together and serve one another.

> Remembering before our God and Father your work of faith and labor of love and steadfastness of hope in our Lord Jesus Christ.
>
> 1 Thessalonians 1:3

The manner in which we serve will be determined by the gifts God has entrusted to us. Paul indicated that each of us have been gifted in such a way as to benefit the common good (1 Corinthians 12:7). Some of us are better gifted to serve, teach, exhort, give, or lead (Romans 12:7-8), but we are all called to serve in some way (Romans 12:10, 13). We use the gifts God has given us to assuage suffering. Therefore, we are called to train ourselves in godliness to impact those around us.

> Therefore, we are ambassadors for Christ, God making his appeal through us. We implore you on behalf of Christ, be reconciled to God.
>
> 2 Corinthians 5:20

Represent

Christians represent God as ambassadors for Christ. An ambassador receives word from his country's government about what the government is willing to do to help. Therefore, we must let Christ's Word dwell within us so we are providing His wishes rather than simply giving our own preference or opinion.

Consider the difference between an ambassador and a tourist. If you are an ambassador, you represent the interest of your country, presenting the position of the government. As a tourist, should a problem arise in the country you are visiting, you might actually leave the country or look for other ways to minimize the impact the problem might have upon you personally. However, as an ambassador, you look for

> Let the word of Christ dwell in you richly, teaching and admonishing one another in all wisdom, singing psalms and hymns and spiritual songs, with thankfulness in your hearts to God.
>
> Colossians 3:16

ways the country you represent might respond and assist with the situation. Therefore, as Christ's ambassador to the world, if we answer our calling, we respond to the problems of the people around us and represent Christ in these situations.

> *For where two or three are gathered in*
> *my name, there am I among them.*
> Matthew 18:20

When Christians are present the Lord is present, but it is critical that we be guided by the Word and the Holy Spirit. The ambassador to another country is not free to "wing it" or express their own opinions while representing their country. Similarly, this kind of helping must be performed by a believer who is guided by the Holy Spirit rather than their own words and opinions. We cannot be careless with our words or resort to our own opinions. Doing so is dangerous and harmful to those we wish to help. The responder must be immersed in the Word of God and come from a heart guided by the Holy Spirit.

The prophet Ezekiel promised that those who followed God would receive a new heart, and that God's Spirit would be within them helping them to walk in His statutes (Ezekiel 36:26-27). Later the writer of Hebrews quoted Jeremiah 31:33 saying that the Holy Spirit bears witness to us, and that He puts His laws on the hearts and minds of believers (Hebrews 10:15-16). This is critical.

> *I myself am satisfied about you, my brothers, that*
> *you yourselves are full of goodness, filled with*
> *all knowledge and able to instruct one another.*
> Romans 15:14

How does the responder know what God wants them to do? Remember, Paul reported his confidence that Christians are able to instruct one another (Romans 15:14) with the important caveat that they are "full of goodness" and "filled with knowledge." In other words, they could instruct one another because the Holy Spirit was at work in their lives and they were students of the

> *Do your best to present yourself to God as one approved, a worker who has no need to be ashamed, rightly handling the word of truth.*
>
> 2 Timothy 2:15

Word (2 Timothy 2:15). These two characteristics are intertwined and inseparable. Therefore, as we provide aid to others, the Holy Spirit will recall teaching that dwells in us (Colossians 3:16). We will even remember hymns and songs that apply to the situation. In short, it is the Word that equips us to help others as well as provides important wisdom, guidance, and comfort to the one we are trying to help (Hebrews 13:20-21).

So, will you answer the call? Jesus lamented that there were many needs but only a few responders or laborers. There was only one Good Samaritan, most passed by the wounded traveler. Will you respond? You may get hurt. It will take time, but responding is the key to seeing changed lives. Answer the call and pray that others will as well. There are many who desperately need the Lord's representative.

In this book, we will try to equip you with what you need to be an emotional first responder. We will also provide you with what you might call an emotional first aid kit of valuable resources so you can help rather than pass by the wounded travelers you meet along the way.

For more resources go to www.FirstAidForEmotionalHurts.com.

Chapter 2

TOOLS OF THE RESPONDER

I will not leave you as orphans; I will come to you.

John 14:18

The Lord has not left us alone to deal with emotional hurts, nor will He leave us without the tools we need to help others. The Christian is given many tools from the Lord to help others.

Many years ago, I had just enjoyed a meal after work with my family at a restaurant in the town of the church I pastor. As I drove away, I received a call on my cell phone about an accident. I was asked to come immediately and told that someone was trapped in a car and I was needed to pray with them. I began to pray as I responded. When I arrived, the accident scene was surreal. There were fire-fighters and law enforcement officers everywhere. As I began to talk to the Fire Chief, a Life Flight helicopter was taking off beside of us. Once the helicopter

> *Now may the God of peace who brought again from the dead our Lord Jesus, the great shepherd of the sheep, by the blood of the eternal covenant, equip you with everything good that you may do his will, working in us that which is pleasing in his sight, through Jesus Christ, to whom be glory forever and ever. Amen.*
>
> Hebrews 13:20-21

took off, the Fire Chief began to lead me through the accident scene. He pointed to a car and said, "the girl in that car has died." As we walked through the scene and by the car he said, "Her parents are over there and we would like for you to talk to them." I have never felt more inadequate and unprepared. My heart sank and my stomach began to hurt. I thought, "I can't do this!" I had taken the first step to provide emotional first aid, and I had responded. I was trying to represent the Lord. Indeed, I had been called to the accident scene because people were looking for God's representative. I was there, but now what? The Fire Chief walked me over to the parents and they began to talk to me. I listened. There were no platitudes or magic words to help in that situation, but I knew the Holy Spirit was there helping me. After a few minutes of listening, I tried to provide for their basic needs, and offered to help them notify other family members. Then we prayed there on the side of the road. Prayer helped me, and I believe it was a comfort to them. Prayer was the most valuable tool I had that night.

> *Therefore, confess your sins to one another and pray for one another, that you may be healed. The prayer of a righteous person has great power as it is working.*
> James 5:16

Prayer

Perhaps the most common (and overused) response to someone in need of emotional aid is "I will pray for you." Our Lord told us to pray often and to be persistent in our prayers (Luke 18:1). He also told us that our prayers help. Therefore, it is important for us to be people of prayer, praying for God's guidance in our own lives. Jesus said, "Abide in me, and I in you. As the branch cannot bear fruit by itself, unless it abides in the

> *For we do not have a high priest who is unable to sympathize with our weaknesses, but one who in every respect has been tempted as we are, yet without sin. Let us then with confidence draw near to the throne of grace, that we may receive mercy and find grace to help in time of need.*
> Hebrews 4:15-16

vine, neither can you, unless you abide in me" (John 15:4). If the Holy Spirit is at work in your life, God hears your prayers. He may not answer your prayers the way you would like, but He hears and He helps.

It is also important that we take the time to pray for those who are hurting. I am convinced that though we tell people we will pray for them, we often forget to do so. Therefore, I encourage you to take the time to pray aloud with the people you are trying to aid. It is important for them to hear you pray for them. That solidifies in their mind that they have been prayed for. It is also a way of demonstrating your belief that Jesus understands and sympathizes with our weaknesses (Hebrews 4:15). Further, you are also modeling for them how they are to pray.

> *And he told them a parable to the effect that*
> *they ought always to pray and not lose heart.*
> Luke 18:1

There is much confusion about prayer. Even the disciples who spent so much time with Jesus asked for guidance about how to pray (Luke 11)—so too do those who need emotional first aid. For some, the issue they struggle with will be spiritual, rather than emotional (Ephesians 6:12). Indeed, every problem will have a spiritual component and there will be some situations (like the one I experienced) where prayer is the only tool that will help. Consider Aaron's prayer in Numbers 6:24-26 as a sample prayer that we may pray at various times. Pray the prayer aloud over the person inserting their name for the word you. There is just something about hearing someone pray over you that brings comfort and strength in times of difficulty.

> *The Lord bless you and keep you; the Lord make his face to shine*
> *upon you and be gracious to you; the Lord lift up his countenance*
> *upon you and give you peace.*
> Numbers 6:24-26
>
> *The Lord bless _____ and keep _____; the Lord make his face*
> *to shine upon _____ and be gracious to _____; the Lord lift*
> *up his countenance upon _____ and give _____ peace.*

We must also prepare ourselves to help those we respond to when they have prayer problems. For example, what happens when prayer does not seem to work? Imagine someone praying Matthew 17:20 ("If you have faith like a grain of mustard seed, you will say to this mountain, 'Move from here to there,' and it will move, and nothing will be impossible for you") while performing CPR on their loved one who did not survive. Did God ignore their prayer? Throughout history people have struggled with whether God hears their prayers. Jesus referred to this kind of problem in Luke 4 where He noted that some saw miracles from Elijah and Elisha and others did not. These words made the Jews who heard Him so angry that they wanted to kill Him. Why? In those days, some of the Jews believed they were superior to other groups of people. Jesus pointed out that Elijah performed a miracle that helped a woman from the hometown of Jezebel, a very evil woman (see 1 and 2 Kings). Jesus also alluded to how a Gentile man named Naaman (2 Kings 5) was healed of the dreaded disease of leprosy. This took place in spite of his poor treatment of Jews (2 Kings 5:2). Why did these two people see miracles while others did not? Indeed, that is the question many people ask, "Why did God seemingly answer their prayer and not mine?"

> But in truth, I tell you, there were many widows in Israel in the days of Elijah, when the heavens were shut up three years and six months, and a great famine came over all the land, and Elijah was sent to none of them but only to Zarephath, in the land of Sidon, to a woman who was a widow. And there were many lepers in Israel in the time of the prophet Elisha, and none of them was cleansed, but only Naaman the Syrian.
>
> **Jesus, Luke 4:25-27**

Sometimes people begin to question their faith when their prayers are not answered in the manner they requested. There are also some who will say to them things like, "All you need is faith and your problems will disappear."

It is easy to see how we can be confused when our prayers are not answered in a manner that we expected. Look back at Jesus' words in Matthew 7. It appears to be a simple

The Formula

Ask = _receive_

Seek = _find_

Knock = _opened_

formula for prayer. If you ask you will receive. If you seek you will find. If you knock the door will be opened. When those we aid do not feel like they have received, found, or seen the doors opened, they often become confused. They pray for depression, persistent grief, or strong cravings to go away, yet these problems persist. They wonder, "Why have I not received?"

Paul's Problem That Did Not Go Away

Three times I pleaded with the Lord about this, that it should leave me. But he said to me, "My grace is sufficient for you, for my power is made perfect in weakness."

2 Corinthians 12:8-9a

Some people seem unaware of situations like that experienced by the Apostle Paul. Paul briefly wrote about a problem he had that he asked God to take away. It is interesting that we do not know Paul's problem. Perhaps God did not provide that information to us because he wanted this situation to be a model for many of the problems we face. At any rate, one might assume that the Apostle Paul was endowed with a great deal of faith, and yet he continued to struggle with this particular problem. As we help people with prayer problems, we must begin by making sure they are a believer. Once that has been established, we will need to help them see that prayer has more to do with our relationship with God than getting what we ask. Many read passages like Matthew 7 and become confused about prayer. Perhaps, they reason, people must have a certain amount of faith to have their prayers answered. Maybe they did not pray "right" or God is punishing them, some wonder.

The Rest of the Story

Or which one of you, if his son asks him for bread, will give him a stone?

Matthew 7:9

An examination of the rest of the story in Matthew 7 indicates that "everyone who asks receives." So, what are we to make of this passage? It is important to look at the rest of the story. Jesus went on to point us to the parental relationship. He asked, "Do good parents give their children everything they ask for?" (My paraphrase). Suppose a child asks a parent for help with homework, hoping the parent will provide the correct answers. The parent looks at the homework and provides some explanation about how to address the problem, but does not provide the answers. How does the child feel after asking for help, but only getting further directions about how to address the problem? Why did the parent not give the child the answer?

> *Or if he asks for a fish, will give him a serpent?*
> *If you then, who are evil, know how to give good*
> *gifts to your children, how much more will your Father*
> *who is in heaven give good things to those who ask him!*
> Matthew 7:10-11

As Jesus said in Matthew 7, a parent does not give a child a serpent when the child asks for a fish. Most parents have the best interest of their child in mind. A parent does not provide the easy answer to homework because the parent wants the child to work to discover the answers, that are best for the child in the long run. In Jesus' words in Matthew 7, He indicated that we, in all of our imperfection, do not ignore the requests of our children and neither does God. Parents who make life too easy for their children are not helping them to develop and mature. In a similar way, God wants His children to develop and mature. Unfortunately, we would often prefer an easy answer or instant miracle rather than work through a process that would help us grow spiritually. We ask God to take our depression away. We expect it to disappear. If we ask God to give us a better marriage, we expect it to miraculously and immediately improve. If we ask God to remove a particular problem, we may expect it to go away without much difficulty. Sometimes there are immediate resolutions to the problems and difficulties that we face, but what is happening when there are none? Perhaps God is allowing us to mature and develop through the difficult situation.

> ### Various Trials & God's Development Plan
>
> *Count it all joy, my brothers, when you meet trials
> of various kinds, for you know that the testing of your
> faith produces steadfastness. And let steadfastness have its full
> effect, that you may be perfect and complete, lacking in nothing.*
>
> James 1:2-4

Did your parents ever discipline you and say it was for your own good? Consider the "development plan" that many coaches have for their athletes. When an athlete is on the receiving end of the development plan, it does not feel good, but he knows it will benefit him if he endures.

We will experience "various" trials in life according to James. In other words, trials are to be expected. In fact, they have a purpose. They develop us into the kind of people God wants us to be. We will all have our trials. The words of James 1 sound similar to the words of Jesus from Matthew. We are told to ask for wisdom. Perhaps when we ask God to help us with our marriage, He whispers to us to apply the message from His Word in 1 Corinthians 13 or Ephesians 5. This will be examined more thoroughly in a later chapter.

> ### God Gives You What You Need
>
> *If any of you lacks wisdom, let him ask God, who gives generously
> to all without reproach, and it will be given him. But let him ask in
> faith, with no doubting, for the one who doubts is like a wave of the
> sea that is driven and tossed by the wind. For that person must not
> suppose that he will receive anything from the Lord; he is a dou-
> ble-minded man, unstable in all his ways.*
>
> James 1:5-8

It is interesting to note that God gives us His wisdom generously. In other words, He gives us all we need. He gives it to us without reproach. You will not hear from Him, "Hey, didn't I teach you that yesterday!" When someone asks God to help him with his marriage, he has at his disposal the Word of God.

After examining James 1, hopefully one leaves with a sense that God will provide what is needed. He will provide you with what you need to help others, and He will give them what they need to address their issue. Perhaps that will be an immediate solution to the problem at hand. Nuggets of wisdom like "a soft answer turns away wrath" and "love your wife as yourself" need to be utilized wisely. Sometimes the answer to a prayer is to apply the Scripture on the subject with wisdom. Maybe it will involve the utilization of an older couple or a professional counselor to further develop wisdom. It could also be taking some type of medication, or an extensive intervention. We must be willing to put our pride away and be open to what God provides. God promises to give us wisdom generously.

The Benefits of Prayer

Is anyone among you suffering? Let him pray. Is anyone cheerful? Let him sing praise. Is anyone among you sick? Let him call for the elders of the church, and let them pray over him, anointing him with oil in the name of the Lord. And the prayer of faith will save the one who is sick, and the Lord will raise him up. And if he has committed sins, he will be forgiven.
James 5:13-15

Prayer is very beneficial in dealing with emotional hurts. For example, prayer as well as church attendance have been found to provide a layer of protection from stress. Research has indicated that prayer can result in healthier blood pressure as well as provide cardiovascular benefits. So, our goal is to help those with whom we work to persist in their prayers. Some of the people we try to help will struggle to pray because they believe God only hears "pretty prayers." Some are confused by what is happening in their lives and may be so upset that they cannot pray a "pretty prayer."

Regularly point those you help to prayers in the book of Psalms. One of the first prayers we find in the book of Psalms is Psalm 3. The caption in many Bibles indicates that it was prayed as David was fleeing from his son Absalom who was trying to kill him. An examination of the prayer indicates the person who prayed the prayer knew what the real world was like.

A Prayer for Help

O LORD, how <u>many</u> are my foes!
<u>Many</u> are rising against me;
<u>many</u> are saying of my soul,
"There is no salvation for him in God." Selah

Psalm 3:1-2

The repetition of the word "many" drives home the point that they had an abundance of problems. We know David had a family in shambles. One of his sons raped his daughter (2 Samuel 13). Then another son killed that son and tried to overthrow his administration (2 Samuel 13, 15). In his prayer, David says people had said there was no salvation or hope for him in God (Perhaps 2 Samuel 16:5-14). We might rephrase that in our terminology to "God saves or helps those who help themselves."

Salvation belongs to the LORD; your blessing be on your people!
Psalm 3:8

You might say that David prayed an ugly prayer. However, as he prayed he concluded, "Salvation belongs to the LORD. Your blessing is upon Your people." It seems that David concluded God helps those who can't help themselves. Perhaps he came to that conclusion because he prayed an ugly prayer. The implication for those we try to help is that it is okay for them to share all their ugly complaints to the Lord; it is likely they will experience a sense of relief at that conclusion as they meditate on the salvation they have in the Lord.

Another ugly prayer is found in Psalm 13. The person who is praying seems to be tired of waiting on God. The word "counsel" in verse 2 is often associated with death. This person is in real pain and they seem to be honestly conveying that to God.

> ## Can You Hear Me?
>
> *How long, O LORD? Will you forget me forever?*
> *How long will you hide your face from me?*
> *How long must I take counsel in my soul*
> *and have sorrow in my heart all the day?*
> *How long shall my enemy be exalted over me?*
>
> Psalm 13:1-2

The prayer also makes reference to an enemy. Who or what is this person's enemy? We don't know. Have you ever wondered why God did not make that clear to us? Perhaps God intends for this prayer from hundreds of years ago to be vague. It is used to teach us how to pray when we feel like God does not hear us or when we deal with an enemy. A woman who is being stalked could pray this prayer while seeing her ex-husband as the enemy. Down the street someone fighting cancer could pray this same prayer while seeing cancer as his enemy. God was vague for a reason.

> *But I have trusted in your steadfast love;*
> *my heart shall rejoice in your salvation.*
> *I will sing to the LORD,*
> *because he has dealt bountifully with me.*
>
> Psalm 13:5-6

Again, the Psalmist concludes that he will trust in God's steadfast love and that God has dealt well with him. And again, the implication is that though one might share some ugly feelings about an enemy, in the end one comes back to the goodness of the Lord and finds relief and comfort. The Psalms are designed to teach us it is okay to pray an ugly prayer. Just make sure you pray. It is key to progressing through emotional hurts.

> *Your word is a lamp to my feet*
> *and a light to my path.*
>
> Psalm 119:105

The Word

Another tool we have to help others is the Bible. It is the Word that equips us and prepares us to help people deal with whatever problems they face, whether it be anger, depression, anxiety, grief, or the chains of addiction. We need to know the Word and what it says about various issues that people encounter. We must be ready to provide those we aid with passages that address grief, depression, entangling sins, and so forth. It helps to be aware of Psalms they can pray as their own and passages they can meditate upon to combat incorrect and negative thoughts and feelings that plague them.

Helping people apply Scripture to their own lives will need to become second nature to the responder as they interact

> **See E. Moody (2013), *First Aid for Your Health: Making 10 Therapeutic Life Changes*. Nashville, TN: Randall House to examine how Bible reading impacts physical and mental health.**

with people at work, school, in their neighborhood, at family gatherings, and church. Interestingly, it appears that as the church was in its infancy it grew with people "preaching the Word" (Acts 8:4) and "proclaiming the Word" (Acts 8:5), resulting in much joy wherever they went "with all wisdom" (Colossians 1:28).

> *Him we proclaim, warning everyone and teaching everyone with all wisdom, that we may present everyone mature in Christ.*
> Colossians 1:28

In other words, as they encountered someone dealing with an entangling sin, the death of a child, or a wayward spouse, they preached and proclaimed the Word. People were changed and helped.

> **Where They Went the Word Went**
>
> *Now those who were scattered went about preaching the word. Philip went down to the city of Samaria and proclaimed to them the Christ. So there was much joy in that city.*
> Acts 8:4-5, 8

If you respond to many mental health issues, you will quickly see there are many myths that get in the way of treating people for depression and other mental illnesses that can be dangerous and detrimental. We must be ready to knock these myths down with the Word of God. Consider the statements in the following box. Many will think if something goes wrong in their life, it is because they have sinned. Some believe their lives will be easier just because they are a Christian. We have already addressed the myth that "It's all about me." We will look at the others in subsequent chapters.

What do you really think?
True or False

1. Bad things only happen to bad people.
2. If people do good things, their lives will be easier.
3. Life should be like a lovely rose garden.
4. It really doesn't matter what you believe.
5. God only hears pretty prayers.
6. God always makes sense to us.
7. All you need is a real dose of faith and your problems will disappear.
8. Real Christians don't get depressed.
9. It's all about me.
10. You don't need a family.

So, what do you think? What you think is very important. It impacts how you live and whether you thrive. Whatever you really believe will come to the forefront when you are placed in a distressful situation. What you think and believe determines your level of resilience. What you believe will also come out as you try to help those who are hurting.

As you try to help people, you will hear many of these myths. Often some are perpetuated by those who otherwise appear to be mature Christians. You will frequently hear statements like, "My Aunt Sally says, 'Christians don't get depressed'" or Pastor Jim said, "Christians enjoy the prosperous life unless they have sin in their life." I have learned to say something like, "All I can tell you is the Bible says in 1 Kings 19 there was a prophet named Elijah who asked God to take his life and he sounds a bit depressed." Patiently point out what Scripture says and teach them how Scripture applies to their particular situation.

> In the day of my trouble I seek the Lord;
> in the night my hand is stretched out without wearying;
> my soul refuses to be comforted.
> I will remember the deeds of the LORD;
> yes, I will remember your wonders of old.
> I will ponder all your work,
> and meditate on your mighty deeds.
>
> Psalm 77:2, 11-12

Even the famed psychologist, Albert Ellis, who was not a fan of Christianity, at least in his early days, noted the value of the Bible to emotional health.[14] It is critical that the hurting people we are trying to aid learn to read and meditate upon the Bible. I think Psalm 77:11-12 is a good guide for learning how to meditate upon God's goodness. Incidentally, the Psalmist makes this statement after saying they cannot be comforted in Psalm 77:2. It is in times like this we learn what passages like Hebrews 4 really mean. As people meditate upon and apply Scripture, they will be changed.

> "I think I can safely say that the Judeo-Christian Bible is a self-help book that probably enabled more people to make more extensive and intensive personality and behavior changes than all professional therapists combined."
> Albert Ellis

> Preach the word; be ready in season and out of season; reprove, rebuke, and exhort, with complete patience and teaching.
>
> 2 Timothy 4:2

We, however, must be ready to teach them and correctly apply Scripture to their situation. For example, we want to learn to match fears a person has to a Scripture on courage or the guilt one struggles with to a Scripture on forgiveness (more on this later). If people will allow the Word to dwell in them, it will teach them and impart wisdom to them (Colossians 3:16).

> *For the word of God is living and active, sharper than any two-edged sword, piercing to the division of soul and of spirit, of joints and of marrow, and discerning the thoughts and intentions of the heart. And no creature is hidden from his sight, but all are naked and exposed to the eyes of him to whom we must give account.*
>
> Hebrews 4:12-13

The Word changes a person so we must think through ways it can be harnessed. Many challenges people experience will be especially difficult; therefore, we may need to help them with various object lessons. Often the faulty thinking people have is so strong they will need to immediately look at Scripture and apply it to their situation. For example, I have often used Philippians 4 with someone who is overcome by anxiety (more on this later). I encourage them to meditate upon and memorize passages from that chapter. I also encourage people to write down and personalize those passages in a notebook they carry around. Then they can read the passages when faced with intense fear. In some way, I think this is what Numbers 15 is describing where the Israelites used items to remind them of the Lord. Instead of a tassel, we can accomplish the same goal with a moleskin notebook or reminder on our smart phone.

> *The LORD said to Moses, "Speak to the people of Israel, and tell them to make tassels on the corners of their garments throughout their generations, and to put a cord of blue on the tassel of each corner. And it shall be a tassel for you to look at and remember all the commandments of the Lord, to do them, not to follow after your own heart and your own eyes, which you are inclined to whore after."*
>
> Numbers 15:37-39

> *With it we curse people who are made in the likeness of God. From the same mouth come blessing and cursing. My brothers, these things ought not to be so.*
>
> James 3:9b-10

Your Words

The words we say to people are very important, and they are another major tool. We can choose to bless or

> *Hear, for I will speak noble things, and from my lips will come what is right.*
> Proverbs 8:6

curse people with them. Our words either help or harm.

Have you ever noticed how one critical comment can take the wind out of your sails? A professor of mine in graduate school told me once that 10 "atta boy's" can be wiped out with one "you stink!" We need to tell people when they do well and when we appreciate them to counteract much of the negativity they hear.

> *Therefore, having put away falsehood, let each one of you <u>speak the truth</u> with his neighbor, for we are members one of another.*
>
> *Let the thief no longer steal, but rather let him labor, doing honest work with his own hands, so that he may have something to share with anyone in need. Let no corrupting talk come out of your mouths, but only such as is good for building up, as fits the occasion, that it may <u>give grace</u> to those who hear.*
> Ephesians 4:25, 28-29

The Christian is called to use the tongue for good and to put away any semblance of corrupting talk. So, what we say, text, tweet, and post can help or harm. We are to use words that build up, fit the occasion, and give grace rather than corrupt (Ephesians 4:28-29). Paul provided direction to us as we answer our calling by speaking the truth and making sure that our words fit the occasion and provide grace. This is a major undertaking.

> *That I may make it clear, which is how I ought to speak.*
> *Walk in wisdom toward outsiders, making the best use of the time. Let your speech always be gracious, seasoned with salt, so that you may know how you ought to answer each person.*
> Colossians 4:4-6

Often, we do not know how dire a situation a person may be in. Sometimes our words can be the difference between life and death. If you confront someone by telling them the truth and they leave an addiction behind, you just might save their life. We can also use our words to knock down debilitating myths. Your words come from your heart, so the key will be to spend time in the Word and talking to the Lord to keep our words true.

> *And let us consider how to stir up one another*
> *to love and good works, not neglecting to meet together,*
> *as is the habit of some, but encouraging one another,*
> *and all the more as you see the Day drawing near.*
> Hebrews 10:24-25

The Church

Church involvement is an important tool to help others. There are many today who are quick to point out that people do not have to go to church to go to Heaven, and many no longer believe that church attendance is important. There is even a myth that it really doesn't matter what you believe. We can't measure what is in a person's heart, but we can measure entities like whether a person goes to church or not and whether a person participates in religious activities.

> See E. Moody (2013), *First Aid for Your Health: Making 10 Therapeutic Life Changes.* Nashville, TN: Randall House to examine how kind of church involvement that impacts physical and mental health.

Active participation in religious activities seems to have a strong health benefit. In fact, in studies that have examined religious involvement and health, 78 percent have indicated that participation reduced the likelihood of disease and disability. "The strongest predictor of the prevention of illness onset is attendance at religious services."[15] Attendance of religious services was also the strongest factor related to longevity. Active participation in religious and spiritual activities has positively influenced the health of older Americans. Notice the phrase "active participation." These people didn't just attend church on Christmas and Easter to get these benefits.

One study examined inpatients that suffered from depression. The symptoms these patients reported were similar in nature. However, the patients who had a "religious affiliation" were less likely to be suicidal.[16] A meta-analysis (a study that looks at a large number of studies) was conducted to examine the impact of "religion and spirituality." The results indicated that subjects who sought assistance from clergy and engaged in religious practices experienced less depression, anxiety, and distress.[17]

Further, faster and more complete recovery from mental illnesses, substance abuse and dependence, as well as depression have been found in those who were associated with religious involvement.[18] Christians do suffer from depression and other metal health disorders. However, the results indicate that engaging in the practice of Christianity can reduce the impact of the symptoms of these disorders.

Interestingly, the benefits of church attendance have been discussed in some surprising places. In a column in the *Monitor on Psychology*, a former President of the American Psychological Association (APA) cited some research on religious involvement. Dr. Koocher said, "Linda Waite and colleagues found frequent attendance at religious services linked to higher emotional satisfaction and pleasure in sex." He was arguing about the importance of looking at research that might not be "politically correct."[19] I doubt you have ever heard that finding in the popular media, but it is well documented.

Marks of a Real Church

Let love be genuine. Abhor what is evil; hold fast to what is good. Love one another with brotherly affection. <u>Outdo one another in showing honor</u>. Do not be slothful in zeal, be fervent in spirit, <u>serve the Lord</u>. Rejoice in hope, be patient in tribulation, <u>be constant in prayer</u>. Contribute to the needs of the saints and <u>seek to show</u> hospitality.

Romans 12:9-13

It appears the health benefit does come from being actively involved in a local church. What does this look like and how does it work? I suspect the reason for the benefit is because of the marks of a real church as seen in Romans 12. People have "brotherly affection" for one another, "constantly pray" for one another, and "show hospitality." For a church to be a tool that helps with emotional hurts, one must know the people in that body and be known.

You might ask a person you are trying to help, "If someone close to you were to die, would the church be there for you?" Are you tied in enough that they would help? For example, I once dealt with a situation where a child drowned at a pond in the community. The grandmother of the child was at the pond and called the first name of the person from the church that appeared in her contacts. That person came to the pond immediately and called others. The first responders tried to revive the child at the pond, but within minutes they rushed the child to a hospital. When the ambulance pulled away from the pond, there were four families from that church already there to support this family. This is the phenomenon that likely leads to the health benefit the researchers find from weekly church attendance. This is the showing of honor and hospitality Paul described as the marks of a real church.

This is exactly the manner in which the early church operated (Acts 4:32-37). Individuals within the church even viewed their own assets as tools that could be used to meet the needs of others and apparently actively engaged in burden bearing and encouragement.

> *A man of many companions may come to ruin,*
> *but there is a friend who sticks closer than a brother.*
> Proverbs 18:24

Your Relationships

Your last major tool is the relationships you have. A myth circulating in our culture is that we don't need other people—we don't need relationships. It seems in vogue to go it alone today and a prevailing sentiment seems to be that family and friends are not all that important. However, research indicates that strong relationships are critical for people to be able to bounce back from difficult circumstances in life.

There are occasional opportunities where we can help strangers (as was the case with the Good Samaritan). But most of the time, you will be responding to people you know. You will also find, it is the people with whom you are in relationship where you can have the greatest impact.

> *Two are better than one, because they have a good reward for their toil. For if they fall, one will lift up his fellow. But woe to him who is alone when he falls and has not another to lift him up! Again, if two lie together, they keep warm, but how can one keep warm alone? And though a man might prevail against one who is alone, two will withstand him—a threefold cord is not quickly broken.*
>
> Ecclesiastes 4:9-12

The impactful relationship of which we should aspire is described in Ecclesiastes 4. We help our friends when they fall. The writer explains that by having a friend, one accomplishes more. Also, if one falls the other can help him up. The writer warns of the danger of falling without having someone to help us up. The passage also speaks of the companionship and camaraderie that emerges from a friendship. Finally, we see that real friends defend one another from attack. In short, wise people find friends to help them through life, and true friends help their companions up when they are down. If you do not help others get up when they are down, you are not a friend.

Positive friendships (often developed in a church setting) have been found to be extremely helpful to people. These relationships help people to cope with problems, but they also help them engage in prosocial or helpful behaviors. In a study of adolescents, it was found that those who have strong and positive friendships were more likely to have prosocial behaviors.

In research on resilience, resilient individuals had better functioning families. Such families were defined as a place where supervision and guidance was received from the parents and other adults. One critical component is that people must have someone with whom they can talk, confide in, and receive guidance. A strong family and good friends provide just the right components.

> *Faithful are the wounds of a friend;*
> *profuse are the kisses of an enemy.*
>
> Proverbs 27:6

In the parable about the Good Samaritan, Jesus explained how He expects us to help our neighbors. How much more would He expect us to help our friends? Real friendship is exhibited when someone experiences a crisis. Real friends look for a way to help or find someone by thinking, "There is someone, somewhere who will know what to do."

When we are in real relationships, we take the time to help someone at the first sign that they are off track. Too often, we wait until a problem has metastasized until we seek treatment or intervene, but we can use the model found in Matthew 18 as a guide to help those with whom we are in relationship. When someone is off track, we are faithful to say something, "faithful are the wounds of a friend." Then we can use our words to guide them by providing "earnest counsel" not to criticize, but to help them to get on track. Being first responders does not mean we are always pleasant. Many people experience problems that require difficult and serious confrontation.

Our counsel works—or has the potential to work—as a result of the mutual investment in each other's lives, the obvious love for one another, and the knowledge of each other's strengths and weaknesses.

> *If your brother sins against you, go and tell him his fault,*
> *between you and him alone. If he listens to you, you*
> *have gained your brother. But if he does not listen, take*
> *one or two others along with you, that every charge may be*
> *established by the evidence of two or three witnesses.*
>
> Matthew 18:15-16

When we confront someone about harmful behavior, they may make a concerted effort to stop the behavior. When they ignore our efforts, it may become necessary to involve others. Jesus told us to do this difficult task (Matthew 18:16). Frequently, confrontation is required with people addicted to alcohol and other drugs. This is often called an intervention

We have a model with Nathan confronting David in 2 Samuel 12. Imagine what might have happened to David had Nathan refused to confront him. Nathan's confrontation was like the Proverb that tells us "Faithful are the wounds of a friend" (Proverbs 27:6). These "wounds" can be unpleasant at the time, but they are necessary if someone is to get better. A true friend helps someone see their errors so they can become better people (Proverbs 27:17).

After we confront a person in private and that individual fails to respond appropriately, we may need to ask the family and friends to become involved in the confrontation and to help arrange for the necessary treatment.

All Scripture is breathed out by God and profitable for teaching, for reproof, for correction, and for training in righteousness, that the man of God may be complete, equipped for every good work.

2 Timothy 3:16-17

We also need to confront people who make damaging comments or promote harmful myths that are destructive to people's lives. In Acts 15:1, a problem developed that hindered the spread of the gospel. People were trying to force the Gentiles to be circumcised. The Bible says Barnabas and Paul were disturbed because they knew this would hinder the spread of the gospel. They confronted those who made the faulty statements to prevent them from causing further damage (Acts 15:7-11). How does this translate in the twenty-first century?

Suppose you were at work as a coworker began discussing the possibility of reconciling with her spouse. Another co-worker (who lives alone and has been divorced five times) says, "If I were you, I'd say good riddance to the man. You don't need him. You ought to sue him for everything you can get out of him." Maybe the co-worker who is considering reconciling with her husband begins to falter. This is an example of a time you might confront those words with truth rather than politely listen.

> *May the God of hope fill you with all joy and peace in believing,*
> *so that by the power of the Holy Spirit you may abound in hope.*
>
> Romans 15:13

It is also important for us to convey hope to those with whom we are in relationship. Sometimes problems seem insurmountable. We might even be shocked or disgusted by the things hurting people share with us. When I was in graduate school, I conducted my internship in a facility where juvenile sex offenders were treated. Many of these youths had committed despicable crimes. In a group counseling session one day, a youth who had molested several children said, "There's no hope for us. Aren't we all doomed to hell?" At that point, the group leader, who knew I was preparing for the ministry, asked me to address their spiritual concerns. I shared with them the principles of Jeremiah 18.

Jeremiah 18:3-6

So I went down to the potter's house, and there he was working at his wheel. And the vessel he was making of clay was spoiled in the potter's hand, and he reworked it into another vessel, as it seemed good to the potter to do.

Then the word of the Lord came to me: "O house of Israel, can I not do with you as this potter has done? declares the Lord. Behold, like the clay in the potter's hand, so are you in my hand, O house of Israel."

The message of Jeremiah 18 is that God forgives those who seek His forgiveness, and He can rework the most spoiled life. Lives spoiled from sin may never be the same, but with God's hand they can be cleansed and reworked into beautiful vessels. As a first responder, it is important to convey hope. Be careful not to be judgmental or condescending with people who have scarred their lives by involvement in sin. Our objective is to help them to sin no more as Jesus demonstrated with the woman who was caught in an adulterous act (John 8:1-11).

In a way, all of these tools are tied together. Your prayer life, time in the Word, your words, the church, and your relationships are interwoven. They can help ameliorate difficulties, but these tools can also be used to make us more resilient. Resilience is "the ability to withstand and rebound from disruptive life challenges. Resilience involves key processes over time that foster the ability to struggle well, surmount obstacles, and go on to live and love fully."[20]

On September 11, 2001, nearly 3,000 Americans lost their lives in the terrorist attacks. Many families lost loved ones. On that day, many people were on the actual sites where the attacks took place. In the immediate aftermath of the attacks, there were staggering estimates of the numbers of people who would suffer from Post Traumatic Stress Disorder (PTSD). However, these estimates have proven to be drastically inaccurate. Many people have coped far better than was expected. In fact, it appears the incidence of PTSD was two-thirds less than predicted.[21]

Why did many cope so well in the aftermath of the September 11, 2001 attacks? In research on Americans as a whole, George Barna found that one-fourth of all adults said their faith was the most important factor in dealing with the attacks of September 11, 2001. In particular, 63 percent of evangelicals indicated their faith was crucial to addressing the difficulty associated with the attacks.[22] These tools help us as we help others because at any moment we can find ourselves as the one needing help. Prayer, the Word of God, your words, the church, and relationships influence how well we recover from a terrible event.

For more resources go to www.FirstAidForEmotionalHurts.com.

Chapter 3

THE CHARACTER AND TECHNIQUES OF THE RESPONDER

But the fruit of the Spirit is love, joy, peace, patience, kindness, goodness, faithfulness, gentleness, self-control; against such things there is no law.

Galatians 5:22-23

Everyone says they want to help people that are hurting, but most people do not really mean it. We have to be people of character who want to help or we will be unable (or unwilling) to respond. Our character, the way we live our lives, determines whether we will have the opportunity to help those who struggle with emotional hurts. Therefore, if the Holy Spirit is not at work in our lives, no one will seek us out for help or listen to us when it is offered. Suppose you came upon a community called Pleasureville, where there are many problems. Children are contracting small-pox and passing it on throughout the schools and neighborhoods. Workers are spreading germs throughout their many workplaces. Many have sores that are visible and constant nagging coughs that needs a good dose of cough syrup. A visitor to Pleasureville might assume there is no medical care in the village, but there is a hospital with plenty of empty beds and stockpiles of vaccines and antibiotics. In addition, there seem to be clinics on every corner. So, you might wonder, "Why are there so many sick people in Pleasureville?"

Unfortunately, Pleasureville describes the spiritual nature of many churches and people who call themselves Christians. Some of our communities seem to have a church on every corner. Outside the walls of these churches there are people who have every conceivable problem. Although the cure is found in the application of biblical teaching and the resources found in these churches, we do not see people racing to the churches to find help. After all, would you go to a doctor who had open

---

What kind of fruit are you?

Where are you on the continuum?

1. I love the hard to love.

X -- X

2. I have joy.

X -- X

3. I'm at peace.

X -- X

4. I am patient.

X -- X

5. I am kind.

X -- X

6. I am good.

X -- X

7. I am faithful (you can count on me!)

X -- X

8. I am gentle.

X -- X

9. I have control of my life and passions.

X -- X

---

and visible sores? Would you want to be examined by a nurse who had a constant cough? Perhaps many do not seek our help because it does not seem all that helpful. It may be that our own lives, families, and marriages do not exhibit the fruit of the Spirit. We cannot help people who do not want our help. So how do we encourage the hurting to let us help them? We embody the fruit of the Spirit. Take the time to examine your own life according to the fruit of the Spirit using the graph in the box above.

We do not know anything about the character of the Good Samaritan. That does not mean that character does not matter. Today, many have concluded that it really does not matter what one believes or how a person lives. Indeed, there are many today who say they are a Christian that do not seem very concerned about their lifestyle. For many years, researcher George Barna examined the ways that Christians and non-believers are similar and different. Among other things, Barna has found that people who say they are Christians divorce at a similar rate as that of non-Christians. One set of researchers have even indicated that the presence of evangelical churches places one at a greater risk for divorce.[23] The problem is some conclude that what one believes is unrelated to the quality of their life or marriage. This is an example of salt losing its saltiness as Jesus described in Matthew 5:13.

> *You are the salt of the earth, but if salt has lost its taste, how shall its saltiness be restored? It is no longer good for anything except to be thrown out and trampled under people's feet.*
>
> Matthew 5:13

No one wants help from an entangling sin (like an addiction to alcohol) from someone who cannot sit and talk to them for 15 minutes without needing a cigarette smoking break. People need believers to be what God has called us to be. They need to see a marriage that works even if it is not perfect. They need to see a godly person mourn, not as a stoic, but as one who is real, dealing with the ups and downs of life. They need to see those who have been entangled in sin leave that sin behind and thrive.

> *You are the light of the world. A city set on a hill cannot be hidden. Nor do people light a lamp and put it under a basket, but on a stand, and it gives light to all in the house. In the same way, let your light shine before others, so that they may see your good works and give glory to your Father who is in heaven.*
>
> Matthew 5:14-16

When we live in this way, we are the light to which Jesus referred. We will naturally attract people and be more likely to be received when we respond. We want people who have demonstrated the ability to apply Scripture to their lives. We must practice what we preach.

> *The words of a whisperer are like delicious morsels;*
> *they go down into the inner parts of the body.*
>
> Proverbs 26:22

Confidentiality

In addition to embodying the fruit of the Spirit, we must be people of character and integrity. We must keep the confidentiality of those we try to help. Confidentiality doesn't sound like a characteristic that is important, but it really is. People are desperate to talk to someone who will not betray them by sharing information with others.

To help others, they must feel safe talking to us. Sometimes when people share something with another person, they walk away and wonder, "What if they tell someone?" Unfortunately, many have been in situations where others did tell someone and there were very negative consequences. As a rule, we should never repeat a matter told in confidence unless we are doing so because someone is in danger. In other words, if someone shares personal information with us, we need to be careful to keep it in confidence even if that person does not specifically say, "Please don't tell this to anyone." People will not honestly share with us unless they feel like they can trust us.

If you are trying to help others, it is best to develop a reputation for not talking about others. In our culture, people are entertained by learning about the problems of others. This drives much of social media and indeed there are some that even make a living sharing gossip about celebrities. We need a different view of gossip.

Why are some people so hesitant to discuss their problems with others? Gossip. So often people do not want to be ridiculed or laughed at or they have experienced others revealing their secrets.

> ### What Are Your Motives for Listening to Someone?
>
> *Whoever goes about slandering reveals secrets,*
> *but he who is trustworthy in spirit keeps a thing covered.*
> *Where there is no guidance, a people falls,*
> *but in an abundance of counselors there is safety.*
>
> Proverbs 11:13-14

Gossip is a cancer. Gossiping is destructive. Suppose you have someone who is depressed and they keep that information to themselves rather than sharing with another. As they suffer in silence, they are not as effective as they could be, and at times that kind of problem has a terrible outcome. Sometimes gossip is at the source of a suicide, destroyed marriage, or broken family.

> *Whoever covers an offense seeks love,*
> *but he who repeats a matter separates close friends.*
>
> Proverbs 17:9

Consider the Proverbs about keeping private information confidential. Hurting people desperately need someone with whom to talk. If they don't find a trustworthy counselor, they might fall (Proverbs 11:14).

For sure, there are some that mean to destroy when they break a confidence, but those people are probably in the minority. Most of the time when a confidence is broken, it is by accident or perhaps when we mean well and are trying to "fix" a situation.

Consider a situation where a person named Jane shares with you that her mother-in-law is giving her a hard time. She feels like her mother-in-law is imposing on her and her new husband's free time. You are an acquaintance of Jane's mother-in-law, and you are tempted to talk to her about Jane's concerns. If we knew her mother-in-law, we might try to "fix" this problem. But Jane doesn't need that; she needs to be heard. We can heed the principle of Proverbs 11:13-14, and give Jane a safe place where she can get counsel. If we betray her and break the confidence, we will probably further separate these two women even if that was not our intent.

Suppose one day over coffee, Jim mentions that he is in terrible debt. He does not know which way to turn and has even considered filing for bankruptcy protection. You know people who could help Jim. Should you tell anyone about Jim's difficulties? The problem Jim is going through is similar in nature. He needs our counsel and someone with whom he can trust and talk. We can listen and help him identify some approaches for dealing with his problems.

On the other hand, consider Helen. She has been extremely depressed since her son died. Her husband left her many years ago. After that event, she poured her life into caring for her son. She tells you she wishes her life were over. She has thoughts of killing herself. Should you tell anyone about this?

This is a more complicated situation. When people visit a professional counselor, psychologist, psychiatrist, health care provider, lawyer, or pastor, what they say is privileged communication.

> **American Counseling Association Code of Ethics (2014)**
> **B.1.c. Respect for Confidentiality**
>
> Counselors protect the confidential information of prospective and current clients. Counselors disclose information only with appropriate consent or with sound legal or ethical justification.

Our system values giving people the opportunity to talk freely and to get counsel and advice without fear of that confidence being betrayed. However, professional ethical codes from the helping professions are informative on this problem. The ethical codes of the American Counseling Association[24] and the American Asso-

> **American Association of Christian Counselors**
> **1-410: Maintaining Client Confidentiality**
>
> Christian counselors maintain client confidentiality, privacy and privileged communication to the fullest extent allowed by law, professional regulations and ethics, and church or organizational rules. Confidential client communications include all verbal, written, telephonic, audio or videotaped, electronic, or Internet and web-based communications arising within the helping relationship. Apart from consented to, regulatory, mandatory or legally required disclosure, counselors shall not break confidentiality regarding client communications without first discussing the intended disclosure and securing written consent from the client or client representative.

ciation of Christian Counselors[25] require that professionals take steps to prevent people from harming themselves or others. Even first responders who are not professionals can glean important lessons from these codes.

Once people become a danger to themselves or others, we must take a more active role. In those cases, the principles of Galatians 6:2 and Jesus' model for confrontation (Matthew 18) need to be applied. We need to insist on people who are a danger to themselves get the proper help, and when they do not, we will need to inform the proper authorities ourselves. This means you will have to involve law enforcement and emergency medical services.

Consider another situation with a person named Lawrence who approaches you and says, "I have something heavy on my heart. I have to share it with someone." You listen to him and he tells you that he is entangled in pornography. He also shares with you that he is attracted to young children. Unfortunately, his wife runs a daycare out of their home, and he has been spending more and more time at home during daycare hours. Should you tell anyone what he has shared with you? This is another situation where we would need to confront the person about their behavior and encourage them to inform those who can help them. When they do not, we may need to break the confidence in this situation.

After thinking it through, we begin to see that character is key to putting a first responder into a position where they may truly help others. How we live and what we believe is critical since responding involves more than a desire to help others. We must have the kind of character that puts us in a position to help. What does this kind of character look like? Consider a case study of a first responder who had the right stuff.

Barnabas: A Case Study

For he was a good man, full of the Holy Spirit and of faith. And a great many people were added to the Lord.

Acts 11:24

Thus Joseph, who was also called by the apostles Barnabas (which means son of encouragement), a Levite, a native of Cyprus.

Acts 4:36

Acts 11:24 describes a man who was extremely helpful to people. His name was Barnabas, and he was said to be "full of the Holy Spirit." He embodied the principles of Galatians 5.

> And when he had come to Jerusalem, he attempted
> to join the disciples. And _they were all afraid of him_,
> for they did not believe that he was a disciple.
>
> Acts 9:26

First, we see that he overcame the barrier of fear to respond. When fear prevented the disciples from helping Saul (later named Paul), Barnabas reached out to him. Saul had changed, but most of the Christians thought his conversion was a trap. No doubt their fears about Saul were based on memories of his role in the death of Stephen. Yet in spite of how others responded to Saul, Barnabas risked his life and brought him to the apostles. When Paul needed someone to be his mentor, Barnabas was there to help and used their relationship as a tool. Barnabas took Paul under his wing and taught him.

What Kind of Character Did Barnabas Have?

_While they were worshiping the Lord and fasting,
the Holy Spirit said, "Set apart for me Barnabas
and Saul for the work to which I have called them."_

Acts 13:2

_And after the meeting of the synagogue broke up, many Jews and
devout converts to Judaism followed Paul and Barnabas, who, as
they spoke with them, urged them to continue in the grace of God._

Acts 13:43

_Barnabas they called Zeus, and Paul,
Hermes, because he was the chief speaker._

Acts 14:12

Barnabas was a man of godly character. Because Barnabas was motivated by love, he was able to focus on Paul's needs. Sometimes we avoid helping people out of self-centeredness. We fear they might get ahead of us or might hold us back. Notice the shift from "Barnabas and Saul" to "Paul and Barnabas" between Acts 13:2 and Acts 13:43. Finally, in Acts 14:12, Paul is referred to as the "chief speaker." Barnabas knew Paul was the better speaker. Instead of sulking at Paul's success, Barnabas helped Paul progress to a position where he could impact many people to follow Christ. True helpers desire to see the best for the person they are helping. They are willing to help others find their place in God's work and work with the selfless attitude of Jesus (Philippians 2:3-4). Barnabas kept his eye on the mission. The gospel benefited from the emergence of Paul, and Barnabas seems to have obediently taken the back seat.

Techniques of the Responder

In addition to the right tools and character, there are certain techniques that are helpful. With physical first aid, there are techniques that make a difference. For example, when one does CPR they are to do 100 to 120 chest compressions a minute (Mayo Clinic). What techniques do we need to know to help someone with emotional first aid?

> When Joseph came to them in the morning, he saw that they were troubled. So he asked Pharaoh's officers who were with him in custody in his master's house, "Why are your faces downcast today?"
>
> Genesis 40:6-7

Observing

The first technique a responder needs is observation. We see an example of observation in Genesis 40 when Joseph observed the demeanor of Pharaoh's officers. The technique of observation is founded in our calling of service, and easily comes if we are using the tool of prayer (watching the people around us and praying for them). When we are focused upon others, we begin to notice differences in their demeanor because we are concerned for their well-being. Look for those who are "downcast" as Joseph observed in Pharaoh's servants. The king for whom Nehemiah worked also used this technique when he noted that Nehemiah appeared to be sad. Look for changes in behavior, disposition, weight, grades, work habits, and other changes that are out of the norm for the person.

> As she continued praying before the Lord, Eli observed her mouth. Hannah was speaking in her heart; only her lips moved, and her voice was not heard. Therefore Eli took her to be a drunken woman. And Eli said to her, "How long will you go on being drunk? Put your wine away from you."
>
> 1 Samuel 1:12-14

As you observe, be careful not to jump to conclusions about what you observe. This is the pitfall Eli fell into when he assumed Hannah was drunk. He was actually observing someone who was praying and in great anguish (1 Samuel 1:12-14), in need of help. He jumped to the wrong conclusion about Hannah. Realize there could be multiple reasons for what you are observing.

Use your observations to check in with people and see how they are doing as did Joseph. He asked, "Why are your faces downcast today?" When we inquire about how someone is doing, it is a way to let them know we are thinking about them and concerned for them, which creates an opportunity to assist them.

> Do not forsake your friend and your father's friend, and do not go to your brother's house in the day of your calamity.
> Better is a neighbor who is near than a brother who is far away.
> Proverbs 27:10

Attending

Earlier we looked at how we are called to respond to those who are hurting. The counseling term for responding is attending. It is the first thing we do by simply being with someone in need. Attending helps more than we could imagine, especially in the aftermath of a traumatic event. A grandmother whose child had drowned at a pond once told me of a family who came to the pond to try to help her in the aftermath. She indicated that this was a comfort to her even though the husband did not appear to have uttered a word. The man was very introverted so she knew this was difficult for him. But his presence was very comforting, knowing how difficult this must have been for him. Being there helps people deal with the initial stress and shock. By being there, one conveys the message that the hurting person is not alone.

Also, do not ask them how they are doing if you do not want to know or don't really care. If we ask, we need to do so because we care and are capable of handling their response.

> *Now when Job's three friends heard of all this evil that had come upon him, they came each from his own place . . . And when they saw him from a distance, they did not recognize him. And they raised their voices and wept, and they tore their robes and sprinkled dust on their heads toward heaven. And they sat with him on the ground seven days and seven nights, and no one spoke a word to him, for they saw that his suffering was very great.*
>
> Job 2:11-13

We often describe the shortcomings of the friends of Job, yet they performed this step well. They spent several days with Job and did not say a word. No magic words are required, there is simply power in presence.

> *Know this, my beloved brothers: let every person be quick to hear, slow to speak, slow to anger.*
>
> James 1:19

Listening

Another technique the responder needs is to simply listen. Unfortunately, we often place little value on listening to other people. Watch a morning talk show or cable news interview and observe the interviewer. Is that person really listening to the individual being interviewed or does it not appear that the interviewer has a preplanned point she is trying to get across? Listening has become a lost art. We like to talk and often we believe we will help people with our many words. When people talk of trying to help someone, they often say, "I don't know what to say," but it is listening to another that is often more helpful than anything anyone may say.

We help people when we listen to them. There is healing in listening. Listening to someone enables them to vent their frustrations. It often provides the opportunity for them to realize they have more alternatives to a situation than they previously thought or the problem may not seem that insurmountable.

When you listen to people, "Actively listen." This means you regularly make eye contact with them. Your body language conveys your interest. Lean forward and show that you are interested in what they have to say. It helps people when those who care about them actively listen to them. But how do you acquire listening skills? Many in the field of business have noted that listening is good for business. As a result, some businesses actually train their staff in the art of listening. Interestingly, one study indicated that self-imposed silence greatly improves listening effectiveness and the development of listening skills.

So, we would do well to develop our listening skills.[26] Practice listening. Go a few hours one day without speaking. When you do interact with people, try to listen to them as intently as possible. What do you learn from your self-imposed silence about the people around you?

If one gives an answer before he hears, it is his folly and shame.

Proverbs 18:13

When we hear about a problem, we often begin to think of advice to give the person. We do not usually fully consider the scope of our friend's problem. If we really thought this through, we would not be so focused on giving advice. Do we really believe we can give a little advice and solve a problem that has been developing for years? Most emotional hurts people have cannot be solved that easily (Proverbs 18:13). We do not feel the pain they are feeling, which makes the problems seem easier to solve than they really are.

> *The simple believes everything, but the*
> *prudent gives thought to his steps.*
> Proverbs 14:15

If you are a student of the Bible, you already know that. The next time someone tells you about a problem and you find yourself itching to give advice, consider the words of James, "Let every person be quick to hear, slow to speak."

Earlier we described how Job's friends attended well to him. As they attended Job, he processed what had happened to him. He said, "I wish I had never been born (3:1-3); I want to die (3:21-22); the thing I feared the most has happened; I can't rest; I have nothing but trouble" (3:25-26). This was very difficult for Job's friends to hear. But it was what Job needed. Job did not need advice or correction. He needed someone with whom to talk. He needed someone who would listen. He needed the presence of someone else in a nonjudgmental way—someone there for him, not there to meet their own needs.

> *The heart of the righteous ponders how to answer,*
> *but the mouth of the wicked pours out evil things.*
> Proverbs 15:28

As we listen, we do not want to jump to conclusions or take sides since we may not be hearing both sides of an issue. Many people have been harmed when someone just believes something that is told to them without thoroughly examining the situation.

The Proverbs also warn us that there are two sides to every story (Proverbs 18:12), and that we should not simply believe everything but carefully examine what we hear (Proverbs 14:15).

Caring (Empathy)

The Compassion of Jesus

And when the Pharisees saw this, they said to his disciples, "Why does your teacher eat with tax collectors and sinners?"

Matthew 9:11

When he saw the crowds, he had compassion for them, because they were harassed and helpless, like sheep without a shepherd.

Matthew 9:36

So Jesus had compassion and touched their eyes. And immediately their eyes received sight, and they followed Him.

Matthew 20:34 (NKJV)

And when the Lord saw her, he had compassion on her and said to her, "Do not weep."

Luke 7:13

And when he drew near and saw the city, he wept over it.

Luke 19:41

When Jesus saw her weeping, and the Jews who had come with her also weeping, he was deeply moved in his spirit and greatly troubled. Jesus wept. So the Jews said, "See how he loved him!"

John 11:33, 35-36

We often see in the Gospels the compassion that Jesus had for hurting people. It led Him to spend time with people who were entangled in sin and hurting for a variety of reasons. Caring or empathy does not sound like a technique, but it is often a process we must put ourselves through to help someone. Many confuse empathy with sympathy. Sympathy or pity for someone can result in the individual becoming dependent upon the helper or repulsed by the helper because they do not want to be seen as a victim. Most people want to be self-reliant, and do not want to feel like they are a burden to anyone.

Empathy is an attempt to comprehend what someone else is going through. An example is imagining what it would be like to learn that you had cancer if you were trying to help someone who had just received this news. Although we cannot truly understand how a person who has just received that news might feel, trying to imagine can prepare us to help that person. Empathy may be the most important component of the helping relationship, and to express it, we must step out of our comfort zone. This is what Paul did.

Paul's Approach With People

For though I am free from all, <u>I have made myself a servant to all</u>, that I might win more of them. <u>To the Jews I became as a Jew</u>, in order to win Jews. To those under the law <u>I became as</u> one under the law (though not being myself under the law) that I might win those under the law. To those outside the law <u>I became as</u> one outside the law (not being outside the law of God but under the law of Christ) that I might win those outside the law. To the weak <u>I became weak</u>, that I might win the weak. <u>I have become all things to all people</u>, that by all means I might save some. I do it all for the sake of the gospel, that I may share with them in its blessings.

1 Corinthians 9:19-23

Paul made himself a servant and became under the law or weak to help others. We must do the same. It is not so much the words we say that help people, but it is their awareness that we are concerned for them. So, as we hear of or see some kind of difficulty come upon a person, it is best to pause and "put ourselves in their shoes" by imagining how we might feel if we experienced something similar to what the person has experienced. This will help us to help them. It will also prevent us from making misguided statements that could be harmful. For example, too many people have tried to say the right thing as they went through a visitation line before a funeral. Often people have quoted Romans 8:28 to those who have just lost a child. Some parents have wondered, "So you are saying this is good that my child has died?" Romans 8:28 is true, but we must remember that Paul told us words should be used "as fits the occasion" (Ephesians 4:29). An empathetic person (one who put themselves in the shoes of another) would not quote that verse on that occasion.

Empathy helps us to be gentle. Paul described how he was gentle to those he helped like a nursing mother to her child, and that he had prepared himself to meet the needs of others because he cared for them (1 Thessalonians 2:7-8). Empathy helps us identify actions we can take to help. Why would someone who is contemplating suicide, hearing voices, or suffering the effects of sexual abuse share that information with another person? That is what James told us to do (James 5). Tell others, and to seek their prayers. Sometimes, the people who talk to us have nowhere else to turn. We can ask ourselves, "If I were experiencing what they are experiencing, how might I feel? What might I want someone to do for me?"

Suppose a co-worker talked to others about the hard time she has had since her mother died. Someone might say, "You should be over your mother's death by now." That response is not empathetic. Someone else might say something like, "You know when my mother died, I..." which is also not empathetic, but it is the one of the responses we tend to give. It is easy to start talking about our own experiences and dispense advice, but this only detracts from helping the hurting person. But if we pause first and ask ourselves, "How might we feel if we were in her situation?" We are more likely to respond empathetically with something like, "That's got to be difficult to deal with." This response acknowledges the hard time she is going through and encourages her to keep talking.

Responding

Helping others goes beyond just listening. There will be a time to carefully respond. It is often best that our first response be a paraphrase or reflection of what has been said to us. This lets the person know we are listening to them and encourages them to keep speaking. Sometimes people need an opportunity to tell their story. As they do, they often talk about their frustrations and pain, which helps them get better. In our fast-paced world, many people do not have the opportunity to share their story. They do not get to be heard.

Fight the urge to ask questions. Sometimes we ask questions as if our gaining of information would somehow solve the problem. If you are not careful, questions will result in people becoming defensive and some will just shut down on you. I have been training professional counselors for over twenty years and I find it hard to convince them of this. Yet, in my own experience doing evaluations on juvenile offenders, I learned that when I asked them too many questions they would shut down, and I was unable to help them. When I coaxed them into telling their story by listening and paraphrasing, I actually did learn valuable information that helped me help them. It is a good idea to think, listen, and clarify. I tell my students, "If you ask a question, make sure you follow with three paraphrases to keep them talking."

Interestingly, as Jesus interacted with a woman from Samaria entangled in sexual sin, He did not ask a single question. We know He was a good counselor—He was Jesus. The prophecies of the Messiah indicated that He would be a Wonderful Counselor (Isaiah 9:6). There are times where Jesus asked clarifying questions of others, which would be like asking, "How long have you had these sleep problems?" To help people with emotional hurts, we will need to ask questions more on the line of Joseph's questions to Pharaoh's servants like, "Why are you so sad today?" We ask questions to get people talking and to help clarify the situation.

We ask open-ended questions that cannot be answered with one-word responses. Open-ended questions are more effective than closed questions like, "Are you doing okay?" which tends to stifle further communication with one word answers like, "Yes." An open question like, "How have you been doing since your mom passed?" is better since it invites them to tell their story.

> But exhort one another every day, as long as it is called "today," that none of you may be hardened by the deceitfulness of sin.
> Hebrews 3:13

As we respond, we try to exhort, teach, and instruct. The writer of Hebrews warns that it is best to seize an opportunity to exhort someone because delay could lead others to become discouraged and hardened.

> Therefore encourage one another and build one another up, just as you are doing.
> 1 Thessalonians 5:11

Through our words, we can also instruct by using Scripture to show how it applies to various problems the people we are trying to help have encountered. You might think of this as Scriptural problem solving where a person defines the problem they are facing, generates alternatives to dealing with it, selects options, and implements a possible solution.

Whether we are dealing with grief, an addiction, or marital problems, Scripture has something to say and the only viable solutions will involve applying Scripture to these difficult situations. We will be looking specifically at what they can do. Remember, Paul expressed his confidence that we are capable of doing this (Romans 15:14).

It is critical though that we stick to the Word rather than our own opinions and conjecture. We do not want to fall into the error of Job's friends who talked too much and jumped to conclusions regarding the source of his problems. Consider some of the statements of Job's "friends." They demonstrate how damaging it can be to fail to listen to the hurting and how ill-given advice can be harmful.

Are these statements generally true?

"Remember: who that was innocent ever perished?
Or where were the upright cut off?
As I have seen, those who plow iniquity
and sow trouble reap the same.

Job 4:7-8

If you are pure and upright,
surely then he will rouse himself for you
and restore your rightful habitation.
And though your beginning was small,
your latter days will be very great.

Job 8:6-7

Job's friends made statements that are generally true, they were just incorrect in this context. Eliphaz's words remind us that we reap what we sow, which sounds like Galatians 6:7. Bildad told us to seek God and we will find Him. Although this is true, this was not the reason Job had trouble. This was an incorrect supposition that assumed Job had sinned and had not sought God. As a result, their words were harmful, and God condemned them, saying, "My anger burns against you and against your two friends, for you have not spoken of me what is right" (Job 42:7). Job also referred to them as "miserable comforters" (Job 16:2). These friends would have been far more helpful to Job if they had left the interpretation to God and concentrated upon listening to their friend and encouraging him.

> *If a brother or sister is poorly clothed and lacking in daily food, and one of you says to them, "Go in peace, be warmed and filled," without giving them the things needed for the body, what good is that?*
>
> James 2:15-16

Acting

Ask the Holy Spirit to guide you in the ways you can help others. Earlier, we looked at the character of Barnabas, which is recorded in the book of Acts. Barnabas was effective because he was a man of action. He saw people who were in need, and to help meet their needs, he sold a field and laid the money at the apostles' feet. We don't know how much Barnabas made when he sold the field, but we do know that the church appreciated his generosity because his actions got a lot of attention. People were pleased with Barnabas; so pleased that Ananias and Sapphira acted like they had done the same thing when they had not. They held some money back because they were trying to impress people and in the process lost their lives (Acts 5:1-11).

Do we have to give people money to help them? Sometimes that is the most helpful thing to give, but at other times there may be something more precious to give—time. The Bible says our life is like a vapor that appears for a little time and then vanishes away (James 4:14). Time is one of the most precious things we can give to others. It takes time to reach out and help the hurting.

Recently, a man whose daughter had died in an accident said, "You know people say, 'Please let me know if there is anything I can do to help,' sometimes as they are backing out the door." Perhaps instead of making a statement like that, it would be better to ask ourselves, "What could I do to help in this situation?" Usually, there are real needs that people have. Consider someone who has experienced a death. They certainly need food, and we tend to take care of that, but many are worried about how their house looks and need someone to tidy up or cut their grass. They may need someone to make a run to the drycleaners or to pick up someone at the airport. If we are present and listening, we will hear their concerns and have opportunities to help them.

Consider this example—suppose a co-worker of yours named Sally has been married for three years and has a new baby. Last week she found out her husband has been having an affair. He has told her he does not love her anymore. It does not sound very spiritual, but Sally needs someone to take care of her baby so she can have some time to figure out what she needs to do. Remember, Jesus commanded us to perform specific acts (e.g., give a cup of water). Another act might be to pay for her to receive counseling or provide for some of the needs of the baby. Like the Good Samaritan, we want to think of specific needs.

> *He went to him and bound up his wounds, pouring on oil and wine. Then he set him on his own animal and brought him to an inn and took care of him.*
> Luke 10:34

Find the Inn

On average, I am contacted 4-5 times a week by someone somewhere looking for professional help. I wrote a booklet on this called *Finding Help* in which I thoroughly discuss this issue. I encourage you to examine that work,

E. Moody (2010). *First Aid for Your Emotional Hurts: Finding Help.* Nashville, TN: Randall House.

that is far more detailed than what we are able to cover here.

I am convinced that some people pass by the wounded traveler because they cannot take them all the way home. In other words, they can bind the wounds as the Good Samaritan did, but they are at a loss about what to do after that. The Good Samaritan did what he could do for the wounded traveler and then he got him to a place where the rest of his needs could be addressed more thoroughly. So, when you do not know what to do, find someone who does and get the one you are trying to help to them.

God has provided people who can help. Sometimes the most helpful thing we can do for hurting people is to find someone who has the knowledge and experience to make a difference in their lives. But it is important for those who need help to get that help soon. One body of research involving long-term mental health problems indicates that when children had difficulties in childhood, they tended to have difficulties later in life. This underscores the importance of intervening early in their lives to reduce the likelihood of problems later in life.

A long-term study conducted by researchers at Harvard Medical School indicated that half of all lifetime cases of mental illness began by age 14. Despite the early onset of those problems, it appeared that most people waited at least ten years before getting treatment. Some waited as long as 20 to 23 years. This was extremely unfortunate since the authors noted that an untreated mental disorder early in a person's life is likely to impact them for the rest of their life. This results in a very adverse impact upon a person.[27]

> *She said to her mistress, "Would that my lord were with the prophet who is in Samaria! He would cure him of his leprosy."*
>
> 2 Kings 5:3

When You Don't Know What to Do, Find Someone Who Does

Consider the servant girl described in 2 Kings 5. Her master, Naaman contracted leprosy. She was not a prophet or a physician. She certainly could not heal Naaman's leprosy, but she knew someone who could—a Jewish prophet. How likely would it be that a proud Syrian general would go to a Jewish prophet for help? Not very likely. But that did not stop the servant girl from sharing the information she had. So how do we get people to someone who can help them? We have to spend some time examining the resources for their particular situation.

For some of the people we are trying to help, we will need to learn more about their particular situation and the professionals available to them. Sometimes it may feel like you are playing alphabet soup, trying to make sense of the various degrees and credentials out there. In this section, we are going to provide you with some basic information about helping professionals. In the subsequent chapters, we will provide information about resources for the specific situations covered there.

Making Sense of Alphabet Soup

We are very fortunate today to have a myriad of professionals who can help people with seemingly insurmountable problems. We have pastors, physicians, psychiatrists, psychologists, professional counselors, nurse practitioners, social workers, and support groups. In this section, we will provide you with an overview of various groups and discuss how to find them.

Pastors

Pastors are a good resource with whom to begin. They should be able to help people apply Scripture to the particular problem they are facing. They should have a referral list of professionals in the area so they can refer people to seek further help. The assistance a pastor is able to provide is determined by their experience and training, which can range from the completion of some college courses through doctoral level studies. Most problems we encounter in hurting people will have a spiritual component to them. Pastors are especially helpful in dealing with the spiritual component and may also be able to help individuals when they are in need of referral to a more advanced helping professional. The type of training and experience a pastor has received will determine the level of expertise he brings to the hurting individual's situation. Some pastors have attended seminary and have received advanced training in counseling. These individuals tend to have a Master of Arts (MA), Master of Divinity (MDiv), or Doctor of Ministry (DMin) degree.

Some pastors and laymen have received training in seminary or through coursework in biblical counseling. Nouthesia is often translated in the New Testament as admonish, correct, or instruct. The goal of nouthetic counselors is to use the Word of God to confront those who are in need of making corrections in their lives. Nouthetic counselors would be beneficial to individuals dealing with home and family problems, spiritual problems, and many other issues that people face.

Alphabet Soup		
Profession	*Degree*	*For more information...*
Physicians	MD, DO	American Medical Association: www.ama-assn.org American Association of Colleges of Osteopathic Medicine: www.osteopathic.org
Psychiatrists	MD, DO	American Psychiatric Association: www.psych.org
Psychologists	MA, MS (Under the direction of a doctoral level) PhD, PsyD	American Psychological Association: www.apa.org American Psycholotical Association: www.asppb.org American Board of Professional Psychology: www.abpp.org
Psychiatric-Mental Health Nurse Practitioner	MSN, DNP, PhD, PMHNP	American Psychiatric Nurses www.apna.org
Professional Counselors	MA, MS, MEd, MFT	American Counseling Association: www.counseling.org National Board for Certified Counselors: www.nbcc.org
Social Workers	BA, MSW	National Association of Social Work: www.socialworkers.org Association of Social Work Boards: www.aswb.org

Physicians (MD and DO)

Physicians are a good resource. There are two types of physicians: An M.D. has a Doctor of Medicine degree while a DO has a Doctor of Osteopathy degree. As you know, physicians with an MD work with a variety of physical ailments. Doctors of osteopathy place special emphasis on the body's musculoskeletal system, preventive medicine, and holistic patient care. Both doctors of medicine and doctors of osteopathy are seen in primary-care situations.[28] Many problems from which people suffer consist of a physical component, so a good place to begin the healing process in many instances is with a physician. A physician can often treat the problem itself and will know the appropriate referrals to make when necessary. An individual suffering from deep depression and the person suffering from schizophrenia would both benefit from the immediate care of a physician. An individual would also benefit from the help of a physician in the immediate aftermath of a sexual assault.

Psychiatrists (MD, DO)

Psychiatrists assess and treat mental illnesses through psychotherapy, psychoanalysis, hospitalization, and medication.[29] Psychiatrists are especially suited to deal with mental illness that requires the use of medication for treatment. We will talk about the use of medication and the medications used in later chapters.

Psychologists

The largest group of psychologists is made up of clinical psychologists. These professionals are trained to help individuals with a variety of serious problems. They can interview clients and administer diagnostic tests to help provide more information about the issue at hand. Counseling psychologists are similar in nature, but often assist people with what are termed "problems of everyday living." The individual who has been sexually abused would benefit from the assistance of a psychologist. These professionals could likely help the individual overcome the trauma and be better able to function normally.

There are many other types of psychologists. Neuropsychologists study the relationship between behavior and the brain. They often work with people who have suffered from a stroke or another brain injury. School psychologists help teachers and parents identify learning disabilities and other school-related problems. They assist in the development of interventions to help with these issues.[30] Psychologists tend to have PhD, EdD, or PsyD degrees. Those with PhD degrees tend to have training from a research-practitioner perspective. Some counseling psychologists have an EdD degree. PsyD degrees (Doctorate of Psychology) tend to have a highly clinical and treatment focus. There are some practitioners who will have a master's degree (MA, MS, MEd) in psychology. In most states, these practitioners work under the supervision of a doctoral-level psychologist. Psychologists are especially helpful when diagnostic testing is necessary.

Psychiatric-Mental Health Nurse Practitioner

Psychiatric-mental health nurse practitioners (PMHNP) are advanced practice nurses with specialized education and training in helping individuals and families with psychiatric conditions. Working in partnership with the patient and family, interventions may include prescribing medications and counseling. All PMHNPs will have a master's degree and many will have a doctorate (e.g., DNP, PhD, EdD). These professionals assess, diagnose, and treat individuals and families with psychiatric disorders or the potential for such disorders using their full scope of therapeutic skills, including the prescription of medication and administration of psychotherapy. Psychiatric Mental Health Advanced Practice Registered Nurses (PMH-APRNs) primarily provide mental health care services. PMH-APRNs often own private practices and corporations as well as consult with groups, communities, legislators, and corporations.[31]

Professional Counselors (MA, MS, MEd, MFT)

Licensed professional counselors generally have a minimum of a master's degree to practice their profession. There are also some doctoral level counselors. They assist individuals with personal, family, mental health, and career decisions and problems. Specialty areas include rehabilitation counselors who work with people with disabilities. Mental-health counselors assist individuals with mental and emotional disorders as well as problems with depression and addiction.

Other types of counselors include substance abuse and behavioral disorder counselors who work with people having problems with alcohol and other drugs as well as gambling and eating disorders. Marriage and family therapists help families with marriage difficulties.[32]

Social Workers (BA, MSW, PhD, DSW)

Most social workers are employed in health-care agencies or with state or local government agencies. They look for ways to help people function well in their environment. They work with individuals with a variety of difficulties. A BSW degree (Bachelors of Social Work) is the minimum requirement for most social workers. However, those working in medial and treatment facilities tend to have an MSW degree (Master of Social Work). Some supervisors of social work have a DSW degree (Doctorate of Social Work) or a PhD.[33] Social workers are especially adept at finding appropriate placements and resources for individuals in crisis. For example, if long-term care becomes needed for an individual suffering from schizophrenia or Alzheimer's disease, a social worker will help to find that resource.

A variety of professionals can usually help with the difficulties people usually experience. It is good to begin with pastors and physicians. The other professionals utilized might be determined by what professionals are available in the particular community where one lives along with considerations of how they will pay for the services offered. Often insurance companies or Employee Assistance Programs (EAP) have particular providers they expect their clients or employees to use. As an important element of this discussion, we need to consider some attributes to look for in a helping professional.

The survey that follows comes from *First Aid for Your Emotional Hurts: Finding Help*.[34] You could use this to help determine the professionals to be utilized for particular issues.

Which items have been experienced during the past 6 months?

_____ 1. Someone close to you died suddenly and unexpectedly (e.g., child, spouse)

_____ 2. Experienced a tragic event and are now "jumpy" and having difficulty relaxing

_____ 3. Experienced a tragic event that you often have dreams about

_____ 4. Have experienced an "anxiety attack" that you initially thought was a major health event

_____ 5. Have thought about hurting yourself

_____ 6. Cry at times for no apparent reason

_____ 7. Most of the time you have difficulty concentrating

_____ 8. Have problems with your sleep (e.g., falling asleep, awakening in the middle of the night or unable to fall back asleep)

_____ 9. Struggle with a chronic illness or disability

_____ 10. Experience pain that cannot be traced to a physical cause

_____ 11. See things others do not see

_____ 12. Hear things others do not hear

_____ 13. Induce yourself to vomit food that you've just eaten

_____ 14. Are often told that you look too thin

_____ 15. Others have told you that you should get some help

_____ 16. Are unsatisfied in your current career

_____ 17. Feel like you are trapped in debt and will never get out

_____ 18. Your marriage is not what it should be (e.g., characterized by bickering, extramarital affair)

_____ 19. You've experienced a divorce and feel overwhelmed

_____ 20. You are in an abusive relationship

This list is by no means exhaustive, but perhaps it will give you an idea of the kind of difficulties professional helpers are accustomed to addressing. Fortunately, there are a variety of helping professionals equipped to address these and many other issues. The chart that follows links these issues with a helping professional or professionals who have been trained to address these issues.

Issues for Which One Might Seek Professional Help	
Issue Number	*Helping Professional(s)*
1, 2, 3, 5, 6, 7, 8, 15, 20	Psychiatrist, Psychologist, Licensed Professional Counselor, Social Worker
4, 10, 11, 12, 13, 14,	Psychiatrist, Psychologist
9	Psychiatrist, Psychologist, Rehabilitation Counselor
16	Career Counselor
17	Financial Counselor
18	Marriage & Family Therapist
19	Marriage & Family Therapist, Licensed Professional Counselor, Psychologist

Looking for Helping Professionals

Like the Good Samaritan or Naaman's servant, sometimes we need to match the person with the problem with a particular helping professional. What do you look for? Fundamentally, we would like to use professionals who are Christian, competent, capable, and caring.

Christian

Today there are colleges and seminaries that specialize in training Christian counselors and psychologists. Also, many Christians who receive

To find Christian counselors go to www.FirstAidForEmotionalHurts.com and select Find a Christian Counselor

training in secular settings often attempt to integrate Christianity into their practice. How does one go about finding a Christian counselor or psychologist? You can find one by looking for professional helpers who explicitly state they are Christians. Keep in mind, however, you will not know if these practitioners are actually members of Christian counseling organizations simply from examining their ads. Second, you can go directly to a Christian Counseling organization to find practitioners.

The American Association of Christian Counselors (AACC) has around 50,000 members from a variety of helping areas. You can use their website to find a counselor in your area. The Christian Association of Psychological Studies (CAPS) is an organization primarily of psychologists, therapists, and academicians. You can find Christian professionals in the online membership directory of this organization. It is important to note that the practitioners listed in the directories of these two organizations are not necessarily screened thoroughly. Another group of Christian counselors is nouthetic or biblical counselors. You can find a nouthetic counselor by going to the website of the National Association for Nouthetic Counselors (NANC). Individuals listed at that website have completed at least a 30-hour Basic Training Course with a minimum of 10 hours of counseling observation by a NANC certified counselor.

Should You Accept Help From a Non-Christian?

Some people will live in places where Christian helping professionals are not available. In these instances, should a professional who is not a Christian be used? Consider the value of the counsel Moses received from Jethro in Exodus 18. Although Jethro was probably not a believer, he provided valuable counsel to Moses. It is important that the hurting person receives the professional help he needs, so it may be necessary to use a non-Christian professional. A client can feel free to ask a prospective therapist about his or her beliefs. The client can then assess whether his own Christian worldview will be respected by the helping professional. In the resources at the end of this chapter, you will find additional information in the ethical statements of professional organizations. Note that these professionals are charged with treating all people respectfully. Each organization allows clients to lodge a complaint against a professional who is negligent or unprofessional. These processes have been designed to protect clients and ensure they receive effective treatment.[35]

Relevant Professional Ethical Standards
American Counseling Association

The Counseling Relationship

A.4. Avoiding Harm and Imposing Values
A.4.a. Avoiding Harm
Counselors act to avoid harming their clients, trainees, and research participants and to minimize or to remedy unavoidable or unanticipated harm.
A.4.b. Personal Values
Counselors are aware of their own values, attitudes, beliefs, and behavior and avoid imposing values that are inconsistent with counseling goals. Counselors respect the diversity of clients, trainees, and research participants.

American Psychiatric Association

Section 1 A physician shall be dedicated to providing competent medical care with compassion and respect for human dignity and rights.

1. A psychiatrist shall not gratify his or her own needs by exploiting the patient. The psychiatrist shall be ever vigilant about the impact that his or her conduct has upon the boundaries of the doctor–patient relationship, and thus upon the well being of the patient. These requirements become particularly important because of the essentially private, highly personal, and sometimes intensely emotional nature of the relationship established with the psychiatrist.
2. A psychiatrist should not be a party to any type of policy that excludes, segregates, or demeans the dignity of any patient because of ethnic origin, race, sex, creed, age, socioeconomic status, or sexual orientation.

Competent

It is of utmost importance that the professionals chosen to help hurting people be competent in their fields. How can you know if a person is competent? One key ingredient is licensure. Appropriate helping professionals will be licensed by the state where they work. In order to be licensed, a professional must have completed the required academic work and field training. The licensed professional will also have taken an examination administered by the states licensure board. If a professional meets the criteria established by the state's licensure board, he or she can be licensed. Some professionals who are licensed at the master's level in their field will have to be supervised for a significant period before they may practice alone. In some fields, professionals who have completed a master's degree will never be allowed to practice on their own without continued supervision. In order for licensed professionals to remain licensed, they will need to maintain ethical and professional behavior and must complete continuing educational credits regularly. Continuing education insures that helping professionals will stay up-to-date in their particular fields.

Capable

A helping professional should also be capable. For example, all licensed psychologists are not capable of effectively treating the individual who is dealing with the aftermath of sexual abuse. A capable professional would be knowledgeable about issues of sexual-abuse survivors and would have experience working with them. This is why I have been somewhat vague about the type of counselor or psychologist a person might see for therapy. Various professionals have diverse capabilities, which are dependent on their experiences and the extra supervision and training they have received.

Caring

It is important that the helping professional utilized be a caring person. Most people have gone into a helping profession because they genuinely care about other people. If you assist someone in obtaining help from a professional, try to assess whether the professional is a caring person. One way potential clients can gauge the level of concern of helping professionals is to ask them why they entered that particular field and why they continue to practice.

> A meta-analysis (study of several studies) has indicated that at the end of treatment, the average individual who has received counseling is better off than 80 percent of the untreated sample.

At some point, deciding whether or not to receive treatment becomes a stewardship issue. As I wrote in the booklet *Finding*

Help, there are a variety of professionals we use to improve our physical health. For example, we use dentists, orthodontist, audiologists, and podiatrists. Could we survive without straight teeth or even any teeth at all? Could we survive without good vision, articulate speech, good hearing, or well-working feet? We could survive, however good teeth, good hearing, adequate vision, and well-working feet sure do enhance our lives. Unfortunately, many miss out on the ways their lives could be enhanced by mental health professionals.[36]

The Apostle Paul to Timothy

No longer drink only water, but use a little wine for the sake of your stomach and your frequent ailments.

1 Timothy 5:23

Utilizing Medication

Another area where you may need to gain information is regarding the use of medication. Clearly there is a proliferation of advertisements for various medications to address the ailments we face, with what seems to be a pill for everything. There is little doubt that some utilize medication as an easy way out of a problem. However, there is also little doubt that many have benefited from medication. Medication has prolonged and enhanced countless lives. Some of the people with whom you will interact with who need help will be struggling with whether they should take medication to address their particular problem.

Should a Christian Take Medication?

Some people you try to help will have a physician suggest they take medicine to alleviate the symptoms of their problems. This is an area where you may be able to help with your words, if you are informed. Some have told those who struggle with mental illness that they lack faith if they take medication. These people are conflicted and confused about using medicine to help believers.

In these situations, you might ask them to consider how other medications have helped them through their life. Often people fear that medications will be habit-forming. From time to time, all of us take medication with this potential. Some time ago, I suffered from a terrible bout with a kidney stone. Immediately after my arrival to the hospital, I was given Morphine. Morphine is an opiate and it is highly addictive. However, used properly under the direction of a physician, it drastically enhanced my life that day.

There are no easy solutions to the problems people encounter in life. There will be some who overuse medications and others who avoid medications they desperately need. The people with whom we work must utilize the wisdom God has promised to decide if medication is appropriate for them. We must be careful about judging others who take medications for problems. Sometimes some of the very people who make such statements themselves may be taking a medication to lower cholesterol or for diabetes—problems for which a proper diet and good exercise regimen could truly reduce their need for those medications. In His graciousness, God has given us many tools that weren't available in the past. We must use wisdom in their utilization. In this section, we will provide an overview of the medications utilized to treat various problems.

A Primer on Medications

In the majority of circumstances, health care providers will combine medication with counseling as the most effective approach. When looking at people who are experiencing difficult problems, professional helpers often try to determine if the source of depression is biological or based on circumstances and life issues. If medication is warranted, a provider may prescribe these medications.

How Do Medications Work?

There is much confusion about the way medications work. Many years ago, I worked as a Clinical Therapist and was working with an individual who had been evaluated by our psychiatrist. The psychiatrist recommended that the person take a particular medication. I too thought they needed the medication (that had led me to refer them to the psychiatrist). As I began to discuss this possibility the person responded, "No way, I am not going to put anything in my mouth that might affect my brain." I had to bite my tongue. The person had a big mountain dew in their hand and smelled as though they had already smoked a pack of cigarettes that morning. I wanted to say, "No, you just don't want to put anything in your mouth that has a good impact upon your brain," but I didn't. Everything that goes into your mouth (everything you eat and drink) impacts your brain. Everything that enters your nose impacts your brain from the scent of lavender (a calming effect) to something negative like snorting cocaine. It helps to look at how medications work.

Within the brain, there are 100 billion neurons. A neuron is a nerve cell. Communication within the neuron takes place electrically and between neurons chemically. These chemical messengers are molecules that are called neurotransmitters. Medications can impact these neurotransmitters. Neurons probably contain many neurotransmitters. Some of the main neurotransmitters are acetylcholine, dopamine, norepinephrine, epinephrine, serotonin, histamine, and gamma-amino-butyric acid. The main neurotransmitters involved with behavior and emotion are dopamine, norepinephrine, and serotonin.[37]

There is an electrical impulse within a neuron that results in the release of neurotransmitters. Neurons also contain receptor sites. When a neuron releases a neurotransmitter, it travels across a space called a synapse to a receptor site on another neuron. These receptor sites are often the targets of medications. When the neurotransmitter is received by a neuron, it receives the chemical cell and the neuron is activated. This allows the neuron to transmit again.[38]

A neurotransmitter and a receptor site act like a key and lock. The neurotransmitter is the key and the receptor site is the lock. In a process called signal transduction, the first messenger of the neurotransmitter binds to the receptor and transmits its message. This process changes the electrical characteristics of the cell. Chemical changes can also take place within a cell when a neurotransmitter binds with a receptor site.[39]

The neurotransmitter dopamine is involved with behavior, mood, and attention. It is believed that overactive dopamine receptors are responsible for the main symptoms of schizophrenia. The neurotransmitter norepinephrine is involved with wakefulness and alertness. It is believed that issues with this neurotransmitter are involved with symptoms of anxiety. The neurotransmitter serotonin is involved with mood, control of eating, and sleeping, as well as pain regulation. The neurotransmitter serotonin is often involved with depression. So, there are medications one can take to impact dopamine. However, activities like gaming and gambling can impact dopamine as well. Everything impacts your brain—what you eat, as well as what you do.[40]

There are three main types of problems that need to be treated with medications. These are depression, psychosis, and anxiety. Each of these sections will be discussed in much more detail in later chapters.

So, how do you feel about guiding someone to a helping professional? Remember, you do not have to help the hurting person all by yourself. You can point the hurting person to a helping professional just as Naaman's servant pointed him to Elisha and the Good Samaritan took the wounded traveler to the innkeeper. Finding a professional to help the hurting is generous behavior that demonstrates God's love. Consider how this behavior shows people the love of God. When you use your time and energy to help someone find a competent and caring helper, you have demonstrated the love of God. This concern for a friend or a coworker helps people see Jesus as the Light of the world.

For more resources go to www.FirstAidForEmotionalHurts.com.

Chapter 4

Helping People Through Grief and Loss

*The Lord is near to the brokenhearted
and saves the crushed in spirit.*

Psalm 34:18

You will not deal with some of the difficulties examined in this book, but everyone (who answers the call) will respond to those who have experienced grief and loss. Further, all of us will experience grief and loss ourselves. Consider the sample case studies that follow. Do you know anyone with difficulties like these?

Jerry and Susan

Jerry and Susan lost their teenage daughter in a tragic automobile accident eight months ago. Needless to say, they have been devastated. Their friends and family are becoming increasingly concerned about them. They never seem to want to go anywhere and sometimes people wonder what to say to them. The situation is exasperated because a habitual drunk driver killed her. He is awaiting trial. Jerry and Susan do not watch television because the event is still in the news as activists discuss strengthening the drunk driving laws in their state.

Howard

Howard lost his wife of thirty years last month to a sudden heart attack. He seems angry with God over her loss. "Why didn't God take me?" he asks his friends. They worked hard much of their lives to save for retirement and had plans to travel the country. "Now I have nothing to do and no one to be with me," he says. He has one daughter who lives on the other side of the country and seems to be becoming increasingly isolated.

James and Helen

James and Helen feel as if their world has crumbled around them. Their son and daughter-in-law had a very rocky marriage that was wrought with acrimony. They seemed well on their way to a divorce, but apparently had an argument about selling the house. It horribly degenerated. Their son allegedly took the life of their daughter-in-law, and then he took his own life. It's been two years and James and Helen continue to struggle with the events and aftermath of that terrible day.

You probably know people who have struggled with some of these problems. We are called to help them and we have tools and techniques that we can use, should we choose to respond.

> *But we do not want you to be uninformed, brothers, about those who are asleep, that you may not grieve as others do who have no hope.*
>
> 1 Thessalonians 4:13

Dealing with Loss

Grief is normal and to be expected. Responses to losses vary in nature. There are emotional responses in which the individual may experience depression, loneliness, guilt, and anger. Intellectually, people may experience occasional confusion, problems with concentration, and a loss of mental sharpness. Physical responses might include aches, pains, headaches, and more serious health complaints. Behavioral responses may include unhealthy behaviors and an attitude like life has no more meaning. Social responses can include disruptions in meaningful relationships and marital strife. Spiritual responses can include doubts, crises of faith, and feelings of hopelessness. The severity of the response is related to the emotional stability and personality characteristics of the person as well as the support received from family and friends.[41]

> *As an example of suffering and patience, brothers, take the prophets who spoke in the name of the Lord. Behold, we consider those blessed who remained steadfast. You have heard of the steadfastness of Job, and you have seen the purpose of the Lord, how the Lord is compassionate and merciful.*
>
> James 5:10-11

A Case Study in Loss

Very easily, tragedy can lead to doubt and discouragement when the wise counsel of a friend is lacking. In chapter 3, we saw how Job's friends were initially helpful to him only to become harmful when they began speaking and trying to fix him. In this section, we will look at the example of Job to better understand how to help those who grieve.

> *Now there was a day when his sons and daughters were eating and drinking wine in their oldest brother's house, and there came a messenger to Job and said, "The oxen were plowing and the donkeys feeding beside them."*
>
> Job 1:13-14

Scripture tells us that the day began normally for Job. There was no ominous music in the background or dark clouds in the sky. In many ways, the description reminds me of September 11, 2001. It was a beautiful day, people were heading off to work and then everything suddenly changed.

The first event was the murder of Job's servants (Job 1:15), which was followed by a tragic lightning strike where Job lost more servants as well as livestock and property (Job 1:16). Then Job was robbed again, camels were taken, and more servants were murdered (Job 1:17). But worst of all, Job's children were together in the oldest brother's home (a sign of a close-knit family), a great wind came, the house collapsed, and they were all killed (Job 1:18-19). It really happened to one man in a very brief span of time.

In what may be the oldest book of the Bible, a perfect storm of grief is described. This event involves all of the situations that make one more susceptible to a complicated grief reaction (e. g., sudden death, no opportunity for anticipatory grief, the loss of a child, the loss of adult children, murder, and multiple losses). Job's coping capability was further compromised when he lost his health. No one would want to trade places with Job. Each individual loss he experienced would have been difficult for him to cope.

> *For the thing that I fear comes upon me,*
> *and what I dread befalls me.*
>
> Job 3:25

Complications From Sudden Death

In a brief moment, Job lost what mattered most. This phenomenon is called sudden death. People who lose someone suddenly have some unique difficulties to deal with. In each of the sample case studies at the beginning of the chapter, the characters dealt with sudden death. They were unable to say goodbye to the person they loved. Sometimes people may be haunted by their last interaction with the person if it involved harsh words or an argument.

People die suddenly more often than we think. It seems we often assume we will have a "death bed" period and see death coming in the future. We expect ample opportunity to be able to say goodbye and to tell those we care about how we feel about them. Actually, having an oppor-

Everyone doesn't get this opportunity

Then Jacob called his sons and said, "Gather yourselves together, that I may tell you what shall happen to you in days to come.

When Jacob finished commanding his sons, he drew up his feet into the bed and breathed his last and was gathered to his people.

Genesis 49:1, 33

tunity to say goodbye to a loved one is a blessing. In reality, most people are deprived of that opportunity and long for it after a loved one has died.

Because sudden death is such a shock, many people who lose a loved one may experience feelings of unreality for a long time. This is what the characters in the sample cases might experience leading to feelings of guilt and "What if" statements like, "What if I had not given her a car when she turned 16?" "What if I'd pushed her to go to the doctor?" "What if we'd become more actively involved in their family?" There may also be complications because others are at fault, as in the opening case involving a drunk driver. Sudden death situations can often involve legal, medical, and insurance authorities as well. There may be a sense of regret over unfinished business—plans that never came to fruition, trips that were never taken. There may also be a need to understand why the incident occurred.

> *Then his servants said to him, "What is this thing that you have done? You fasted and wept for the child while he was alive; but when the child died, you arose and ate food."*
>
> 2 Samuel 12:21

Anticipatory Grief

Job did not have the benefit of anticipatory grief. Death is always painful, but when it is without anticipation it is especially hard. Anticipatory grief can help soften the blow. An example is recorded in Scripture as David dealt with the death of his baby. It helps, even if it is ever so little, to be somewhat prepared for what is coming.

It is not surprising to see this verified in many studies. For example, the suddenness in perinatal death was found to lead to a poorer outcome after the death of a baby[42] and the feeling of recovery was found to be diminished when a child was lost suddenly via suicide or tragic accident.[43] Another study indicated that the more parents were able to engage in anticipatory grief before their child died, the more prepared they were for the death. Parents whose child was sick for more than 6 months and less than

95

18 months had better adjustment after the child's death. However, those who had a child that experienced a prolonged illness and a long period of suffering (defined as longer than 18 months) had the most difficult time after their child's death.[44]

> We are afflicted in every way, but not crushed;
> perplexed, but not driven to despair; persecuted,
> but not forsaken; struck down, but not destroyed.
>
> 2 Corinthians 4:8-9

Losses and Their Impact

The Loss of a Child

Not only did Job not have the opportunity for anticipatory grief, but he also lost children. Two of the sample cases involved the loss of children. The loss of a child is widely recognized as the most difficult loss with which to cope. We do not expect to have to bury our children. It is impossible to enumerate or describe what is lost or the pain that is felt when a child dies. In addition, many children die in tragic circumstances.

More than 9,000 children aged 12 and younger die in an automobile accident every year.

The leading cause of death for children ages 1-14 is unintentional accidents. Others die from congenital anomalies and malignant neoplasms.[45] So, in addition to losing a child, the majority of these parents are suffering from the suddenness of accidental death, homicide, or prolonged death and suffering through lengthy illness.

There is a level of pain that never seems to go away after the death of a child. Situations unique to the loss of a child are searching for meaning, guilt, and trouble dealing with social situations like family reunions and holidays with families. There is a crisis of meaning where the way one once existed is changed.[46] For example, many who have lost an only child especially struggle on Father's Day or Mother's Day wondering, "What am I to do now?"

Additionally, many husbands and wives grieve differently. This may have played a role in the tension between Job and his wife that was exhibited when she told him to curse God and die. Some husbands try to take care of their wives, while many wives are concerned when their husbands do not appear to demonstrate feelings of sorrow. In many ways, losing a child is a loss

> Then his wife said to him, "Do you still hold fast your integrity? Curse God and die."
>
> Job 2:9

of the future, which impacts parents and grandparents alike.[47] Grandparents in particular suffer when their grandchildren die.[48]

The loss of an unborn child can also be extremely painful. Studies about the impact of grief indicate that grief reactions of women who miscarry are similar to the experience of people who lose a close relative.[49] Women who have had abortions also appear to have grief reactions, as do people who put their child up for adoption. Infertility can also include mourning for the child that never was. There are few rituals or support for those who are unable to have children. This too is a loss, especially if it comes at the conclusion of multiple tests and failed efforts to have a child.[50]

> And the king was deeply moved and went up to the chamber over the gate and wept. And as he went, he said, "O my son Absalom, my son, my son Absalom! Would I had died instead of you, O Absalom, my son, my son!"
>
> 2 Samuel 18:33

Loss of an Adult Child

When the child that dies is an adult—as was the case with Job's children—coping is even more difficult. In studies comparing parents who lost young children and those who lost an adult son in war, 10 years after the death, the parents of adult children reported more pronounced mourning. The loss of an adult child is incredibly difficult. There are many reasons for this. The loss of one's future must be considered and can include the pain of not having grandchildren or being separated from them. The death of an adult child may also include concern over the loss of a potential caretaker in old age. This bonding opportunity is lost in the death of an adult child.[51] Parents who lose a child tend to measure time in terms of what their child would be doing now. For example, "They'd be graduating from college now."

One difficulty parents face who have lost children is to deal with people who give well-meaning advice and platitudes and who urge them to get on with life. Put yourself in the shoes of people who have suffered loss before you speak to them . . . and then speak carefully.

> And the LORD said, "What have you done? The voice of your brother's blood is crying to me from the ground.
>
> Genesis 4:10

Complications From Murder

Perhaps the most difficult sudden death situation is that of murder. Job lost friends and servants (some say as many as 400). Many of these were murdered. Murder is especially complicated because it is a personal violation. Someone is responsible for the terrible act. Many murders go unsolved, which means the assailant(s) are free and are not required to give an account for their offense. A trial is especially difficult because the details of the death are often described and their character is sometimes assailed. Feelings specific to the loss of a loved one through murder are different from feelings associated with the loss of a loved one from war.[52] Trials are excruciating. If the assailant was arrested immediately after the act, the trial can be around the anniversary of the event. Thoughts or conversations about the murderer intrude into the lives of those grieving over the loss. In some ways, those who are grieving become the murderer's victims themselves.

> And he said, "Naked I came from my mother's womb, and naked shall I return. The Lord gave, and the Lord has taken away; blessed be the name of the Lord."
>
> Job 1:21

Multiple Losses

Grieving can be complicated by multiple losses. Job experienced multiple losses—he lost his children, friends and servants, financial stability, and health. We often find ourselves helping people who have lost a child and sibling or the loss of a spouse and a close friend. The losses have a cumulative effect.

> *And Sarah died at Kiriath-arba (that is, Hebron)*
> *in the land of Canaan, and Abraham went*
> *in to mourn for Sarah and to weep for her.*
> Genesis 23:2

Loss of a Spouse

One of the cases at the beginning of the chapter involved Howard who suddenly lost his wife of 30 years. This kind of loss can be devastating to the person left behind. In each marriage, it is inevitable that one spouse will pass before the other. Obviously, this is a difficult time for the surviving spouse. Initially, the surviving spouse goes through a crisis-loss phase, typically with a lot of support from family and friends. This phase is exacerbated when the death was not anticipated. After this initial phase, the spouse goes through a transition phase of creating a new life. A final phase involves continuation of this new lifestyle. For wives, the pattern of continuation is often that of a single widowed person, but husbands are more likely to remarry.[53]

Men and women who lose a spouse early in life have been found to suffer from more physical complaints than those who do not lose a spouse. There may also be a higher rate of death for older men who lose a spouse.[54]

Consider the extensive losses when someone loses a spouse. In addition to the spouse, the surviving spouse is also losing a friend, handyperson, lover, gardener, companion, partner, bookkeeper, housekeeper, mechanic, cook, organizer, and much more. No one knows better than a widow or widower the value of a marriage partner's life.[55]

> *When Ahithophel saw that his counsel was not followed,*
> *he saddled his donkey and went off home to his own city.*
> *He set his house in order and hanged himself, and he*
> *died and was buried in the tomb of his father.*
>
> 2 Samuel 17:23

Complications From Suicide

Suicide has been described as the most difficult of all losses. Families who lose a loved one through suicide suffer in terrible ways. Parents who lose a child this way often blame one another and may become overprotective of any surviving children. There may also be a conspiracy of silence about the event, and the family can become ostracized from the community. The stigma associated with suicide can separate surviving loved ones from people they need the most.[56]

People who lose a loved one through suicide experience a high degree of confusion and anger. Surviving family and friends wonder, "What kind of relationship did we really have if he would do this?" There is a sense that family members should have anticipated and perhaps even prevented the event, and then there is confusion about what to tell people who inquire about the loved one.[57] Often those who lose family members to suicide do not feel like they really fit in any support groups that may be available in the community.[58]

Some time ago, I was helping a family after their loved one committed suicide. I met a man at the information desk of the hospital who was trying to find the young man who had taken his life. The individual was not listed as a patient at the hospital because he was pronounced dead upon arrival to the hospital. I offered to take the man I met at the information desk to the family. The individual was actually in the intensive care unit on life support because he was an organ donor. As soon as we got on the elevator, the man looked at me and said, "This was an accident, right?" I responded, "No, he did this to himself." The reaction of the man tells you everything you need to know about suicide. As hard as it may be to believe, in some way he would have been relieved if the young man had died in an accident rather than taken his own life.

> *And the sons of the prophets who were in Bethel came out to Elisha and said to him, "Do you know that today the LORD will take away your master from over you?" And he said, "Yes, I know it; keep quiet."*
>
> *The sons of the prophets who were at Jericho drew near to Elisha and said to him, "Do you know that today the LORD will take away your master from over you?" And he answered, "Yes, I know it; keep quiet."*
>
> 2 Kings 2:3, 5

Death of a Sibling or Friend

Elijah did not die: instead God took him to Heaven. Yet, his mentee Elisha could not bear to talk about it. This is the pain of losing a close friend or sibling. Never underestimate the pain felt from this kind of loss. The impact of a sibling's death is nearly universal. Typically, it is the longest relationship people experience. In adulthood, death of a sibling can trigger a personal vulnerability to death in surviving siblings. The death of a sibling who has been a lifelong companion can result in feelings of emptiness and loneliness. A sibling's death can also threaten family unity as the family is never the same again.[59]

> *There is a friend who sticks closer than a brother.*
>
> Proverbs 18:24b

One of the major differences between friends and siblings is that we get to choose our friends. The death of a close friend, especially in adolescence, can cause difficulties as severe as those suffered from the loss of a family member. Often, friends grieve without the social support of family members and may have an especially difficult time.[60]

> *So Satan went out from the presence of the LORD and struck Job with loathsome sores from the sole of his foot to the crown of his head. And he took a piece of broken pottery with which to scrape himself while he sat in the ashes.*
>
> Job 2:7-8

Illness

Interestingly, the last loss Job experienced was that of his health. We do not understand completely why some people combat diseases and survive, while others lose the battle. Sometimes people lose

> A tool you can use to provide more information about grief is the booklet, *First Aid for Your Emotional Hurts: Grief.* Nashville, TN: Randall House.

their loved ones in the struggle against disease. It can seem that death happens right before their eyes. Some are able to combat the disease and survive. Acknowledging that someone we love is dying and transferring from cure to care is a major leap. It is quite a transfer for the person as well, as they are leaving their goals and dreams behind to face other decisions and become focused on the needs of surviving family members.[61]

Chronic illnesses, such as multiple sclerosis, heart disease, cancer, fibromyalgia, and disabilities like blindness bring drastic and often permanent changes to a person's life. Before people are diagnosed with these types of illnesses, they may feel frustrated because others do not believe their complaints about ill health and tell them, instead, that they are imagining the symptoms. Initially, those who are ill are often relieved once a diagnosis is made. However, the difficulties and challenges soon increase as they learn about medical treatments and begin working with physicians and insurance companies.

> *Oh, that I were as in the months of old, as in the days when God watched over me.*
>
> Job 29:2

Inevitably, those who suffer debilitating illness must answer the questions of family and friends. They will also experience the loss of the image of what they are or might have become. We hear this in the voice of Job. Relationships can become strained as family members take on new roles. The only constant is continued change and unpredictability.[62]

> And the LORD said, "You pity the plant, for which you did not labor, nor did you make it grow, which came into being in a night and perished in a night."
>
> Jonah 4:10

Other Losses Hurt as Well

Depending on the person, other types of losses can be devastating as well. For example, the loss of a house, a favorite pet, a rewarding career, or any part of one's health can result in a period of grief.[63] Jonah even mourned the loss of a plant!

Family conflict can result in loss through separation or divorce. Up-rootedness, which is often caused by natural disasters or changes in family structure, can result in grief through broken life dreams, and the loss of dignity or integrity.[64]

> A man's spirit will endure sickness,
> but a crushed spirit who can bear?
>
> Proverbs 18:14

Use Your Tools

You and I do not want those wounded by loss to remain in a state of a crushed spirit. Therefore, we want to utilize the serving gifts that God has granted us and get busy using the tools we have at our disposal. We can begin with prayer.

> Likewise the Spirit helps us in our weakness. For we do not know what to pray for as we ought, but the Spirit himself intercedes for us with groanings too deep for words.
>
> Romans 8:26

Pray

God has given us the tools and techniques we need to serve those who are grieving. As we discussed in Chapter 2, if you are a believer, you have the Holy Spirit with you, so we must pray for those who grieve. When we do not know how to pray for them, the Holy Spirit intercedes for us. We must also remember that it will get better, if not in this life, then in the next one. God will end all mourning (Revelation 21:4).

It is important that we pray for those who grieve as we discussed in Chapter 2, and that they hear us pray for them. Often, the Psalms can be a comfort to them. Take the time to use the psalms to pray with them (so they learn to do this). For example, pray Psalm 147:3, and pray it for Jerry and Susan as mentioned at the beginning of this chapter. Pray like this, "Father, you have told us that you heal those who are brokenhearted and that you bind up their wounds. Father, please heal Jerry and Susan, please bind up the wounds they have as a result of the tragic death of their daughter Samantha. Heal them from the hurts they receive when they are reminded of Samantha's loss when it appears in the news. Help them to know that you have not left them nor forsaken them. In the name of your Son, Jesus Christ, I ask this. Amen."

For all his rules were before me, and his statutes I did not put away from me.
Psalm 18:22

Use the Word

Use the Word to comfort. You may encourage the person you are trying to help to write the verse or verses in a moleskin notebook and to bring them out to read and mediate upon as they go through their day. For example, a good passage to mediate upon is 2 Corinthians 1:3-7.

> *Blessed be the God and Father of our Lord Jesus Christ, the Father of mercies and God of all comfort, who comforts us in all our affliction, so that we may be able to comfort those who are in any affliction, with the comfort with which we ourselves are comforted by God. For as we share abundantly in Christ's sufferings, so through Christ we share abundantly in comfort too. If we are afflicted, it is for your comfort and salvation; and if we are comforted, it is for your comfort, which you experience when you patiently endure the same sufferings that we suffer. Our hope for you is unshaken, for we know that as you share in our sufferings, you will also share in our comfort.*
>
> 2 Corinthians 1:3-7

The passage reminds us that our God comforts us in pain. As one journeys through grief they often wonder, "Will I ever get better?" You will, and this is implied in the passage. There will be a day when you will comfort others as you yourself have been comforted by the Lord.

Another favorite passage of mine is Revelation 21:3-4. This is a promise that there will be a day when the grieving will end. God will wipe all tears away and there will be no more pain. This will end one day.

> *And I heard a loud voice from the throne saying, "Behold, the dwelling place of God is with man. He will dwell with them, and they will be his people, and God himself will be with them as their God. He will wipe away every tear from their eyes, and death shall be no more, neither shall there be mourning, nor crying, nor pain anymore, for the former things have passed away."*
>
> Revelation 21:3-4

Everyone will grieve or be grieved over. Even Jesus experienced grief, as He was "deeply moved" and "greatly troubled" after the passing of Lazarus, a man He was about to raise from the dead. No matter the circumstances, death is a difficult loss. The disciples also grieved.

> *When Jesus saw her weeping, and the Jews who had come with her also weeping, he was deeply moved in his spirit and greatly troubled. And he said, "Where have you laid him?" They said to him, "Lord, come and see." Jesus wept. So the Jews said, "See how he loved him!"*
>
> *Then Jesus, deeply moved again, came to the tomb.*
>
> John 11:33-36, 38a

We must use the Word and our words to knock down the myths people often have about grief. There will be some that will say the Christian should not grieve, since the loved one is in Heaven. Some will make statements indicating one should not mourn, making statements like, "This was part of God's perfect plan."

> *Devout men buried Stephen and made great lamentation over him.*
>
> Acts 8:2

If there ever were a Romans 8:28 moment ("all things work together for good"), it was the aftermath of the death of Stephen. But it did not feel that way. Stephen was murdered (Acts 7:6). Christians scattered (Acts 8:1), wherever Christians went, the gospel went with them (Acts 8:4-8), and eventually the world was turned upside down (Acts 17:6). Yet these devout men "made great lamentation" (Acts 8:2). The grief of Jesus and these devout men show that good Christians grieve even when they know their loved one is in Heaven, and that death was part of God's plan.

> *As I have seen, those who plow iniquity*
> *and sow trouble reap the same.*
>
> Job 4:8

Is Life Fair?

Someone like we see in the case of John, who suddenly lost his wife, may struggle especially if he has lived by an unwritten rule that "life is fair." Some think, if I do what I am supposed to do (tithe, treat people well, follow Christ), then nothing bad will happen to me or the people I love. Sometimes it seems as if some view doing good as a kind of insurance policy against bad things. It's as if we think bad things only happen to bad people and we have control over our lives. After all, the Bible does teach that you reap what you sow. If I do good, then good will come my way and if I do bad, I can expect bad to come. Truly, we will be blessed for following God, but that does not preclude us from experiencing grief and tragedy. There is nothing new about this type of thinking.

In Chapter 2, we mentioned the error of Job's friends when they assumed his trouble was the result of some unconfessed sin he had committed. In other words, Job had brought the death of his own children upon himself.

> *Jesus answered, "It was not that this man sinned, or his parents, but that the works of God might be displayed in him."*
> John 9:3

Hundreds of years later, the disciples of Jesus saw a blind man and they asked Jesus who was responsible for the man's disability. They assumed his problems stemmed from his sin or the sins of his parents. The man had been born blind. Jesus told them their assumption was wrong. The man was not blind because of sin. He was blind so God's works could be displayed through his healing. In other words, as mentioned earlier, bad things happen to bad people. Bad things happen to good people. Bad things can happen to anyone. We want to be prepared to stress this as we deal with those who mourn.

Is This God's Plan?

Sometimes, you will have to help those who are going through grief with their own prayer lives, which can be complicated because of what has happened to them. In a tragic event like that faced by James and Helen, they may struggle when they hear people say things like, "This is part of God's plan" regarding the loss. Those who have experienced loss may begin to wonder, "Is this God's plan?" They may become disillusioned when they do not understand how the tragedy fits into God's plan. One of the myths listed in chapter 2 was that God always makes sense. We should probably rephrase that. Actually, God knows all and does have His own plan and purpose. However, we can become confused if we think we will always understand God's plan in this life.

For example, consider the plight of Abraham. He was called and told to leave his homeland to travel to another country (Genesis 12:1). He was told that God would make a nation out of him even though he and Sarah did not have a child (Genesis 12:2; 15:4; 17:17). He erred by having a child with another woman (Genesis 16). God finally gave Abraham and Sarah a son when he was 100 and Sarah was 90 (Genesis 21). Then God gave the command we read in Genesis 22. Do you think Abraham might have been confused?

What did Abraham think?

After these things God tested Abraham and said to him, "Abraham!" And he said, "Here I am." He said, "Take your son, your only son Isaac, whom you love, and go to the land of Moriah, and offer him there as a burnt offering on one of the mountains of which I shall tell you."

Genesis 22:1-2

We know Abraham thought carefully about this command. He reasoned that if he sacrificed his son as God commanded, God could raise his son from the dead (Hebrews 11:19). Scripture tells us this was a test for Abraham (Genesis 22:1). However, we also know that all of this was part of a bigger plan—a plan Abraham did not understand completely at that time. God stopped Abraham from offering his son as a sacrifice and provided him a ram instead (Genesis 22:13). Abraham named the place "the LORD will provide" (Genesis 22:14). Incidentally, Mount Moriah, where this sacrifice took place, is where Solomon's Temple was placed, and it is adjacent to Golgotha where Jesus was crucified.

As we work with those we are trying to help, we want to encourage them to keep praying. There are many who have gone before them (and will come behind) who have been confused by what has happened in their lives, but it is important to keep talking to the Lord.

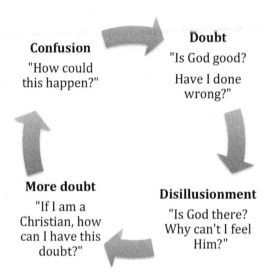

Confusion
"How could
this happen?"

Doubt
"Is God good?
Have I done
wrong?"

More doubt
"If I am a
Christian, how
can I have this
doubt?"

Disillusionment
"Is God there?
Why can't I feel
Him?"

> *"Are you the one who is to come, or shall we look for another."*
> Luke 7:19b

Why Do I Struggle With Doubt?

We can also prepare to help others with our tool, the Word. We may have to keep going back to the Scripture. In the midst of loss, people can begin to have doubts as exhibited in the figure above. Doubt leads to disillusionment and more doubt like, "If I were a good Christian, I would not have doubt." Sometimes, it can be helpful to look at some of the godly people from the past who have experienced loss, and examine how they dealt with those experiences.

The world had come down around John the Baptist. He was a man who loved the freedom of the outdoors (Luke 3), however, he found himself confined to a dark prison dungeon (Matthew 11:2). He thought he had done what God wanted him to do, and yet a wicked man named Herod was enjoying sinful pleasure while a righteous man like John was suffering (Matthew 14:3-4).

John may have sensed his days on earth were numbered (Matthew 14:10). The man who had boldly proclaimed, "Behold the Lamb of God" (John 1:36) now bluntly asked Jesus via a messenger, "Are you the One?" (Matthew 11:3). In other words, "Did I waste my life following something that doesn't exist?" People are vulnerable to discouragement and confusion when dramatic events happen in their world. Notice Jesus' response. "How dare you doubt that I'm the Messiah!" Well, He didn't say that did He? Jesus did not ask, "How could you of all people ask that?" No, Jesus simply reminded John of the truth.

> And he answered them, "Go and tell John what you have seen and heard: the blind receive their sight, the lame walk, lepers are cleansed, and the deaf hear, the dead are raised up, the poor have good news preached to them.
>
> Luke 7:22

Jesus reminded John of the Holy Scriptures such as Isaiah 61 and Malachi 3. Often people say things like, "I should know better. I should not have doubts." But, if a godly man like John the Baptist could doubt, it is understandable that those who suffer loss today will also have doubts. We want to encourage those we help to take doubt directly to Jesus and pray to Him about their concern. We also want to look to Scripture for the answers. That is how Jesus dealt with John's concerns.

> ...blessed is the one who is not offended by me.
>
> Jesus to John the Baptist, Matthew 11:6

Note, the most direct words Jesus gave to John in Matthew 11:6. In other words, you have been called to walk a difficult road, blessed are you as you walk it and are not offended by what I have called you to do.

Also, use the Word to knock down these myths. Myths can mess up people. If our beliefs are incorrect, they can impair thoughts, emotions, and our lives. We can defeat myths by immersing ourselves in Scripture that deals with these kinds of problems. A common myth is that bad things only happen to bad people. We want to quickly knock this myth down when we get a sense that it has emerged.

As we read the Bible, we find examples where those who followed God and were blessed, emerge. However, the example of Job really helps us defeat this myth. We know why bad came his way, God bragged about him (Job 1:8), and his worst nightmare had come true (Job 3:25). Job 1 and 2 make it clear that Job actually suffered these problems because of his faithfulness to God.

> And the Lord said to Satan, "Have you considered my servant Job, that there is none like him on the earth, a blameless and upright man, who fears God and turns away from evil?"
>
> Job 1:8

Sometimes I think we instinctively think, "I hope God does not brag on me" because we do not want any trouble to come upon us. Yet, Job's insistence on continuing to hold onto his integrity was something that pleased the Lord, and led God to brag on him again.

> And the Lord said to Satan, "Have you considered my servant Job, that there is none like him on the earth, a blameless and upright man, who fears God and turns away from evil? He still holds fast his integrity, although you incited me against him to destroy him without reason." Then Satan answered the Lord and said, "Skin for skin! All that a man has he will give for his life."
>
> Job 2:3-4

Ultimately, Job disproved Satan's claim that he was only serving God because God had blessed him. We should all be prepared for the bad that may come our way and use the Word to inform ourselves of how we can honor God by remaining faithful in the midst of great difficulty.

Your Words

Our words are another tool that can help people grieve. Grieving is not sinful, unspiritual, or a sign of weakness. We can use our words to reinforce that people need to grieve in order to move beyond their loss. Although no two people grieve alike, there are some similarities that can help us reach out to those who experience loss. Grief often has a pattern of peaks and valleys. The pain and grief actually intensify in the first three months after the loss and may gradually subside. Birthdays, anniversaries, holidays, and other special days like Mother's and Father's Day are difficult. On the one-year anniversary of the death, the grief often rivals that experienced on the day of the loss. People never really "get over" the loss of a loved one. Eventually, they may experience periods of happiness, but they may be brought to tears in moments after seeing something that triggers a memory, even decades after the loss.

The Rocky Road to Recovery

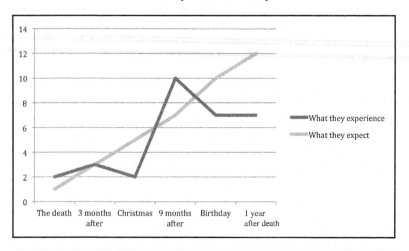

> *Rejoice with those who rejoice, weep with those who weep.*
> Romans 12:15

The Church and Your Relationships

Be ready to use your church and the relationships you have to help in the wake of a loss. People who suffer from loss will certainly be coming your way. In a study of parents who lost a child as a result of a violent death, researchers found that prayer was the most frequent resource used to cope with the loss (75 percent). The next two most frequent resources were church attendance

(50 percent), and family prayer (30 percent). People look to God in the wake of a loss, and if you are His ambassador, that means they will be looking to you.[65] Indeed, I have experienced this as a pastor. Years ago, I was looking at the communication cards completed by visitors after a service. One family wrote, "God sent us to this church." I was taken back a little. I followed up with them later and learned their son had been killed days earlier in an automobile accident. The church was the tool they used to cope with their loss. They seemed comforted by the people of the church and blessed by their involvement. The church was good for them and they were good for the church. Similarly, there is no time a person needs a friend more than in the aftermath of a loss. There is nothing that ties people together more than going through a crisis together. Many grieving people are quick to state, "We do not know where we would be without our church, family, and friends," as they have endured a significant loss.

Using Your Techniques

We can be assured that if we use our techniques well, those we try to help will get better. In fact, most who experience grief emerge as more adaptive, empathetic, and creative with a capacity to overcome.[66] In other words, Romans 8:28 is borne out in the research. Though great pain is experienced, those who grieve develop in ways that are inexplicable.

> **Don't Let This Be You!**
>
> *Reproaches have broken my heart, so that I am in despair. I looked for pity, but there was none, and for comforters, but I found none. They gave me poison for food, and for my thirst they gave me sour wine to drink.*
>
> Psalm 69:20-21

Observe

> It is estimated that as many as 10-20 percent of bereaved individuals experience a syndrome of complicated grief.

We can help with growth by using the tool of observation. After someone has experienced a loss, it is best for us to observe them and pray for them. In particular, we want to determine if they exhibit characteristics of complex bereavement. In the latest edition of the Diagnostic and Statistical Manual of Mental Disorders (DSM-5), persistent complex bereavement disorder (a proposed syndrome) has been estimated to impact 2.4 percent to 4.8 percent of the population.[67] It is good for us to be on the lookout for signs someone is experiencing complex bereavement so we can assist those who experience it. For this to be a concern, the characteristics would persist for at least 12 months and 6 months in a child. The individual would experience a persistent longing for the person who has passed away, intense sorrow and pain in response to the death, and preoccupation with the deceased, and the circumstances of the death.[68]

Note the following table from my booklet on grief,[69] which was adapted from the work of Hillman.[70]

One of the reactions that persists is difficulty accepting the death. In a child, we become concerned when they continue to struggle to comprehend the permanence of the death. There may be numbness over loss, and difficulty with positive reminiscing about the loved one. Other problems include bitterness or anger related to the death as well as blaming oneself for the death. Finally, there may be avoidance of anything that might remind one of the person that died.[71]

Signs Someone Is in Trouble

How do you know if you are at risk for a complicated grief reaction?

_____Cannot speak of the lost loved one without experiencing fresh and intense grief

_____A relatively minor event triggers an intense grief reaction

_____Cannot remove personal possessions of the lost loved one

_____Radical change in lifestyle that excludes family, friends, activities, and places associated with the deceased

_____Long period of depression following the death

_____Suicidal thoughts

_____A desire to reconstruct the events surrounding the death

_____More focus upon the death than upon the complete span of the relationship

_____Continual desire to fix blame and assign responsibility for the death

---

Some of the social problems include a desire to be with the person who has passed away and difficulty trusting others after the death. Feelings of being detached from other people as well as feeling empty are characteristic of complex bereavement. There may also be confusion about one's role in life and a reluctance to plan for the future.[72]

Sometimes, it may seem like those struggling with grief are depressed. There are major differences between grief and clinical depression. The chart below is derived from the DSM-5 footnote that is used to aid clinicians in determining the difference between grief reactions and clinical depression.[73]

Is it Grief or Depression?

Characteristic	*Grief*	*Depression*
Feelings	Emptiness and loss	Inability to experience happiness
Dysphoria	Occurs in waves Tied to thoughts of the deceased	Persistent Not tied to specific thoughts
Thought content	Memories of the deceased	Self-critical
Self-esteem	Preserved	Feelings of worthlessness
Thoughts of death	Associated with wanting to join the decised	Associated with unable to cope with pain of depression

Attend

Go to the person after a loss has been experienced. Job's friends attended to him well (Job 2:11). Jesus requested the disciples attend to Him as He was preparing for death in Gethsemane. If Jesus needed someone to attend to Him, so will those with whom we work.

> **Attend**
>
> *Then he said to them, "My soul is very sorrowful, even to death: remain here, and watch with me."*
>
> Matthew 26:38

Go to the funeral. One of the best ways to help those suffering loss is to attend the funeral of their loved one. On average, Americans attend less than one funeral per year. This is down from 1.5

funerals per year over a decade ago. Many now live into their 40s and 50s before they experience a close personal loss. Today, two-thirds of deaths in the United States happen to people 65 or older. In the early 1900s, most children had been to many funerals by the age of ten. In 1900 over half of all deaths in the United States each year were children 15 and younger. Our grandparents were far more adept at grieving with others than we are.

It is better to go to the house of mourning
than to go to the house of feasting,
for this is the end of all mankind,
and the living will lay it to heart.
Sorrow is better than laughter,
for by sadness of face the heart is made glad.
The heart of the wise is in the house of mourning,
but the heart of fools is in the house of mirth.

Ecclesiastes 7:2-4

Attending the funeral is good for the person we are trying to help, but sometimes they are too dazed to remember anything said. Attending the funeral is good for us as well. It prepares us to help the person by being better informed of the challenges they are facing. It also helps us to prepare for our own death, as the writer of Ecclesiastes states.

Attending continues in the months (and even years) after a loss. We can help by sending a private message, text, or card on the anniversary of a death, or the birthday of the one who has died.

Listen

As we attend, we need not talk but listen, and let the person tell their story. Be willing to let those who have experienced a loss talk about their situation. Be careful not to begin speaking about your own experiences. Be careful not to give advice. Remember, that is where Job's friends went wrong. Do not try to fix them, just listen.

> *Who comforts us in all our affliction, so that we may be able to comfort those who are in any affliction, with the comfort with which we ourselves are comforted by God.*
>
> 2 Corinthians 1:4

Care (Empathize)

Everything that has happened to us can be used by God to prepare you to help others. Think of the losses you have experienced. You usually do not want to launch into your own hurts as someone is telling their story, but thinking of your own difficulties can help you help others. Just trying to have empathy for others as Paul described in 1 Corinthians 9 (see Chapter 3) will help you help others and prevent you from doing harm. Consider our sample cases. Put yourself in the shoes of someone who has lost a child. How would you feel if someone approached you (as discussed in Chapter 3) and quoted Romans 8:28? Instead, we want to look at a person and answer some questions about them.

What unique struggles await them?

What will holidays be like in the future?

What hopes and dreams have they lost?

What might they be asking "What if?" about?

Why might they be feeling guilty?

Thinking through this will help us to be sensitive to their needs and better prepared to help them.

Respond

Answering these questions will also help us respond to them as well. Also, think about what the person might have thought before the loss was experienced. For example, isn't the Christian life to be lived on the mountaintop? Some believe that by becoming a follower of Christ they will be free of major struggles. Today there is a type of prosperity gospel that is very prevalent. It goes like this: follow God and the blessed life will come to you. In essence, one lives on the mountaintop or the victorious life. Too bad it isn't true. We will have times when we are on the mountaintop, but we will all have times when we walk through the valley of the shadow of death. To someone who expects the Christian life to be nothing but bliss, the normal struggles of life can be disconcerting. According to Ecclesiastes 3:1-8, every phase of life has its difficulties.

> *For everything there is a season, and a time for every matter under heaven: a time to weep, and a time to laugh;*
> *a time to mourn, and a time to dance.*
> Ecclesiastes 3:1, 4

Life is a rollercoaster. There are ups and downs; good times and bad. There are weddings and funerals. For every birth, there is a death. Each generation has its particular struggles. In childhood, there are issues with bullies and academic concerns. Then the teenage years bring a whole new set of problems. Acceptance and identity become critically important, and each decision seems to carry an enormous consequence. Young adulthood involves critical decisions about school, career, marriage, and children. It is when we feel we have finally arrived in the "real world," that the struggles of middle adulthood arise. Getting kids through college and losing the stamina one used to possess become the focus. Then there is the process of getting adjusted to an empty home. Adulthood can become complicated by family problems and illnesses. Then one becomes a senior citizen. At that point, we should feel like we have finally arrived. Instead there is a pill to take for every limb, and we face health concerns of every kind. A spouse may be lost as well as siblings. Then there are friends with their own struggles.

In many ways, life is a rollercoaster, but in other ways it is a rose garden too. It will help us to keep a good prospective on life if we remember that where there are roses there are also thorns.

How we deal with those thorns makes a big difference in the kind of life we live.

You may have to instruct and exhort those you help about what the Bible actually says about grief. As you listen and spend time with those who have lost someone, there will be times to respond with instruction. At times, people begin to get impatient as it seems like the grieving process is taking too long. Be prepared to respond when people become confused about their life thinking, "I should be over this by now."

Our culture encourages us to suppress our emotions and to avoid crying over loss. However, there are many incidents in Scripture where people who lost a loved one were moved to tears. Abraham wept over Sarah (Genesis 23:2), Israel grieved for Moses for 30 days (Deuteronomy 34:8). When Jacob died, Joseph threw himself on the body and wept (Genesis 50:1). He lamented loudly. The Egyptians wept for Jacob for 70 days. Joseph was comfortable with tears as you can see in Genesis 42-50.

A Case Study in Grieving

Then he turned away from them and wept. And he returned to them and spoke to them. And he took Simeon from them and bound him before their eyes.

Genesis 42:24

And he lifted up his eyes and saw his brother Benjamin, his mother's son, and said, "Is this your youngest brother, of whom you spoke to me? God be gracious to you, my son!" Then Joseph hurried out, for his compassion grew warm for his brother, and he sought a place to weep. And he entered his chamber and wept there.

Genesis 43:29-30

> *Then Joseph could not control himself before all those who stood by him. He cried, "Make everyone go out from me." So no one stayed with him when Joseph made himself known to his brothers. And he <u>wept aloud</u>, so that the Egyptians heard it, and the household of Pharaoh heard it.*
> Genesis 45:1-2

When Joseph saw his brothers in Egypt and had Simeon bound, it probably reminded Joseph of the time he was bound as he was sold into slavery (Genesis 37; Psalm 105:17-19). For us this would be like seeing an accident on the same road where one's child died in an accident. Weeping in that situation is very normal. Later Joseph wept upon seeing Benjamin, something which reminded him of his mother and life before he was sold into slavery. Judah's pleading (Genesis 44) for Benjamin clearly brought all of the pain and grief of that day to his mind.

> *Then he fell upon his brother Benjamin's neck and <u>wept</u>, and Benjamin wept upon his neck. And he kissed all his brothers and <u>wept</u> upon them. After that his brothers talked with him.*
> Genesis 45:14-15

Joseph even wept when he was reunited, after so many years, with his father.

> *Then Joseph prepared his chariot and went up to meet Israel his father in Goshen. He presented himself to him and fell on his neck and <u>wept</u> on his neck a good while.*
> Genesis 46:29

Again, he wept after his father's death.

> *Then Joseph fell on his father's face and wept over him and kissed him.*
> Genesis 50:1

Clearly, Joseph had learned that tears are a source of healing. What great sorrow would have been bottled up inside of Joseph if he had not found release by weeping. We must help people understand that people who have suffered a loss do not simply "get over it." One last event of weeping is found in Genesis 50 when Joseph's brothers mention selling him into slavery.

> *Then Midianite traders passed by. And they drew Joseph up and lifted him out of the pit, and sold him to the Ishmaelites for twenty shekels of silver. They took Joseph to Egypt.*
> Genesis 37:28
>
> *Say to Joseph, "Please forgive the transgression of your brothers and their sin, because they did evil to you. And now, please forgive the transgression of the servants of the God of your father." Joseph wept when they spoke to him.*
> Genesis 50:17

Decades had passed between the time Joseph's brothers sold him into slavery and the time of the event, yet the mention of it brought him to tears—even though he realized God had used the event for good (Genesis 50:20). For us, this is like seeing the reminder of a loved one who passed years ago and being moved to tears. Though we are in a better place, the pain is still present.

> *Therefore encourage one another with these words.*
> 1 Thessalonians 4:18
>
> *Even in laughter the heart may ache, and the end of joy may be grief.*
> Proverbs 14:13

Stuck in Grief

Sometimes, people who have lost a love one become stuck in grief. We can see this in Jacob's response to the loss of his son Joseph in Genesis 37:34-35. The loss of Joseph was unanticipated and, as we know, unresolved. Some people become stuck in the recovery process simply because they refuse to grieve. They refuse to cry and work through the grieving process to assimilate what has happened to them. Getting stuck in grief can result in physical complaints and problems. Those who are stuck can become conflicted, feeling guilty over moments of happiness or any appearance of living a normal life. People can also become stuck if they displace their grief with anger or bitterness. Be alert to the use of denial, "sanctification" of the person lost, and excessive blaming.

Activities to Help

There are activities that can be used to help people grieve. These are listed below. We need to help those who grieve feel and experience the range of emotions that arise. They need to say good-bye to what was lost, and to invest in other areas of their lives. One sign that people are moving successfully through the grieving process is when they are able to see reminders of the deceased without being completely overwhelmed.[74]

Programmed Cry

One way to help those who are stuck in grief is to encourage them to participate in a programmed cry. The grieving individual selects a time to be alone. During that time, the person listens to music, reads Scripture, and looks through photos or videos of the lost loved one. While doing these things, the person contemplates the meaning of the relationship and what he or she has lost, before ending with a period of prayer for God's comfort.

Memory Book

Another way to move through the grieving process is to develop a memory book of the lost loved one. The cover might be made from the fabric of an article of clothing of the one who has died. The book could include items such as their birth certificate, photographs, menus from favorite restaurants, reminders of vacations taken, favorite passages of Scripture, newspaper announcements, letters sent and received, the funeral program, and sympathy cards.

It might be helpful to include all surviving family members in creating the memory book with different people contributing material based on the various roles of the lost loved one (e.g., husband, father, worker, leisure, church). Every other page can be left blank to allow for future additions or comments. The book can be placed in a special place.[75]

Grief Recovery Letter

You can also help people move through grief by encouraging them to write a completion letter. Have them write the letter in the span of an hour. One of the purposes of the letter is to give them an opportunity to write down any apologies they would like to make to the person who has died. Beyond this, they can write anything they wish they had discussed with the loved one prior to his or her death. They might wish to include statements of forgiveness to the loved one, especially in situations where the loved one was lost as a result of a suicide. The letter can close with a summary and a note of farewell.[76]

Acting

In H. Norman Wright's book *Recovering from the Losses of Life,*[77] he described some good actions to engage in and some to avoid to help others. Wright noted we should not withdraw from them. Sometimes, because we do not know what to say, we avoid the person who has experienced a loss. Job referred to this (Job 30:29). It seems his family and

> I am a brother of jackals and a companion of ostriches.
>
> Job 30:29

friends either hurt him with their words or avoided him, ignoring his pain. We also do not want to compare, evaluate, or judge their response. People respond in different ways, and we should not judge them—we really have no idea how we would respond since every experience is unique. Some look for sympathy for themselves, and begin to talk about their own losses. We want to keep the focus on the loss the person has experienced. Do not patronize or pity the person. People want empathy, not pity. If they want pity, that is actually unhealthy for them. Lastly, do not forget them. People move on with life quickly. Do your best to remember those who have experienced a loss through cards, texts, and visits.

> *Religion that is pure and undefiled before God the Father is this: to visit orphans and widows in their affliction, and to keep oneself unstained from the world.*
> James 1:27

Wright also provided us with some very important tasks in which we should engage. He noted one should discover the grieving person's personal situation and needs. Look for specific actions one can take to help. He also said to decide what you are willing and able to do for them, realizing you cannot nor should you do all things. Remember, you have others who can help and at times, we simply need to get them to the inn. We can help them with practical problems and assist in preventing them from making unwise decisions. Lastly, we must remember, it's not about us, but about the one who is grieving.

Find the Inn

In some situations, especially in complicated grieving circumstances, you will need to help the person find more substantial help. Support groups for the bereaved are a source of additional information and advice. Encourage those who are grieving to find meaningful support through groups such as Alive Alone, (for parents who have lost an only child), Compassionate Friends (for parents who lost a child of any age), Mothers in Sympathy and Support (for parents who have lost an infant), Parents of Murdered Children, and Mothers Against Drunk Driving.

Some of the people you help through the grieving process will need professional helpers. Some would benefit from medications such as antidepressants, especially if they have difficulty sleeping. Some couples might benefit from a professional helper who will guide them as they experience differences in mourning, give them guidance, or help as they navigate the legal system when that is necessary.

Sometimes those who become "stuck" in their grief develop some maladaptive patterns that are difficult to break. The implication is that when people experience especially egregious losses, it might be proactive to seek treatment early. It appears that grief therapy is most effective when someone seeks treatment early in the grieving process. A meta-analysis (a study that examines the finding of numerous studies) indicated that clients who went to grief therapy over 2 years after the death only demonstrated moderate improvement. However, those who sought treatment in a range within three to four months of the death, demonstrated more progress. Those who waited twenty-four months or more demonstrated limited progress.[78]

It is also good to become as informed as you can about the particular loss the one you are trying to help is experiencing. Some sample resources follow as well as material on the book website.

For more information go to www.FirstAidForEmotionalHurts.com.

Resources

Alive Alone
(for parents who have lost their only child or all of their children)
P.O. Box 182
Van Wert, OH 45891
Website: www.alivealone.org
E-mail: alivalon@bright.net

American Association of Suicidology
Central Office
5221 Wisconsin Avenue, NW
Washington, DC 20015
Phone: 202.237.2280
Fax: 202.237.2282
Website: www.suicidology.org

Compassionate Friends
(Grief support for parents and grandparents after the death of a child)
1000 Jorie Blvd., Suite 140
Oak Brook, IL 60523
Phone: 630.990.0010
Fax: 630.990.0246
Toll Free: 1.877.969.0010
Website: www.compassionatefriends.org

National Grief Support Services, Inc.
West Hills, CA 91307
Phone: 818.521.3696
Website: www.griefsupportservices.org

National Hospice & Palliative Care Organization (NHPCO)
1731 King Street
Alexandria, VA 22314
Toll Free: 1.800.658.8898
Phone: 703.837.1500
Fax: 703.837.1233
Website: www.nhpco.org/

National Parents of Murdered Children
4960 Ridge Avenue, Suite # 2
Cincinnati, Ohio 45209
E-mail: natlpomc@pomc.org
Phone: 513.721.5683
Fax: 513.345.4489
Toll Free: 888.818.7662
Website: www.pomc.com

National Sudden Infant Death Resource Center
SIDS Resources, Inc.
1120 South Sixth Street, Suite 100
St. Louis, MO 63104
Phone: 314.241.SIDS (7437)
Fax: 314.588.0850
Toll free: 800.421.3511
Website: www.infantlossresources.org

SHARE
(for parents who have lost a child during pregnancy and still birth)
P.O. Box 9195
Austin, TX 78766
E-mail: info@missfoundation.org
Toll Free: 888.455.MISS (6477)
Website: www.missfoundation.org

WidowNet
(Support for widows and widowers)
Website: www.widownet.org

Books

Dobson, J. (1993). *When God Doesn't Make Sense*. Wheaton, IL: Tyndale House Publishing, Inc.

Lewis, C. S. (1961). *A Grief Observed*. New York, NY: HarperCollins.

Wolfelt, A. D. (2006). *Companioning the Bereaved*. Fort Collins, CO: Companion Press.

Wolflet, A. (1983). *Helping Children Cope with Grief*. New York, NY: Routledge (Taylor & Francis Group).

Worden, J. W. (1996). *Children and Grief: When a Parent Dies*. New York, NY: Guilford Press.

Chapter 5

When Down Gets Dangerous

Elijah was a man with a nature like ours, and he prayed fervently that it might not rain, and for three years and six months it did not rain on the earth.

James 5:17

In this chapter, we will look at depression and examine what to do to help those who struggle with it. Consider the cases that are described below. Do you know anyone with difficulties like these?

Lenny

Lenny's wife left him six months ago. When she left, he began to blame himself and think of himself as a worthless person. Lenny does not feel like doing anything with his six-month old child. He has trouble working. He cannot concentrate. He goes to church and he tries to read his Bible, but he just does not seem to get anything out of it.

Laura

Laura is having a hard time. She increasingly has difficulty going to sleep at night. Her husband says she does not seem to want to do anything with the children. She seems tired all of the time, cannot concentrate, and feels like she is worthless.

Jim

For as long as he can remember, Jim has been depressed. As a teenager growing up, Jim says he "felt down a lot." He says he often lacked the energy to go places. As an adult, he finds it difficult to have the energy to work and often has trouble concentrating.

Joan

Joan often experiences sadness to the point that she does not want to go on with her life. When this period happens, she feels so bad that she cannot get out of bed or do anything. It seems like she is the complete opposite a few months later. She will get to the point where she cannot sleep because she has so many things she wants to do. Often, she does not eat because she cannot seem to slow down.

All of these people suffer from something more than "the blues." Their problems go much further than that. Many of them suffer from depression. All kinds of people become depressed. Seven percent of the population in the United States will struggle with major depressive disorder every year.[79] Our first step is to try to understand what depression really is.

What is depression?

A Clinical Picture

Depression is not just the blues. A person who is clinically depressed or meets the criteria for a major depressive episode must have at least five major symptoms of depression during the same two-week period. One of the symptoms must be depressed mood or a loss of interest or pleasure in almost all activities.[80] In this chapter, we will look at what depression really is and how you can help someone who suffers from depression. Even if you have never suffered from depression, you have seen a picture of it if you have ever read the book of Psalms.

> *I am weary with my moaning; every night I flood my*
> *bed with tears; I drench my couch with my weeping.*
>
> Psalm 6:6

Depressed Mood Most of the Day Nearly Every Day

The most obvious sign of depression is that people constantly feel bad. Often, they cry frequently for no apparent reason. The Psalmist reported this, saying his couch was drenched with his tears. People who struggle with depression report feeling sad and empty. They do not just have a bad day; they have bad weeks and even bad months. The problems persist despite their best efforts to alleviate them. Children may experience this symptom as irritability.

> *Be gracious to me, O Lord, for I am languishing; heal me,*
> *O Lord, for my bones are troubled.*
> *My soul also is greatly troubled. But you, O Lord—how long?*
>
> Psalm 6:2-3

Diminished Interest in Pleasure

Another major symptom is an inhibition to engage in pleasurable activities. People suffering from depression feel their souls are "languishing." Their troubles consume them to a point they cannot really imagine doing anything others would consider fun. They do not experience any pleasure or happiness. This symptom is nearly always present, and it is like an avid golfer who no longer wishes to play golf.

> *My heart is struck down like grass and has withered;*
> *I forget to eat my bread. Because of my loud*
> *groaning my bones cling to my flesh.*
>
> Psalm 102:4-5

Significant Weight Loss or Gain

The weight of those who experience depression is often significantly impacted. They tend to gain or lose up to more than five percent of their weight. Some people lose their appetite and find it hard to eat, reporting they must force themselves to eat. On the other hand, depression can also result in people overeating as a way to address their distress. Some crave certain foods like sweets or carbohydrates. Children who are depressed may fail to make the expected weight gains for their age.[81]

> *I lie awake; I am like a lonely sparrow on the housetop.*
> Psalm 102:7

Insomnia or Hypersomnia

Depression often impacts how well people sleep. In fact, there have been at least nine studies that show insomnia to be a significant risk factor for developing major depression.[82] As the Psalmist said, "I lie awake." Some are not able to fall asleep, while others fall asleep only to awaken and find themselves unable to fall back asleep. Depression may have the opposite effect. Some depressed people have difficulty wakening from sleep. They find themselves oversleeping and sleeping more and more throughout the day.

> Sometimes it is good to complete a 2-week sleep-wake diary that can be shown to a professional.

The most common problem is to wake up in the middle of the night and be unable to fall back asleep or to wake up early and be unable to go back to sleep. Initially, there may be difficulty falling asleep. Often, it is sleep difficulty that leads someone struggling with depression to seek treatment.[83]

> *Tremble, and do not sin;*
> *Meditate in your heart upon your bed, and be still. Selah.*
> Psalm 4:4 NASB

Psychomotor Agitation or Retardation

This symptom is less common and includes agitation as well as the inability to sit still. Some who are depressed may pace or rub their skin or clothes if they become agitated. When retardation is present, the individual may move, speak, and think slower. There may be long pauses before responding to a question or even trouble speaking at all.[84]

> *For my days pass away like smoke,*
> *and my bones burn like a furnace.*
> Psalm 102:3

Fatigue

This is a very common symptom where one wonders, "Where does the day go?" The person may be tired even though they have not engaged in any activity. They feel as if they can hardly get through the day. They have trouble getting up in the morning and experience a general lack of energy. Fatigue can result in a lack of energy to do the basic things throughout a day that most people take for granted like bathing or dressing, which can take more time than usual and be exhausting.[85]

> *And he asked that he might die, saying, "It is enough; now,*
> *O Lord, take away my life, for I am no better than my fathers."*
> 1 Kings 19:4b

Feelings of Worthlessness

A more frightening symptom of depression is when people begin to feel worthless. Elijah made a statement like that, "I'm no better than my fathers." There is a sense that one is not what they ought to be or that one is not worthy of living. This may be an unrealistic negative evaluation where an individual blames themselves for that which they had little or no control. They think often or ruminate upon past failures.[86]

> *These things I remember, as I pour out my soul: how I would go with the throng and lead them in procession to the house of God with glad shouts and songs of praise, a multitude keeping festival.*
>
> Psalm 42:4

Diminished Ability to Think or Concentrate

People who suffer from depression may experience an inability to remember, concentrate, and focus. These symptoms impact the success and effectiveness of people at work or in school. Eventually the impact can be felt in other spheres of their lives and can affect even their relationships with their families.

> *For my soul is full of troubles, and my life draws near to <u>Sheol</u>. I am counted among those who go down to the <u>pit</u>; I am a man who has no strength, like one set loose among the <u>dead</u>, like the <u>slain</u> that lie in the <u>grave</u>, like those whom you remember no more, for they are <u>cut off</u> from your hand. You have put me in the depths of the pit, in the regions dark and deep.*
>
> Psalm 88:3-6

Recurrent Thoughts of Death or Suicide

There may also be frequent thoughts of death. Notice in Psalm 88 how many times the Psalmist refers to death (e.g., Sheol, the pit, the grave). At its worst, depression results in people wishing they could die. A person can become suicidal and even act on that ideation by making a suicide attempt. Later, we will look closer at suicide so we are better prepared to prevent it.

Depression and Related Difficulties

Problem	Prevalence
Major depression	7 percent
Bipolar disorder (I, II & unspecified)	1.8 percent
Cyclothymic disorder	0.4-1 percent
Dysthymia	0.5 percent

Types and Causes of Depression

There is no single type of depression. The most common type of depression is major depression which impacts 7 percent of the population.[87] The type of depression a person has is often related to the particular cause of the depression.

Major Depressive Disorder

In the cases we examined, Laura may be experiencing symptoms of major depressive disorder. This type of depression often has a biological basis. People who suffer from major depression often have issues with the neurotransmitter serotonin. Up to 20-25 percent of people who suffer from medical conditions like diabetes, stroke, and carcinomas experience major depressive disorder. More than 60 percent of those who suffer from an episode of major depression will suffer from a second episode. Those with first-degree biological relatives with the disorder are 1.5-3 times more likely to experience it.[88] Major depressive disorder can appear at any age, but the likelihood of onset increases greatly with puberty. The incidence in the United States peaks in the 20s though it is not unusual for one to have their first episode of depression later in life.[89] Only half of individuals with major depression in the general population and 33 percent of depressed patients in primary care settings receive any treatment for depression.[90]

Bipolar Disorder

The problems experienced by Joan would best be described as bipolar disorder. Bipolar disoder can be very debilitating. Those who

---

A Difficult Diagnosis

15 percent of individuals with bipolar disorder also have an eating disorder with binge eating disorder being the most common.

Half of the people who struggle with bipolar disorder also abuse illicit substances, which greatly complicates their treatment.

Anxiety disorders are commonly comorbid with bipolar disorders. Up to one-third of patients with bipolar disorder are diagnosed with comorbid anxiety disorders.

---

struggle with bipolar disorder often struggle with other problems like eating disorders,[91] substance abuse problems,[92] and anxiety.[93]

This disorder can be quite confusing to those around the person who suffers with this problem. At one point, the person may be about as low as he can go with symptoms of depression. At a later point, he finds himself "flying high." Some refer to this problem as manic-depression. The person can be extremely depressed and over a period of weeks or months followed by a period of mania, at which point he describes himself as feeling great.

During the manic period, the person may have inflated self-esteem, a decreased need for sleep, pressure to keep talking, racing thoughts, distractibility, significant goal directed activity, and excessive involvement in pleasurable activities.[94] Some of these activities may be positive in nature even though they may not be well planned or organized. However, they may also engage in some very dangerous behaviors during this period (e.g., fast driving). There can also be excessive spending and sexual hyperactivity.

Bipolar disorder seems to be caused by a problem with the neurotransmitter dopamine. Many people who suffer from bipolar disorder have a family history of bipolar or schizophrenia or some other psychiatric disorder in their background. Bipolar disorder is often treated with a mood stabilizer medication. Individuals who suffer from bipolar disorder can face dire consequences for failing to take their medication. Although Saul was struck with depression because of his disobedience, his account recorded in the Bible sounds like a description of bipolar disorder.

The average age at onset of bipolar disorder is about age 25, and symptoms typically start between ages 15 and 30 years.[95] Mania and hypomania are often forgotten by patients or are not perceived as problematic.[96] How-

> On average bipolar patients will experience 4 depressive episodes for every 1 manic episode, and the depressive episodes will last longer than the manic episodes.

ever, one is more likely to experience periods of depression than mania as they struggle with bipolar disorder.[97]

The lifetime risk of suicide in individuals with bipolar disorder is 15 times that of the general population.[98] Anywhere from 10-15 percent of those people who suffer from bipolar disorder commit suicide. Children who experience bipolar disorder tend to have difficulty with school attendance and their grades. Thirty percent of adults tend to suffer from occupational problems and have a high divorce rate.[99]

Persistent Depressive-Disorder (Dysthymia)

The disorder that plagued Jim is called dysthymia. Dysthymia is a type of depression that lasts for at least two years in adults and at least one year in children. The symptoms tend to be the milder symptoms of depression like poor appetite or overeating, insomnia or hypersomnia, low energy or fatigue, low self-esteem, poor concentration, and feelings of helplessness. The more dangerous symptoms like feelings of worthlessness and preoccupation with death are usually absent. It would be very difficult for a person to experience the harshest symptoms for a two-year period and survive. A person who suffers from dysthymia would likely require treatment with psychotropic medication in addition to other types of interventions.

Right after I finished my master's degree, I began working on getting licensed as a counselor. I had to videotape a session each week for my supervisor. One of my teenage clients agreed to let me tape a session with him because he could watch the tape with me. That gave me a chance to critique my own skills and he got a chance to see himself on videotape. He was excited, and even dressed up for the session. I taped it and took it to my supervisor. As soon as the tape began rolling, she looked at him and said, "Wow, now that guy is depressed!" He had dysthymia, even on his best day he appeared depressed.

Cyclothymic Disorder

Similarly, when one has numerous symptoms for at least 2 years (1 year in children and adolescents), they can meet the criteria for cyclothymic disorder. This problem usually begins in adolescence or early adult life. Individuals with this condition also frequently struggle with substance abuse problems and sleep difficulties.[100]

Situational Factors

Health problems can make us very susceptible to depression as can be seen in the chart below, which is also in the *First Aid for Your Emotional Hurts: Depression* booklet.[101]

Medical Illness and Susceptibility to Depression	
Illness or Medical Condition	*Prevalence of Depression*
Stroke	10-27%
Alzheimer's Disease	Unclear
Parkinson's Disease	50%
Diabetes	15%
Coronary Heart Disease	40-65%
Cancer	25%
Chronic Fatigue Syndrome	46-75%
Fibromyalgia	40%

There are many health problems that make one more susceptible to depression.[102] Life events can lead to depression. For example, in one study one third of the women who received an abnormal mammogram reported symptoms of depression in the month following the report.[103] In the case of Lenny, his depression was triggered by an event. Although he may have had a natural predisposition toward depression, the stress of his wife leaving would certainly exasperate his situation. He might also meet the criteria for adjustment disorder with depressed mood, especially if his depression subsides in the wake of his wife leaving him. The description of Elijah in 1 Kings 19 sounds like an individual who is suffering from major depression. The person who prayed some of the Psalms like Psalm 88 also seems to suffer from major depression.

In my booklet on depression, we tried to show how depression or mania can impact all areas of a person's life, the way they feel, think, behave, function, and relate to others.[104]

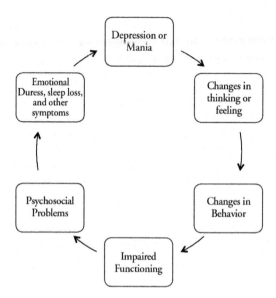

A Case Study of Depression

How do situations lead to depression? Perhaps we can get an idea by examining the life of Elijah. Imagine going from what was arguably the best day of your life to your worst in just twenty-four hours. That is what happened to Elijah. One day he was praying to God and fire was coming down from Heaven (1 Kings 18:38). The next he was running for his life (1 Kings 19:3). His experience helps us see how events can trigger major depression.

The Event

Then Jezebel sent a messenger to Elijah, saying,
"So may the gods do to me and more also, if I do not make
your life as the life of one of them by this time tomorrow."

1 Kings 19:2

What Happened to Elijah?

Elijah got scared. Fear can shake up a person. A lump in a breast, hearing about layoffs, and many other events can send someone spiraling down into depression. Jezebel sent a message to Elijah threatening his life. Those words sent fear down Elijah's spine. It's the kind of fear you feel when you are in a parking garage late at night and you hear footsteps behind you. It is the fear you experience when your child is late coming home at night and you get a call from someone identifying themselves as a trauma doctor at your local hospital. Elijah's fear was real.

But this was Elijah. Why would a prophet like Elijah get so scared? Why did this impact him so adversely? He had seen God bring a drought and miraculously meet his needs throughout the drought (1 Kings 17:6). He had seen God miraculously provide for a widow and her son (1 Kings 17:16). He had seen God miraculously raise that son from the dead (1 Kings 17:23). He had seen God miraculously defeat the prophets of Baal (1 Kings 18:40), but when Jezebel threatened him, he ran for his life.

The Reaction

Then he was afraid, and he arose and ran for his life and came to Beersheba, which belongs to Judah, and left his servant there. But he himself went a day's journey into the wilderness and came and sat down under a broom tree. And he asked that he might die, saying, "It is enough; now, O Lord, take away my life, for I am no better than my fathers."

1 Kings 19:3-4

Elijah responded by running 90 miles. This was like running more than three Boston Marathon's in one day! Elijah exasperated his problems by becoming exhausted and leaving his servant behind. When people become tired, their thinking can become clouded and their judgment impaired. They can begin to see everything in a negative light. Elijah ate some food, but then he went on another trip. He traveled down to Horeb and didn't eat for 40 days or 40 nights.

If you have ever fasted, you have an idea of what Elijah experienced. During a fast, people often experience fatigue, weakness, and intense headaches. Can you imagine how you would feel after fasting for 40 days? Then Elijah went into a cave.

Going into a cave was one of the worst things Elijah could do. It compounded the problem. When Elijah closed himself off from the world. He just made his depression worse. He was not realistic.

Using Your Tools

How would you help Elijah? How would you help depressed people like him that you encounter today? There is hope for those who struggle with depression. In a large Canadian study of individuals who had a history of depression, about two in five adults completely recovered. However, those who recovered were more likely to have good social support, good physical health, exercise regularly, and use spirituality to cope.[105]

> *How long, O LORD? Will you forget me forever?*
> *How long will you hide your face from me?*
> Psalm 13:1

Prayer

Often people who are depressed experience prayer problems with which we need to help them. For example, Jim who was described at the beginning of the chapter, has been dealing with depression for as long as he can remember. In his youth, he became a follower of Christ. He is active in his church and studies his Bible, yet his depression remains. He has prayed for God to remove the problem from his life more times than he can count. Does he lack faith? If you were helping him, you might say something like, "As difficult as this must be, I know God is hearing you and will help you." We cannot judge whether a person is praying properly or possesses the requisite level of faith. It is important to pray for the one who is depressed and to affirm the promises contained in the Bible that God listens to us, and He answers our prayers.

The Word and Your Word

Years ago, when I was working as a Clinical Therapist, I listened to a young lady as she described her symptoms to me. She was having trouble sleeping, eating, and concentrating, as well as other symptoms of depression. As I pointed this out to her she responded, "Oh no, I can't be depressed!" "You can't?" I asked, "Yes," she continued, "Christians don't get depressed?" I said, "Oh, really." She went on to indicate that a family member of hers, that was a "solid Christian," told her that "real Christians don't get depressed." This family member, and the young lady with whom I was working seemed ignorant about what the Bible says about godly people from the past and depression.

Sometimes people believe that a "real" Christian does not get depressed. Consider the statements below by some Old Testament prophets.

Do Believers Get Depressed?

Therefore now, O Lord, please take my life
from me, for it is better for me to die than to live.

Jonah 4:3, Jonah

Cursed be the day
on which I was born!
The day when my mother bore me,
let it not be blessed!

Jeremiah 20:14, Jeremiah

And he prayed that he might die, and said, "It is enough!
Now, Lord, take my life, for I am no better than my fathers!"

1 Kings 19:4b (NKJV), Elijah

Was Jonah depressed, even suicidal? When he asked to be thrown overboard during a storm (Jonah 1:12), it was akin to trying to open the exit window on an aloft airplane—there was not going to be a good outcome. But you might say, he had brought it all upon himself, which would be true. Jeremiah indicated he wished he had not been born. If you make that kind of statement in front of health care professionals today, you may be spending at least one night in the hospital to make sure you are okay. Jeremiah is clearly discouraged. However, it is clear that Jeremiah endured an especially difficult time in the ministry. Elijah is a classic case. He says he has quit, wants to die, and is "no better than his fathers." It sounds like something major is going on underneath his concerns. James reminded us that Elijah had a "nature like ours" (James 5:17). In other words, if Elijah could become depressed not to mention Jonah, Jeremiah, and the Psalmist so can many others. You can use the Word, and your own words to refute some of the myths about depression.

Those who struggle with depression often feel defective, hopeless, abandoned, and guilty. Attack these thoughts with Scripture. For example, use Psalm 139:13-14 to attack thoughts about being defective. Second Corinthians 4:17 can be helpful with dealing with hopelessness, and Hebrews 13:5 helps as one deals with abandonment. For those who feel guilt, remind the person to pray passages like 1 John 1:9 and Romans 10:9-10, 13.

> *Because your steadfast love is better than life,*
> *my lips will praise you.*
> *So I will bless you as long as I live;*
> *In your name I will lift up my hands.*
> Psalm 63:3-4

You can also use the Word to comfort and help those who struggle with depression. Consider Psalm 63. The Psalmist writes about how they seek and thirst for the Lord (Psalm 63:1). He also notes the wonder of the steadfast love of God (Psalm 63:3). Later, we will look at the impact of rumination on those who struggle with depression. Meditation is the opposite of rumination, and it can be very helpful in defeating depression.

This is a good passage to memorize and read throughout the day. You can encourage those you try to help to read a Scripture like this when you get up in the morning and before you go to bed at night.

> *When I remember you upon my bed, and*
> *mediate on you in the watches of the night.*
> Psalm 63:6

There is research that indicates that as one sleeps at night, their brain ponders whatever they were exposed to in the hour or two before they went to bed.

> *Therefore, confess your sins to one another and pray for*
> *one another, that you may be healed. The prayer of a*
> *righteous person has great power as it is working.*
> James 5:16

The Church and Relationships

The church, a friend, family member, or co-worker can do a lot personally to help someone that is depressed. This statement is based in strong research. For example, in a study that followed a large sample of individuals (2,676) for 29 years, it was found that those who were depressed at the beginning of the study who attended church at least weekly were 2.3 times less likely to be depressed at follow-up.[106] Another study examined patients who were struggling with medical problems (e.g., heart failure) who were also depressed. The depression remitted significantly faster for those who attended services and participated in group related activities.[107] Church attendance has also been found to significantly reduce depression and the risk of suicide.[108]

> In one study that compared people who had committed suicide to those who had died of natural causes. Those who committed suicide were four times more likely to have never participated in religious activities.

Why does church attendance help with depression? In addition to dispelling myths about depression, church attendance can combat faulty thinking, and provide critical social support. In fact, we want to do our best to accomplish this in our church activities and relationships. For example, when someone claims that no one cares about him or her, we can ask him or her to explain the statement. This is similar to God's repeated questions to Elijah ("Elijah, what are you doing here?"). We will talk more about this later. We can help by just being someone to talk to, which can decrease feelings of isolation, as Elisha must have done for Elijah.

Use Your Techniques

Observe

As you interact with others, be on the lookout for those who struggle with depression. Often, we may miss them because we do not see them. They often withdraw so we do not have the same access to them that we had prior to the episode of depression. When we are with them, we may notice they seem downcast or we may observe changes in their behavior where they may be more lethargic.

Our worst fear for depressed people is that they could become so depressed they might try to take their own lives. If you come into contact with individuals who express the desire to commit suicide, it is critical that you take direct action and get help from the appropriate professionals and authorities immediately. How do you know if a person is in danger?

Every year on average 44,193 people take their lives in the United States (an average of 121 a day).

Suicide 101

Prepare yourself to prevent suicide. It is believed that 121 people take their lives every day. Twenty-two veterans take their lives every day,[109] and suicide is the third leading cause of adolescent deaths in the United States.[110] Suicide can be an impulsive act, but it seems that most of the time

Risk Factors for Suicide

Recent trauma
Specific suicide plan
Preoccupation with earlier abuse
Family destabilization
Giving away prized possessions
Radical change in behavior
Isolating from others
Reading material about methods to commit suicide
References to what life will be like after death
Demeaning statements (e.g., "I am no good.")
Making arrangement for death, like making a will

people have thought it through and communicated their difficulties to others. Anytime you hear someone begin to talk of harming themselves, you must take them seriously. Some fear that by talking to someone about suicide that they are putting the thought of suicide in their mind. However, talking to someone about suicide shows that you are taking their pain seriously and allows steps to be taken to help the person. Women attempt suicide twice as often as men, but men commit suicide twice as often as women because they use more lethal means. Often suicidal people are ambivalent. The suicidal person may not decide until the last minute whether they will go through with the act. Often, they hope others will find them after making a suicide attempt. Note that the risk of suicide is greatest when depression lifts. It may be that the person now has energy to follow through with their suicide plan once they are less depressed.

There are many risk factors that can lead to a person trying to take their life.[111] It is important to be aware of their situation and to take steps to intervene. A depressed person who is suicidal should be taken to a hospital and placed under the care of a primary care provider. If a suicidal person refuses to go to a hospital, you need to enlist the help of law enforcement officials to get the type of help he or she needs.

The research indicates that people who are likely to continue to try to kill themselves tend to have certain characteristics in common. Multiple suicide attempters are more likely than single suicide attempters to report childhood emotional abuse, family mental illness, or substance abuse. They are also more likely to have family members who had attempted suicide. Not surprisingly, they have more frequent and intense suicidal ideation.[112]

Those who attempt suicide and wish they had died are more likely to commit suicide in the future. An examination of individuals who had engaged in a suicide attempt indicated that 40 percent of those who wished they had died eventually did kill themselves. In other words, a person's response to a failed suicide attempt is a key predictor as to whether they will eventually kill themselves.[113]

I once worked with a young man who had attempted suicide many times. Some of his attempts had been superficial. Finally, he horded the medication of many of the students at his correctional institution and took them all at once. I asked him about this since he conveyed his desire to live to me after the incident. He said, "You don't understand. Everyone knew I had those pills. I wanted to live, but I didn't see any way out." That's typical of many who are suicidal. They do not see any other way out of their inner turmoil. We have to help them find a different way out.

How did God deal with Elijah?

There he came to a cave and lodged in it. And behold, the word of the LORD came to him, and he said to him,
"What are you doing here, Elijah?"
1 Kings 19:9

Attend

There is no doubt about it, usually someone struggling with depression would not be considered the life of the party. I am, of course, excluding the person in the manic phase of bipolar disorder. It is often difficult to attend to someone who is struggling with depression. Therefore, we must go out of our way to attend to them. We can learn much from the Lord's response to Elijah. The first thing we see God doing is responding. "The Lord came to him," which is what we are called to do as well.

Listen

God used an opened ended question, "What are you doing here?" to get Elijah talking. Notice that God did not tell Elijah to "buck up" or "be a man." God simply got Elijah talking. If God had made statements to Elijah, he may not have listened. By asking a question that required Elijah to think, it required him to use his brain. God was already intervening by asking Elijah an open-ended question.

God's questioning of Elijah showed that the depressed prophet was ruminating. Note how similar verses 10 and 14 are.

Rumination

He said, "I have been very jealous for the LORD, the God of hosts. For the people of Israel have forsaken your covenant, thrown down your altars, and killed your prophets with the sword, and I, even I only, am left, and they seek my life, to take it away."

1 Kings 19:10

He said, "I have been very jealous for the LORD, the God of hosts. For the people of Israel have forsaken your covenant, thrown down your altars, and killed your prophets with the sword, and I, even I only, am left, and they seek my life, to take it away."

1 Kings 19:14

The term ruminate comes from the Latin word for "chewing the cud." When people ruminate on an issue, they mull it at length. Ruminating about problems can fuel depression. It can also impair thinking and problem solving and drive away people who might be supportive to the individual. Elijah could not stop thinking about the perceived injustice he had received.

Ruminating → Negative Beliefs → Depression

You might say that rumination is a root of depression.[114] Longitudinal studies have indicated numerous negative effects of rumination. For example, a study that examined residents who experienced the 1989 San Francisco earthquake found that those who ruminated about the experience were more likely to have symptoms of depression and post-traumatic stress disorder. Another study examined people who lost a family member due to terminal illness. Those who ruminated tended to become depressed more often and remain depressed for long periods. Another study indicated that people who ruminated over their problems were four times more likely to develop major depression than those who did not ruminate.[115]

Why is rumination so debilitating? Ruminators express little confidence in their solutions. The rumination tends to induce immobilization, which makes it hard for the person to move on. Elijah was immobilized. He had separated from others and was hiding in a cave, where his symptoms persisted. Ruminators tend to hear people tell them to "buck up and get on with your life" and "Pull yourself together." As a result, they become hostile and withdraw from others. They then wonder, "Why is everyone abandoning me? Why are they being so critical of me?"

Caring

Often, we can become frustrated as we listen to those who are depressed. It will help us to listen when we have empathy for them. Consider how you might feel if you were trying to help Elijah. How could someone who had seen God move in such a way become so frightened?

Why was Jezebel so frightening?

Has it not been told my lord what I did when Jezebel killed the prophets of the LORD, how I hid a hundred men of the LORD's prophets by fifties in a cave and fed them with bread and water?

1 Kings 18:13

Jezebel's actions had led to the murder of Naboth to take his vineyard. She'd killed many prophets as well.

When Jehu came to Jezreel, Jezebel heard of it. And she painted her eyes and adorned her head and looked out of the window. And as Jehu entered the gate, she said, "Is it peace, you Zimri, murderer of your master?"

2 Kings 9:30-31

When death approached for Jezebel, she taunted the man who had her life in his hands. She was mean and threatening and unafraid of anyone.

It's one thing to be threatened by someone, but it is quite another thing to be threatened by a killer. How would you feel if Charles Manson threatened to kill you? Jezebel was mean and she was not confined to a maximum-security prison. In later years, Jehu approached Jezebel to take her life. Did she repent or seek lenience? No! She called him Zimri (2 Kings 9:31). Zimri was a man who was known as a traitor. Years earlier he had killed a king and took over his reign, but it only lasted for seven days (1 Kings 16:15). Jezebel looked death in the face and insulted the executioner. So, Elijah had good reason to be scared. She was one mean lady. If one thinks about what Elijah was up against, it is easier to have empathy for him. Similarly, some we will try to help have experienced all kinds of hardships associated with depression and other areas of their lives. If we can think about that, it will help us to empathize with them and help them.

Respond

We can help people by asking questions like "What are you saying to yourself? How are feeling? What are you thinking? Is it true?" As we listen to people, we learn about their thoughts and their needs. God allowed Elijah to speak for what seemed like a long time. When God responded, He was helpful. Listen for cognitive distortions that are often present when someone struggles with depression.

Elijah responded irrationally and made his problems sound bigger than they were. Often, people who experience depression begin to think thoughts like, "I'm alone" or "I'm the only one trying here." They "catastrophize" their situation. These kinds of cognitive distortions can be extremely debilitating.[116]

Examples of Cognitive Distortions

All or nothing thinking: For example, a performance is either perfect or a failure.
Mental Filter: Dwelling on one negative detail exclusively.
Jumping to Conclusions: Interpreting something
negatively without having all of the facts.
Catastrophizing: Exaggerating the importance of something.

As we listen, we can make paraphrase responses like, "All alone?" and probe further. The Lord listened to the cognitive distortions of Elijah. Elijah said he was the only one that served God, though he had interacted with Obadiah (1 Kings 18:17), a godly man (1 Kings 18:3) who had saved the lives of 100 prophets (1 Kings 18:4).

The Truth

Yet I will leave seven thousand in Israel, all the knees that have not bowed to Baal, and every mouth that has not kissed him."

1 Kings 19:18

God confronted that distortion with truth. We too want to gently knock down cognitive distortions as we respond to others.

The Regimen

And he lay down and slept under a broom tree. And behold, an angel touched him and said to him, "Arise and eat." And he looked, and behold, there was at his head a cake baked on hot stones and a jar of water. And he ate and drank and lay down again.

1 Kings 19:5-6

Act

How does one overcome rumination? People need to be distracted by taking small actions toward solving their problems. God took action. God told Elijah to eat. Elijah might not have felt like it, but he ate. When you are helping people who are depressed, it is wise to help them do the things they need to do. They need to eat even if they don't feel like it. They need to get out of bed in the morning and begin moving around even if it is hard. All Elijah wanted to do was sleep, but God made him get up and eat.

> See the process in *First Aid for Your Emotional Hurts: Depression.*

The tendency is for someone to become depressed, then feel fatigue, which leads them to be inactive. The result can be a feeling of hopelessness, and then more depression and the cycle continues.[117]

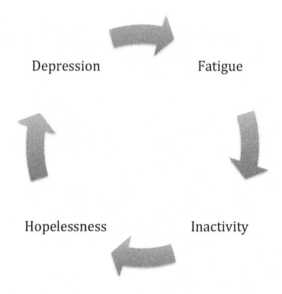

Depression

Fatigue

Hopelessness

Inactivity

The Lord intervened by putting Elijah on a regimen where he would get up at a certain time, eat, and go to bed. You can help someone by helping them to get on a regimen where they increase their activity. You might do this by taking them walking, to a sporting event, to church, or anything that gets them active.

One of the best things someone who is depressed can do is to exercise. In fact, some research has indicated that exercise is more effective than antidepressant medication. The types of activities that seem to be the most beneficial are activities like biking and swimming. You could offer to do these activities with someone who is depressed. When individuals engage in these types of exercises, they should concentrate on their breathing to calm their nervous system and deliver the maximum amount of oxygen to their body. For maximum benefits, a person should exercise 150 minutes a week (30 minutes a day, five days a week). To help someone assess the effectiveness of their exercise, ask them to rate how they feel on a scale of 1 to 10 before they begin. Then ask them to rate how they feel again after exercising. Exercising can also be an effective tool in breaking the cycle of rumination[118] and increasing energy and mood.

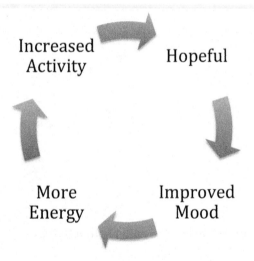

Increased Activity → Hopeful → Improved Mood → More Energy → Increased Activity

It is also important to note that when people are depressed, they have peaks and valleys through the day. On average, the peak in positive mood occurs nearly 2 hours later for depressed individuals (5:22 p.m.) than for healthy individuals (3:35 p.m.). On the other hand, negative feelings peak in the late morning, with these feelings decreasing steadily throughout the day. Why is this helpful to know? It is important for depressed people to be aware of their mood fluctuations to keep from catastrophizing during the negative feelings and to take advantage of the time of elevated mood.[119]

Formerly depressed individuals are vulnerable to changes in mood and may have a diminished ability to engage in problem-solving skills. One should pay close attention to someone who has been suicidal in the past. Should that person have a mood disturbance, their problem solving skills might be diminished placing them at greater risk.

In the example of Elijah, he ate, drank, and rested. God's plan included rest and rejuvenation for him. The process sounds like some of the treatment very depressed people get when they enter a hospital. They get rest, appropriate medication, a good diet, and are nursed back to a state of equilibrium.

Each step of action God gave dealt with Elijah's depression. Hazael would defeat Ahab. Jehu would execute Jezebel, and Elisha would take over Elijah's responsibilities. God made Elijah get busy with some goal-directed problem-solving activities. God also gave Elijah a friend in Elisha, who would lend support and encouragement. Notice that God's directions came without argument and it would be decades before they would be completed.

The Plan

And the LORD said to him, "Go, return on your way to the wilderness of Damascus. And when you arrive, you shall anoint Hazael to be king over Syria. And Jehu the son of Nimshi you shall anoint to be king over Israel, and Elisha the son of Shaphat of Abel-meholah you shall anoint to be prophet in your place. And the one who escapes from the sword of Hazael shall Jehu put to death, and the one who escapes from the sword of Jehu shall Elisha put to death.

1 Kings 19:15-17

When we work with someone, walking them through problem-solving steps to address their issues, we are following the plan God used with Elijah. Step by step, the problem is addressed.

As we examine the case of Elijah and his depression, we can see that God used many of the techniques described in chapter 3. One way we may help people is by helping them find a professional who can more effectively treat depression. Out of those who report being depressed. It is believed that only 30 percent will seek treatment, and despite what is often perceived, less than 20 percent will be treated with antidepressant medication.[120]

The kind of professional needed will be determined by the type of depression that individual experiences and its severity. As described in chapter 3, there are a myriad of professionals that can help with this process.

Since the etiology of many types of depression is a particular disease or illness, a health care professional is a good place to start. People who are dangerously depressed may need to be hospitalized. Others may be capable of being treated as an outpatient, but they might require medication. For people who struggle with persistent depression, a professional counselor or psychologist would also be necessary.

Cognitive behavioral interventions seem to be particularly effective. Cognitive therapy has been found to significantly reduce the relapse of depression for individuals who have experienced five or more episodes of depression. Cognitive therapy has also been found to be an effective prevention approach for less depressed individuals.[121]

Some depression will need to be treated with medication. It may help you to be acquainted with different types of medications that are used. The oldest type of antidepressants are tricyclics (TCA). These have been used for more than fifty years, and they are effective. Depression is believed to result from a depletion of a neurotransmitter (serotonin, dopamine, or norepinephrine). TCAs address this problem. However, they can have a negative impact on the body. Common side effects for these medications include sedation, weight gain, difficulty urinating, dizziness, dry mouth, constipation, sexual dysfunction, and blurred vision. These medications are usually considered unsafe for children and adolescents. They are usually avoided with suicidal individuals since they can cause death if overdosed.[122] The elderly and those with serious health problems may also avoid them.

A newer type of antidepressant that was introduced in the late 1980s is called selective serotonin reuptake inhibitors (SSRIs). As the name suggests, these medications are believed to block the reuptake of serotonin, thereby eliminating the problem of serotonin depletion. These medications appear to be quite effective. The side effects of SSRIs are significantly less drastic than the tricyclics. However, there are still some side effects that include headache, nausea, diarrhea, dry mouth, anorexia, weight gain, restlessness, insomnia, tremor, sweating, yawning, dizziness, and inhibited sexual desire.[123]

Typically Used Tricyclic Antidepressant Medications		
Trade Name	*Generic Name*	*Level of Sedation*
Adapin	doxepin	Heavy
Anafranil	clomipramine	Heavy
Asendin	amoxapine	Moderate-heavy
Elavil	amitriptyline	Heavy
Ludiomil	maprotiline	Moderate
Norpramin	desipramine	Light
Pamelor	nortriptyline	Moderate-heavy
Sinequan	doxepin	Heavy
Surmontil	trimipramine	Moderate
Tofranil	imipramine	Light-moderate
Vivactil	protriptyline	Light

Typically Used Selective Serotonin Reuptake Inhibitors		
Trade Name	*Generic Name*	*Level of Sedation*
Celexa	citalopram	Light
Lexapro	escitalopram	None
Luvox	fluvoxamine	Light
Paxil	paroxetine	Moderate-heavy
Prozac	fluoxetine	None
Zoloft	sertraline	None

Other medications that have been of help are serotonin-norepinephrine reuptake inhibitors. Also, trazodone is often used, which is an antidepressant of the serotonin antagonist and reuptake inhibitor (SARI) class. This medication helps with depression and anxiety.

Typically Used Serotonin-Norepinephrine Reuptake Inhibitors	
Trade Name	*Generic Name*
Pristiq	desvenlafaxine
Cymbalta	duloxetine
Fetzima	levomilnacipran
Effexor XR	venlafaxine

Another classification of antidepressants is monamine oxidase inhibitors (MAOIs). MAOIs include marplan, nardil, and parnate. These medications inhibit the enzyme that breaks down neurotransmitters and makes them ineffective. The side effects are similar to those of TCAs. People who take them must adhere to important diet regulations. When people do not respond well to other medications, MAOIs often work as a last resort.[124] These are rarely used and there can be withdrawal symptoms if one stops using these suddenly.

Sometimes, no medication is particularly effective in cases of severe depression. If the individual is suicidal, they may be referred for electroconvulsive therapy. The patient is given anesthesia and electrodes are placed on the scalp. Electricity is administered resulting in a seizure. Many patients will receive three treatments per week for up to four weeks or until they improve. The main side effect is memory loss.[125] Many clinicians believe the risks are preferable to many of the medications used for depression.[126]

Some individuals who suffer from depression will have bipolar disorder. Typically, this disorder is treated with lithium or some type of anticonvulsant. Some of these medications also have side effects like increased thirst, weight gain, and dry mouth among others.[127]

Typical Mood Stabilizers

Trade and Generic	Most common side effects
Lithobid (lithium)	Increased thirst, increased urination, rash, tremor, dry mouth, increased appetite, weight gain, nausea, bloating, diarrhea, edema, and thyroid dysfunction.
Depakote (divalproex sodium)	Nausea, diarrhea, hair loss, weight gain, and tremor.
Tegretol (carbamazepine)	Rash, fatigue, nausea, dizziness, and sedation.
Neurontin (gabapentin)	Sedation, tremors, nausea, dizziness, and weight gain.
Topamax (topiramate)	Weight loss, sedation, cognitive dulling, fatigue, headache, and numbness in extremities.

Despite these side effects, it is critical that those who struggle with bipolar take their medication. Failing to do so probably has a greater

> See *First Aid for Your Emotional Hurts: Depression* for approaches that can be used to alleviate the side effects of taking psychotropic medications.

adverse impact upon them than that felt by those who struggle with other types of depression.

Treatments prescribed for Majesty Fernado VI (1713-1759) by Dr. Andreu Piquer Arrufat

Donkey's milk
Syrup of cochlear and water pimpernel
Broth with turtles, frogs, veal, and vipers
Enemas
Lime blossom and cherry infusion
Mother of pearl powder
Fumitory
Head baths
Gelatin of deer antler and young viper
Violets
Diet
Syrup of heliotrope scorzonera
Anise
Agrimony

It is important to remember it can take some time for antidepressants to work (typically eight to twelve weeks). When people begin to complain about the side effects from their medications, it is important to encourage them to keep taking the medicine until they talk with their provider. Abruptly stopping medications can result in withdrawal symptoms. By consulting with their provider, they understand how to safely address the side effects.[128]

Consider the medications that King Fernado VI was prescribed in the 18th century listed on the previous page. Though we do have some difficult side effects to our medications, they do not compare to what people have contended with in the past.[129]

There are many complicated problems that people we care about can experience today. Let those who share their problems with you know that there are probably many others who share the kind of difficulties they have. It is also important to convey the hope that comes from Jesus Christ and His Word. Jesus has invited those who struggle to come to Him. Jesus has promised to answer our prayers and provide wisdom to those who ask it of Him and believe He will provide it.

> Now the word of the LORD came to Jonah the son of Amittai, saying,
> "Arise, go to Nineveh, that great city, and call
> out against it, for their evil has come up before me."
> But Jonah rose to flee to Tarshish from the presence of the
> LORD. He went down to Joppa and found a ship going to Tarshish.
> So he paid the fare and went down into it, to go with them to
> Tarshish, away from the presence of the LORD.
>
> Jonah 1:1-3

A Case Study in Bad Decisions

We would be remiss if we did not discuss the case of the Prophet Jonah as it relates to depression. There are some who are depressed because of the sin they have committed, an affair, refusal to forgive someone, or unwillingness to give up a particular sin. Jonah is an example of someone who became depressed because of situational factors. He lived some 2800 years ago, but he has a lot in common with many people today. Anyone who has ever felt trapped has a lot in common with Jonah. Traps are often the result of multiple bad decisions that can lead to problem after problem. Finally, the person might bottom out and feel like they have no way out. That describes Jonah. Many feel the same way. They are involved in a bad relationship, debt, or addicted to some terrible substance or activity and they see no way out.

Rebellion

Jonah did not want to do what God wanted him to do. God told
him to go to Nineveh, so he did the exact opposite. God tells us to
honor our parents; people chose to disrespect theirs. God tells us
to live pure lives; people chose to be as promiscuous as they can.
God tells us to love our wives as ourselves; people chose to abuse
their spouse. Jonah is a picture of rebellion.

Jonah probably felt trapped. The people of Nineveh were very
wicked and violent. They murdered and enslaved people and were
known for their cruelty. Apparently, Jonah would rather die than
go and help them.

Rebellion Turns Us Into People We Don't Know

Have you ever noticed how a bad decision can lead to rebellion that results in a person becoming someone we would never recognize? That is what happened to Jonah. He ran from God, and pretty soon he did not even care about his own life.

Any map will show you that Jonah did the opposite of what God called on him to do. Notice that Jonah got on a ship. We may not think much about that, but in those days getting on a ship was a lot like getting on an airplane might be for us—except it was far more dangerous as one journeyed out into the rough Mediterranean. A big storm arrived. All the sailors were praying, but Jonah was below the deck fast asleep. The sailors learned that Jonah was the probable cause of the storm. What did Jonah do? He asked to be thrown overboard. Jonah did not know that a big fish was waiting. He thought he was committing suicide. He probably did not think anyone could survive being thrown into the sea. No doubt the sailors also thought this as they begged God not to hold Jonah's blood against them (Jonah 1:14).

Sin Takes You Where You Don't Want to Go

Sometimes people would rather persist in their sin than repent. They do not realize where their sin can take them. Jonah certainly did not. He found himself in the belly of a big fish. Imagine what that was like. It might be like being in a jumbo jet that repeatedly rolled over. Jonah hit the bottom. When we get stubborn and rebellious toward God, we go places we never wanted to go. We can get in a far worse situation than we ever bargained for. Maybe those you are trying to help are feeling like God has asked too much of them. Maybe they feel God is being unreasonable. He has asked them to love the unlovable, forgive the unforgivable, or stop the unstoppable. Until they deal with their stubbornness and submit to God, they will remain depressed.

Yet, there is hope. Who wrote Jonah's story? I suppose it was Jonah. That might mean he repented and got on the same page with God. If he could do that, so could those we help as well. If a prophet like Jonah could find himself suicidal, then so could those around us. God can help those around us who are down and depressed. We need to be ready to be His ambassador to them. We will definitely encounter people who are depressed. God has given us a good model with which to help them before being down gets dangerous.

For more information go to www.FirstAidForEmotionalHurts.com.

Resources for Dealing With Depression

SUICIDE
American Association of Suicidology
5221 Wisconsin Avenue, NW
Washington, DC 20015
Phone: 202.237.2280
Fax: 202.237.2282
Website: www.suicidology.org
E-mail: ajkulp0124@ix.netcom.com

American Foundation for Suicide Prevention
120 Wall Street, 22nd Floor
New York, NY 1005
Phone: 888.333.AFSP
Website: www.afsp.org
Crisis hotline: 1.800.SUICIDE

BEHAVIOR THERAPY
Association for Behavioral and Cognitive Therapies
305 Seventh Ave., 16th Floor
New York, NY 10001
Voice: 212.647.1890
Fax: 212.647.1865
Website: www.aabt.org
E-mail: referral@aabt.org

DEPRESSION/MANIC DEPRESSION
National Alliance for Research on Schizophrenia and Depression (NARSAD)
60 Cutter Mill Rd., Suite 404
Great Neck, NY 11021
Voice: 800.829.8289
Fax: 516.487.6930
Website: www.bbrfoundation.org

Depression and Bipolar Support Alliance
730 N. Franklin, #501
Chicago, IL 60610
Voice: 800.826.3632
Fax: 312.642.7243
Website: www.ndmda.org
E-mail: myrtis@aol.com

The International Foundation for Research and Education on Depression (iFRED)
2017-D Renard Ct.
Annapolis, MD 21401
Voice: 410.268.0044
Fax: 443.782.0739
Website: www.ifred.org
E-mail: info@ifred.org

POSTPARTUM DEPRESSION
Postpartum Support, International
91 E. Somerset St.
Raritan, NJ 08869
Voice: 800.944.4773
Website: www.postpartum.net

Chapter 6

Helping People Survive and Thrive

Fear not, for I am with you; be not dismayed,
for I am your God; I will strengthen you, I will help you,
I will uphold you with my righteous right hand.

Isaiah 41:10

In this chapter, we will look at some conditions that have fear at the root. Consider the cases that are described below. Do you know anyone with difficulties like these?

Larry

Larry is a United States army sergeant who returned home after two tours of duty in Iraq. He has become withdrawn from his family. He has trouble sleeping, and is very irritable. He is "jumpy" and says he cannot forget what he saw in Iraq. He even dreams about it and cannot get certain images out of his head. His friends and family say, "He just isn't himself anymore."

Samantha

Samantha was sexually assaulted after leaving a mall last year. She does not go to the mall anymore. In fact, she does not go to very many places. Sometimes, she has a hard time concentrating and she cannot seem to forget about what happened to her. She has trouble sleeping and has recurring nightmares about the incident.

Howard

Last week Howard thought he was having a heart attack. He was on vacation at a fairly secluded island resort. The only way to reach the island is by ferry, which means there is no easy access to the hospital. While he was there, he began to sweat profusely and feel like he was having a heart attack. He started thinking to himself, "There is nothing they can do for me here." However, the emergency medical technicians arrived quickly and transported him on the ferry to a hospital on the mainland. When he arrived at the hospital, the medical staff told him he had just had an "anxiety attack." This is the fourth time he has had an "anxiety attack."

Julie

Julie is 36 years old. She lives with a persistent fear of getting cancer because her mother died with cancer, as did her grandmother and her great-grandmother. Julie spends a lot of her time focusing on good health and eating habits.

Jerome

Jerome is a father of three and the only wage earner in his family. He is afraid he might lose his job. At night, he cannot sleep. He wonders what would happen to his children and his wife if he were unable to support them. The family's financial situation is difficult right now, but if he loses his job, they might not be able to buy food.

Sarah

Sarah seems to be nothing but skin and bones. She was a vibrant teenager who now appears to be seriously ill. Her parents continually encourage her to eat, but she says, "I'm cutting back." She thinks she is fat. She is becoming terribly thin and her parents are concerned for her health.

The difficulties these individuals are experiencing are different in nature. We could write a chapter on each of these cases, but time and space do not allow for it. Though each case is very different, at the root of each there is fear and anxiety.

Some people are predisposed to be anxious. For example, it has been estimated that 10 to 15 percent of children grow up with behavioral inhibition, which makes them more susceptible to anxiety. Children who struggle with behavioral inhibition are more fearful and have a tendency toward extreme cautiousness. Left unaddressed this could lead to anxiety.[130]

Behavioral Inhibition ➤ Anxiety

Anxiety can have a terrible impact upon a person. One study has indicated that struggling with chronic anxiety increases the likelihood of an individual having a heart attack by 43 percent,[131] and another study indicates that anxiety more than doubles their risk of death from lung cancer.[132]

However, it seems that everyone is afraid of something. Some people are afraid of flying. Others fear closed-in places, and some are afraid of snakes or dogs. Some people live with more fear than others. They fear getting sick, being rejected, or being harmed by others. Some people have reasons to be afraid because of their experiences and living situations. Others have allowed fear to overtake them and to rule their lives. We know God is concerned with our fears because the phrase "fear not" appears at least 158 times in the Bible. We can conclude that God does not want us to be paralyzed by fear or for fear to dominate our lives.

Some fear is rational, such as fear that results from certain medical tests. Sometimes our worst fears are realized. Many years ago, Charles Swindoll told the story of a man who was afraid something might happen to his child. He constructed all types of devices and set up procedures to protect his child. He had created a situation in which the child did not have to go anywhere close to the road because he was afraid he might get run over. One morning, the father backed his car out of his garage and ran over his own son, killing him. His greatest fear had been realized despite all of his precautions.

> The fear of the LORD is the beginning of knowledge.
> Proverbs 1:7a
>
> But the LORD takes pleasure in those who fear him.
> Psalm 147:11a

Some fear is healthy. The Bible says, "The fear of the Lord is the beginning of knowledge." Fear of the consequences of sin can help us avoid sin. Fear can keep us from danger. My mother used to say, "Fear of the ocean is good." She meant respect for the ocean could keep a person safe. Someone who has respect for the ocean does not swim out too far or swim during a storm. When the Bible talks of fear in reference to God, it is also pointing us to look at God with awe and wonder, hence He takes pleasure in those who do so.

> Do not be afraid of sudden terror . . . for the LORD will be your confidence and will keep your foot from being caught.
> Proverbs 3:25a-26

Fear can lead to anxiety. Some anxiety is to be expected in life. Paul said, "There is the daily pressure on me of my anxiety for all the churches" (2 Corinthians 11:28b.) Paul also said of Timothy, "For I have no one like him, who will be genuinely concerned for your welfare (Philippians 2:20). Both Paul and Timothy were anxious over the well-being of other Christians. Some anxiety can motivate us to take important action, like studying more for fear of failing a class or to perform at our optimal level. However, too much anxiety can overwhelm us, and it is unhealthy, like those who live with a constant sense of unease. Perhaps, it is because they have been traumatized by a terrible event. Some people live with fears that make it difficult for them to thrive. Some fear can cause people to bring harm to themselves. In this chapter, we will examine several problems together. We will address each of these areas, and once we have done so, we will examine how you can use your tools and techniques to help those who struggle in this area.

Surviving Trauma

In the opening cases, both Larry and Samantha were struggling with trauma. When people experience trauma, they can have an adverse reaction called post-traumatic stress disorder (PTSD). PTSD is diagnosed after an individual has experienced stressful symptoms for more than one month. A person who has experienced stressful symptoms for at least 3 days and up to a month are diagnosed with acute stress disorder. I hesitate to call this a disorder because as discussed in *First Aid for Your Emotional Hurts— Veterans*, these kinds of reactions are actually normal when one has experienced trauma.

> See E. Moody & D. Trogdon (2016), *First Aid for Your Emotional Hurts: Veterans*. Nashville, TN: Randall House.

For example, a defense department study found that of soldiers returning from Iraq and Afghanistan, 1 in 6 reported symptoms of severe depression, PTSD, or other problems[133] so this is very common among service personnel who have experienced combat. PTSD can impact anyone who has experienced a trauma.

> **The Prevalence of Sexual Assault**
>
> From 7 to 8 percent of America's youth report being sexually victimized between the ages of 12 and 17

It is not unusual for someone as in the case of Samantha to be impacted by PTSD. In addition to sexual assault or rape, many children suffer stressful reactions to sexual abuse. Sexual abuse is being forced, threatened, or deceived into sexual activities ranging from looking to intercourse or rape.

> **PTSD is Rare, Right?**
>
> It has been suggested that between 5 and 10 percent of Americans will suffer from post-traumatic stress disorder (PTSD) at some time in their lives.

What is PTSD?

PTSD is more common than we often think.[134] PTSD can result after an individual experiences a traumatic event or events. Accidents involving fatalities or situations where people are physically trapped can result in PTSD. The trauma experienced from storms, like violent hurricanes, can inflict trauma. Military combat (like the case of Larry), and violent personal assault (as is the case of Samantha) can lead to PTSD. The event is outside of the realm of usual human experience and results in fear, helplessness, or horror. People often have dreams about the event. In these cases, there is a feeling of numbness or shock. Survivors often experience a state of disequilibrium that results in disorganized thoughts and behaviors. There can be a sense of loss and a belief that the world, which was usually safe, secure, and predictable, is gone as well.[135]

The slightest cues associated with the event can stimulate recurrent thoughts about it. Despite their best efforts, people with PTSD continue to struggle with the symptoms.[136]

The common symptoms of post-traumatic stress disorder include intrusions, as in nightmares, about a traumatic event and intrusive thoughts that cannot be avoided. There is also avoidance. For example, someone who has experienced an improvised explosion around a bridge while driving might avoid bridges and driving. There are also negative alterations in thinking and mood where one may feel depressed and detached. Finally, there is arousal or excessive vigilance. One may be easily startled by loud noises.[137]

And Moses lifted up his hand and struck the rock with his staff twice, and water came out abundantly, and the congregation drank, and their livestock.

Numbers 20:11

Noah began to be a man of the soil, and he planted a vineyard. He drank of the wine and became drunk...

Genesis 9:20-21a

Biblical Example

As noted in *First Aid for Your Emotional Hurts—Veterans*, it is believed that Moses suffered post-traumatic stress in the aftermath of the rebellion of Korah (Numbers 16-17), where there were 14,700 people killed. There were another 24,000 deaths from a plague at Peor after the people engaged in Baal worship. This would have resulted in 1 to 2 percent of the population dying. Perhaps, it was this irritability at play when Moses struck the rock (Numbers 20) after the death of Miriam.

Noah also exhibited stressful symptoms with his intoxication after the flood. The flood, where the world was destroyed resulting in many deaths, would have certainly been traumatic. Many have improperly coped with stress through the use of alcohol (Genesis 9:20-26).[138]

> Every two and a half minutes, someone is sexually assaulted in the United States. As many as 1 in 6 American women and 1 and 33 men are victims of sexual assault.

Surviving Sexual Abuse

Sexual abuse is far too common[139] so we would do well to learn more about it in order to help people who have experienced it. It is believed that childhood sexual abuse affects approximately 20 percent of women and 8 percent of men worldwide.[140] Children with disabilities seem to be at greater risk because of their increased vulnerability.[141]

A sexual abuse survivor with whom I once worked wrote this poem to help others understand what survi-

The Experience of Sexual Abuse

I lay here and it's late at night
Granny's just shut off the light.
Pretty soon he will be here
Telling me not to fear.

I hear him creeping in the night
and what he does I know ain't right.
He's my uncle, I must obey
So once again he has his way.

I'd tell daddy, but He'd be blue
Most likely say it ain't true.
No one knows how much I've tried
To keep this secret that I hide.

When morning comes he'll go to work
I'll take a bath wash off this dirt.
I think that I should run away.
But that's no use where would I stay?

vors of sexual abuse feel at the time of the abuse. As the poem indicates, most sexual assaults take place at the hands of people the survivor knows personally. In this example, an uncle assaulted this girl. She was afraid to tell her family because she doubted they would believe her. She was correct; initially they doubted the truthfulness of her story. She also indicated that she felt dirty or guilty as well as trapped. Usually, the offender blames the sexual-assault survivor for what happened. This girl eventually ran away and traveled across several states. As she tried to escape the abuse, she was placed in further danger. She was finally placed in a treatment facility when she was 15 years old, she was there to be treated for depression and stress resulting from the repeated abuse. How others react to someone who has experienced trauma goes a long way toward determining how well they will cope.

> *Then Amnon hated her with very great hatred, so that the hatred with which he hated her was greater than the love with which he had loved her. And Amnon said to her, "Get up! Go! But she said to him, "No, my brother, for this wrong in sending me away is greater than the other that you did to me."*
> 2 Samuel 13:15-16

Biblical Example

A biblical example of sexual assault is found in 2 Samuel 13. It is much like the assaults that many experience today. Amnon plotted with a peer to find a way that he might be alone with Tamar (2 Samuel 13:5). When Amnon got Tamar alone, he assaulted her (2 Samuel 13:11-14). The way Amnon treated Tamar (with hatred) is similar to what many who have been assaulted experience (2 Samuel 13:15). Unfortunately, the assault does not appear to have been handled well, and she was never the same again (2 Samuel 13:20).

Surviving Panic

Howard, in the opening case study, is struggling with panic disorder. It is estimated that 2-3 percent of individuals in the United States and several European countries struggle with panic disorder, and that as many as 11.2 percent of the population of the United States will experience a panic attack once a year. The median onset of panic disorder is between the ages of 20 and 24. Most individuals will struggle with attacks throughout their lives. Panic disorder refers to recurrent panic attacks. A panic attack involves a surge in intense fear when one experiences an accelerated heart rate, sweating, shaking, and feeling as if they are short of breath. They may have feelings of choking, nausea, dizziness, chills or heat sensation, numbness, feelings of unreality, losing control, and fear of dying. Sometimes a panic attack has an obvious cue and at other times the panic attack may occur without any cue. Anywhere from one-quarter to one-third of people who struggle with panic disorder will have an event where they wake from sleep in a state of panic.[142]

But when the disciples saw him walking on the sea, <u>they were terrified</u>, and said, "It is a ghost!" and they cried out in fear. But when he saw the wind, <u>he was afraid</u>, and beginning to sink he cried out, "Lord, save me."

Matthew 14:26, 30

Biblical Example

One of my favorite examples of panic in the Bible is when Jesus' disciples were terrified when they saw Jesus walking on water. Later, Peter experienced great fear as he began to sink in the water. These events were sudden, unexpected, and led to great fear among the disciples. A solution to fear and panic is also provided in the case. As long as Peter had his eyes on Jesus, he did well (Matthew 14:29). When Peter focused on the storm (Matthew 14:30), he began to sink.

Anxiety Difficulties	
Problem	Prevalence
Specific phobia	7-9 percent
Social phobia	7 percent
Panic disorder	2-3 percent
Panic attacks	11.2 percent
Agoraphobia	1.7 percent
Generalized anxiety disorder	2.9 percent
Obsessive compulsive disorder	1.2 percent
Post-Traumatic Stress Disorder	3.5 percent
Somatic symptom disorder	5-7 percent

Surviving Phobias and Anxiety

There are numerous anxiety disorders with which people struggle (e.g., separation anxiety disorder, generalized anxiety disorder, specific phobia). We address anxiety disorders as well as obsessive compulsive disorder in the booklet *First Aid for Your Emotional Hurts: Helping Children with Emotional Problems.* In general, these difficulties stem from fear as an emotional response to a real or perceived threat. Anxiety is anticipation of a future threat.

> See E. Moody (2011), *First Aid for Your Emotional Hurts: Helping Children with Emotional Problems.* Nashville, TN: Randall House.

Some people struggle with a fear of flying or animals as is the case of specific phobia, or a fear of social situations like giving a speech or eating in front of others (as is the case of social phobia).[143] Most people with specific phobia fear more than one object or situation.[144]

In the sample case, Julie has illness anxiety disorder. Illness anxiety disorder is the preoccupation and fear of having various serious diseases. People with illness anxiety disorder tend to do a lot of "doctor shopping." It is believed that 1.3 percent to 10 percent of the general population suffer from illness anxiety disorder. Often people with this type of problem interpret their aches and pains to be serious illness. It also seems that these perceived illnesses bring a high level of attention to the individual that they would not receive otherwise.

In the new DSM, obsessive-compulsive and related disorders are now in their own category. However, these problems also often have a fear component that permeate every aspect of a person's life. The chart below is used to demonstrate how this kind of problem can impact one's thoughts, behavior, and way of relating.[145]

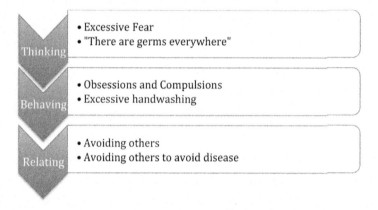

Thinking	• Excessive Fear
	• "There are germs everywhere"
Behaving	• Obsessions and Compulsions
	• Excessive handwashing
Relating	• Avoiding others
	• Avoiding others to avoid disease

The case involving Jerome is of an individual who does not meet the criteria for a particular disorder, although his situation would be described as an emotional hurt. He would benefit from the tools and techniques we will examine later.

> *And there we saw the Nephilim (the sons of Anak, who come from the Nephilim), and we seemed to ourselves like grasshoppers, and so we seemed to them.*
> Numbers 13:33

Biblical Example

It appears that the Judge, Gideon, struggled with fear. God appeared to him and specifically told him, "Do not fear." Yet he needed prodding and signs to perform the calling that God gave to him, and would eventually be transformed into a courageous man (Judges 7).

Another good example of fear and anxiety that led to inaction is the story of the twelve spies who returned from Canaan. They had been given a charge to spy out the land and report back to Israel their findings (Numbers 13:17-18). They did report the beauty of the land (Numbers 13:16), but they chose to focus upon the obstacles they faced, which led to inaction. They had already been warned they would need to have courage (Numbers 13:20). Rather than focusing upon the opportunity available to them, they focused on the obstacles and were stopped by their fear. A prescription for handling this kind of fear was presented by Caleb, "Let us go up at once" (Numbers 13:30). Sometimes when one faces a fear, the best thing they can do is immediately act, lest the fear overtake them.

> The incidence for anorexia nervosa is 8 cases per 100,000 people and the incidence for bulimia is 12 cases per 100,000 people per year.

Surviving Eating Disorders

Sometimes our fears of what other people may think of us can place our lives at great risk. Sarah is at great risk. She has anorexia nervosa. There are many who struggle with eating disorders and anorexia nervosa and bulimia nervosa in particular.[146] People who have anorexia nervosa refuse to maintain their normal body weight. Their weight is generally less than 85 percent of what is healthy. They have an intense fear of becoming fat and live in denial about their low body weight. Because there is a distorted body image, they genuinely do not see how malnourished they appear. The disorder often begins between the ages of 14 to 18 and onset rarely occurs in females over age 40. More than 90 percent of the cases occur in females.[147] When the illness does occur in males, they are usually athletes like swimmers, divers, bodybuilders, and gymnasts.

Eating disorders cause serious cardiovascular and neurological complications. In fact, 5 percent of those who are diagnosed with anorexia nervosa will die within a decade.[148]

Another eating disorder is bulimia nervosa. This disorder involves binge-eating followed by self-induced vomiting; the misuse of laxatives, diuretics, enemas, or other medications; and fasting or excessive exercise. People with bulimia are also unduly influenced by their body shape and weight. There may be times of binge eating followed by vomiting to get rid of the food they have consumed.[149]

Eating Difficulties	
Problem	Prevalence
Anorexia nervosa	0.4 percent
Bulimia nervosa	1-1.5 percent
Binge-eating disorder	1.6 percent (females) and 0.8 percent (males)

A study examined what medicine is used by people suffering from bulimia nervosa. Sixty-seven percent of the patients reported using laxatives, 64 percent used diet pills, 31 percent used diuretics, and 18 percent used ipecac (a nonprescription emetic that induces vomiting).[150] The mortality rate for bulimia nervosa is nearly 2 percent per decade.[151]

How do people become trapped in these unhealthy habits? It appears to involve an internalization of Western culture's ideal image of the female body. Anorexia nervosa and bulimia typically occur in adolescence when media influence is the greatest. It is also apparent that the female body images portrayed in the media have an effect on how satisfied or dissatisfied people are with their bodies.[152]

There also appears to be a link between eating disorders and childhood sexual abuse. For example, the Remuda Ranch is a nationally known, biblically based, eating-disorders treatment facility. Since 1990, they have treated over 7,000 women and girls for eating disorders. They have found that 49 percent of their clients report being sexually abused. This is 20 percent higher than the general population.[153]

Each of these unique difficulties can be debilitating. Fortunately, God has given us the tools and techniques to help those who struggle in these areas.

> *Cast your burden on the* Lord,
> *and he will sustain you;*
> *he will never permit*
> *the righteous to be moved.*
>
> Psalm 55:22

Using Your Tools

Prayer

Prayer is the key to fighting back against fear and anxiety. Unfortunately, you will encounter (or have already encountered) many who will have problems praying. For example, consider the case of Howard who we discussed earlier who has a long history of panic attacks. He has prayed for God to take away his problem. Sometimes he feels as if God has heard his prayer. He can go weeks, in some cases months, without a panic attack. Then suddenly he will experience a panic attack again. He does not know what to do. He follows Christ, goes to church, and reads his Bible. Specifically, he prays that God will remove this problem. He has heard of people being healed instantaneously, but that has not been his experience. This is an example where you will have to help Howard using the actions discussed in chapter 3. However, whatever Howard does, he must keep praying.

The Psalms are a good place to start. Pray a verse like Psalm 55:22, and entire Psalms such as Psalm 121 for someone like Howard, or anyone who is inhibited by fear. You could begin by praying and inserting the name of the person you are praying over. Then ask Howard to make the Psalm his own, praying it after he rises in the morning, throughout the day, and before going to bed at night.

> *I lift up my eyes to the hills*
> *From where does my help come?*
> *My help comes from the LORD,*
> *who made heaven and earth.*
> *He will not let your foot be moved;*
> *he who keeps you will not slumber.*
> *Behold, he who keeps Israel*
> *will neither slumber nor sleep.*
> *The LORD is your keeper;*
> *the LORD is your shade on your right hand.*
> *The sun shall not strike you by day,*
> *nor the moon by night.*
> *The LORD will keep you from all evil;*
> *he will keep your life.*
> *The LORD will keep*
> *your going out and your coming in*
> *from this time forth and forevermore.*
>
> Psalm 121

Psalm 23 is another passage that can be prayed especially focusing on "the valley of the shadow of death." Psalm 46 is helpful as a worst-case scenario Psalm with focus upon how the Lord is with us "though the mountains fall into the middle of the sea." Psalm 91 is also a psalm to pray.

> For more on the use of prayer see *Therapeutic Life Changes, First Aid for Children with Emotional Problems,* and *First Aid for Veterans.*

The Word and Your Word

Meditation upon Scripture can really help reduce fear and anxiety. Find passages that focus as closely upon the fear as one can. For eating disorders, one might focus on Psalm 139. For many fears, consider passages like Matthew 6. You can encourage those you help to read these passages and prepare to explain these passages to them. Consider the different parts of the passage. First, Jesus specifically forbade anxiety and indicated that it was not helpful.

> *Therefore I tell you, do not be anxious about your life, what you will eat or what you will drink, nor about your body, what you will put on. Is not life more than food, and the body more than clothing?*
>
> Matthew 6:25

Jesus used the environment as a tool. As you are out and about, look at the birds, look at the flowers, and you can see God is at work.

> *Look at the birds of the air: they neither sow nor reap nor gather into barns, and yet your heavenly Father feeds them. Are you not of more value than they?*
>
> Matthew 6:26

The passage points out to us that we are valuable. If God thinks about the bird in your park or in your backyard, you know He is thinking about you.

> *And which of you by being anxious can add a single hour to his span of life?*
>
> Matthew 6:27

Jesus reminds us that the anxiety we deal with does nothing to solve our problem. The threat or danger is still there. We would be better suited to focus upon solutions to our problems.

> *Therefore do not be anxious about tomorrow, for tomorrow will be anxious for itself. Sufficient for the day is its own trouble.*
>
> Matthew 6:34

Jesus ends by telling us the best thing we can do is to focus upon Him. As a person focuses upon God, many fears melt away. The last phrase reminds us to just focus on today. Today has enough trouble without getting bogged down on something else.[154]

> *But seek first the kingdom of God and his righteousness,*
> *and all these things will be added to you.*
>
> Matthew 6:33

An outward focus is especially helpful in defeating fear. An attitude of selflessness goes a long way toward helping a person be resilient. The side-bar is from an interview with a former gang member that survived leaving the gang. Notice how he says he was able to leave the gang and thrive.[155]

Resilient People Are Dead to Christ.

"I joined the gang. And after that I found out that the only way out of a gang is through death. So I died to Christ. We went to church after a big gang fight, and I guess the sermon was directed towards me. The guy was talking about violence. And this sermon opened my eyes, and instead of fighting a guy I was mad at, I went up to him and I shook his hand. The Bible has a lot to do with it because there are words in there that express what you feel, and what you think, and what's going on around you."

For to me to live is Christ, and to die is gain.

Philippians 1:21

Eventually, the former gang member concluded that he won if he lived and if he died. This is an important understanding. In other words, "If I survive, I win. If I do not, I am with the Lord in Heaven." For example, consider Julie, in the case of the individual who was fearful of developing cancer. You might ask, "What if you do get cancer?" The goal is to help her realize even if her worst fear does come true, God will get her through it.

> *I tell you, my friends, do not fear those who kill the body,*
> *and after that have nothing more that they can do.*
>
> Luke 12:4

As you help people meditate upon Scripture, the opportunity for the Holy Spirit to ease people's minds is provided. This will help them address their fears. Sometimes, it helps to question people about their specific fears.

Jerome does not appear to need the help of a professional; he needs a friend. How might you help Jerome? You can use the tools and techniques discussed earlier. Help Jerome examine his concern in light of the Word. What would happen if his fear was realized? For example, Jerome is afraid of losing his job. What would happen if he lost his job? If he did lose his job, it would be difficult, but he and his family would survive. Julie is afraid of getting cancer and dying. You could discuss with her what would happen if she got cancer? What would happen if she died? If she is a believer, she has hope. As we help anxious people face their fears, we can also remind them that God will help them overcome the very things they fear most. Encourage them to focus on passages like Psalm 46, and Luke 12:4.

> *There is no fear in love, but perfect love casts out fear.*
> *For fear has to do with punishment, and whoever*
> *fears has not been perfected in love.*
> 1 John 4:18

Other key passages are 1 John 4:18, which reminds us that the more we focus upon Christ, the more He casts out our fears.

> *Let not your hearts be troubled. Believe in God; believe also in me.*
> *In my Father's house are many rooms. If it were not so, would*
> *I have told you that I go to prepare a place for you? And if I go*
> *and prepare a place for you, I will come again and will take*
> *you to myself, that where I am you may be also.*
> John 14:1-3

All of John 14 is helpful, but especially the first three verses where we focus upon Heaven. If all else fails, and life falls apart, we know we will be in Heaven one day if Christ is our focus.

The Church and Relationships

The support of the church and other relationships can be extremely helpful. Consider the help that could be provided to Larry and Samantha. In a study examining the coping strategies of individuals who had been involved in serious injury, of all of the coping strategies used, religious coping was the only strategy that predicted lower PTSD symptoms.[156] In fact, it has been estimated that anywhere from one-half to two-thirds of people who experience a trauma will have post-traumatic growth. The areas where growth is most likely to be observed are: appreciation of life, relationships with others, new possibilities in life, personal strength, and spiritual change.[157]

Julie's friends and family can go a long way toward helping her, by encouraging her to face her fears. They can also encourage her to get help from a professional counselor. Counseling with cognitive behavioral techniques could be helpful for her. People with Illness Anxiety Disorder (IAD) and similar difficulties often "doctor shop," and undergo many unnecessary procedures and take medications unnecessarily. This can cause an illness, which results in the realization of their worst fears.

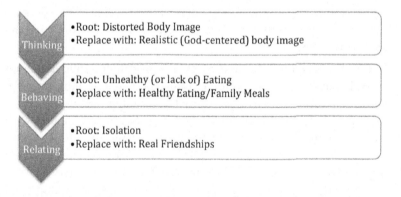

Thinking
- Root: Distorted Body Image
- Replace with: Realistic (God-centered) body image

Behaving
- Root: Unhealthy (or lack of) Eating
- Replace with: Healthy Eating/Family Meals

Relating
- Root: Isolation
- Replace with: Real Friendships

These problems are pervasive. They impact how one thinks, behaves, and relates. But, it is surprising how much good relationships can help. Just being in relationships can defeat these problems. For example, research on relationships within families has indicated that when a family takes the time to eat together, the risk for anxiety disorders and eating problems diminish. Further, for those who struggle with eating problems, their distress is greatly reduced when they have just one friend with whom they can confide.[158]

Using Your Techniques

Though these problems are very different in many ways, some of the same techniques can be used to address each difficulty.

> *And Tamar put ashes on her head and tore the long robe that she wore. And she laid her hand on her head and went away, crying aloud as she went.*
>
> 2 Samuel 13:19

Observe

Use the technique of observation to identify when someone is struggling in these areas. Scripture indicates that it was obvious something traumatic had occurred to Tamar. We should be able to spot those who are having difficulty, if we are looking for it. For someone struggling with post-traumatic stress, you would look for restlessness, fatigue, symptoms of tension, changes in personality, tremors, trouble concentrating, and preoccupation with the traumatic event.[159]

For childhood sexual abuse, you are looking for sudden changes in behavior. For example, a child who was outgoing now appears to be withdrawn. There may be a sudden decline in grades and participation in hobbies. They may experience difficulty with wetting themselves or soiling themselves long after toilet training has been mastered. As in the poem addressed earlier, there may be feelings of guilt or descriptions of oneself as dirty.

Panic disorder should be easy to spot. The individual will have events when they become very ill. Often, they will seek medical attention, and eventually a health care professional will suggest they may be struggling with anxiety.

It should also be obvious when someone is struggling with a phobia or other type of anxiety, as they will have an adverse reaction around the feared object or event. This could result in them avoiding important activities because of the fear.

Regarding eating difficulties, look for a preoccupation with food and weight, disappearing to the bathroom after meals, and excessive exercising. Look for signs of voiding food, like use of diuretics and laxatives. Sometimes one can smell the odor of vomit after food has been voided or see a change in the enamel on a person's teeth.[160]

> *Jesus immediately reached out his hand and took hold of him.*
> Matthew 14:31a

Attend

In the aftermath of a trauma, one of the most helpful things we can do is to promote a sense of safety and calm. When you talk to people in these situations, do not judge them. In the wake of trauma, people will sometimes say things they would not normally say. Keep your comments brief and sincere. It is fine if you do not agree with everything they say, but this is not the time to argue with them.

Your presence after someone has been sexually assaulted is also valuable. Absalom appears to have initially responded and Scripture indicates that David was very upset when he heard of the assault. Yet, it appears David did nothing. Knowing is not enough. We must act.

> *So Tamar lived, a desolate woman, in her brother Absalom's house. When King David heard of all these things, he was very angry.*
> 2 Samuel 13:20b-21

When dealing with a child who has been sexually abused, report the abuse immediately to the Department of Social Services and your local law enforcement agency. In cases where rape has occurred, encourage the person to get examined at a local hospital immediately (before showering). Offer to go with them and advocate for them if needed. In the case of a rape, a "rape kit" can be completed. Encourage the person to have the rape kit completed, even if they do not wish to press charges against the perpetrator.

Your presence with someone who struggles with panic, phobia, or some other anxiety will help them get through those difficult moments. This may also lead to other opportunities to help them further since you have been with them at the peak of their difficulty.

You can attend to those struggling with eating problems by doing your best to support and encourage them. Your presence can be extremely helpful to them.

> *Then Gideon said to God, "Let not your anger*
> *burn against me; let me speak just once more."*
> Judges 6:39a

Listen

Taking the time to listen to someone share about their fears is helpful. Regarding the veteran or someone experiencing stress after an assault, you also want to be calm with them. Many people are unaware of the kind of evil that exists in the world and are not willing to take time to be with those who have endured it. Attending to someone who has experienced trauma can be very helpful to them.

It can be extremely uncomfortable to listen to the terrible things that have happened to many people, but they need to share it. Be willing to let them talk about these things without judging so they can release their feelings. Be understanding of those who have waited for a long time to tell others what has happened to them. Often survivors have been threatened to keep them silent. For example, when children are sexually abused, they initially feel shock and may even deny what has happened to them. They become fearful and anxious and then experience shame and guilt. In most cases, the abuse was at the hands of someone they knew, which results in feelings of betrayal and confusion. Especially in the cases of children, there can be feelings of helplessness and hopelessness—after all, what can children do? They can feel trapped. They will no doubt feel sadness and anger. You can help by letting them tell you their experience.

> *When the cares of my heart are many,*
> *your consolations cheer my soul.*
> Psalm 94:19

Care

As a culture, we like to move on quickly after a tragedy. We want everything to get back to normal as soon as possible. If you are going to help those who survive trauma, you will need to set aside this tendency and put yourself in their shoes. We also have a tendency to want to talk about ourselves or someone we know who had a similar experience. Neither of those behaviors are helpful to those suffering from trauma. The best thing we can do is listen to them and let them tell their story.

> But Caleb quieted the people before Moses and said, "Let us go up at once and occupy it, for we are well able to overcome it."
>
> Numbers 13:30

Respond

As you listen, you can look for opportunities to encourage those you are trying to help. Instead of asking, "Why me?" after a tragic event, you can seek to help them look for steps they can take to deal effectively with their situation, encouraging them to learn from their experiences rather than be defeated by them.[161]

You can also stress the danger of concentrating on obstacles. In the account of the twelve spies, after detailing the opportunity before the people (Numbers 13:25-27), the spies said, "However" and began to enumerate all of the obstacles before them. This is what happens when a person is overcome by fear. They focus on the barriers and challenges and tend to overstate them. The spies referred to themselves as grasshoppers when compared to the enemy (Numbers 13:33). As we listen to people, we can encourage them to act quickly before their fears overwhelm them. As Caleb said, "Let us go up at once."

Courage Confidence Independence

Our goal is to break the chain of fear, timidity, and overdependence with courage, confidence, and independence.[162] As part of this process, we may begin to think of and refer to people as

what we hope they will become rather than how they are present-
ly. Consider the manner in which God dealt with Gideon, a man
prone to fear.

> *And the angel of the LORD appeared to him and said to him,
> "The LORD is with you, O mighty man of valor."*
> Judges 6:12

With all of the cases we have examined, it would be good to
focus upon the application of Philippians 4 as a prescription for
dealing with fear. It is interesting to consider the context of the
passage. Paul begins by encouraging two ladies within the church
to work together and for others to help them. Church conflict,
always a source of anxiety, is in the background of the passage.

A Prescription for Handling Anxiety

> *Rejoice in the Lord always; again I will say, rejoice.*
> Philippians 4:4

Step 1: Concentrate on God's Goodness.

As this verse suggests, one good way to keep anxiety in perspective is to focus on God's goodness and generosity. This re-
moves the focus from ourselves and the many obstacles we encounter. We can encourage those with whom we work to make a
list of the character traits of God as they read their Bibles to help
them focus upon God's goodness.

> *Let your reasonableness be known to everyone.
> The Lord is at hand.*
> Philippians 4:5

Step 2: Concentrate on Others.

Next, Paul tells the reader to focus on others. We can overcome
fear by focusing on reaching out and helping others. This moves
the focus of our thoughts from ourselves and our own anxiety to

the needs of others. It is also implied that one notes the closeness of the Lord to them.

> *Do not be anxious about anything, but in everything by prayer and supplication with thanksgiving let your requests be made known to God.*
>
> Philippians 4:6

Step 3: Pray.

The little things create a great deal of stress in those who struggle with fear. We need to remind them that no problem or concern is too big or small for us to share with God. When people are fearful and anxious, we can encourage them to pray about the things that are bothering them. Encourage those struggling with fear to immediately go to God whenever they experience stress.

We want people to become very focused in their praying by concentrating on Scriptures such as Isaiah 41:10 and 13.

> *Fear not, for I am with you;
> be not dismayed, for I am your God;
> I will strengthen you, I will help you,
> I will uphold you with my righteous right hand.
> For I, the LORD your God,
> hold your right hand;
> it is I who say to you, "Fear not,
> I am the one who helps you."*

It might also help to write these and similar verses on note cards that they keep with them at all times. When they feel anxious thoughts returning, they can read the cards to renew their faith and replace the anxiety with assuring Scripture. This exercise will help them develop the habit of concentrating on truth, rather than feelings or speculations. In addition, it helps to personalize the verses. For example, Larry could personalize the verse this way:

> *Larry, do not be afraid, for I am with you;*
> *be not dismayed, for I am your God;*
> *I will strengthen you, I will help you,*
> *I will uphold you, Larry, with my righteous right hand.*
> *For I, the LORD your God,*
> *hold your right hand;*
> *it is I who say to you, "Fear not,*
> *Larry, I am the one who helps you."*

> *Finally, brothers, whatever is true, whatever is honorable,*
> *whatever is just, whatever is pure, whatever is lovely,*
> *whatever is commendable, if there is any excellence, if there*
> *is anything worthy of praise, think about these things.*
>
> Philippians 4:8

Step 4: Concentrate on Your Thoughts.

It is not sufficient to wait until one becomes fearful. Paul instructed the Philippians to be intentional about what they spent their time thinking. All of those in the cases we have examined need to seek to control their thoughts. By getting their minds focused on that which is positive, a person can be helped. A major project, a hobby, some type of work, or a new area of study could all be commendable and items of excellence.

> *What you have learned and received and heard and seen in me—*
> *practice these things, and the God of peace will be with you.*
>
> Philippians 4:9

Step 5: Act.

We can all learn from each other, and especially those who have experienced problems similar to those with which we deal. Paul encouraged the Philippians to imitate him. We can help people identify veterans, survivors of sexual abuse, and others who have dealt well with their difficulties. As they imitate others and simply act upon the teaching of Scripture many issues will be resolved. They cannot simply consider these steps or talk about them—they must actually do them! That is what Paul did. What was the result? Peace

> And the peace of God, which surpasses all understanding, will guard your hearts and your minds in Christ Jesus.
>
> Philippians 4:7

The Result = Peace

Essentially Paul said, "This works." This is the prescription to real peace. There will always be times when a problem pops up, but as one applies the prescription, the fear will wilt away.

Act

You can take important actions to help. Help the trauma survivors identify things they can do and promote connectedness to other people while instilling hope. For example, try to reconnect them with friends, family, and church. The more socially isolated they are, the more potential for danger to them. Help them get "grounded." Make it clear there is nothing wrong with them. It is normal to have an adverse reaction after seeing and experiencing something adverse. Help them problem solve and set achievable goals.[163]

For individuals who have survived sexual abuse or assault, you may have to be with them at different times as they deal with this process. Some individuals will have to prepare to confront the abuser; for example, when trauma survivors need to testify against those who raped them or when they witnessed a crime. You can help by being there when they make statements like, "I'm going crazy," or "I can't do anything about this."

Find the Inn

Many of these issues can be effectively addressed by helping professionals. It is important for trauma survivors to see a professional helper. Larry could get services from his local veteran's administration center and Samantha would need to see a professional counselor. This will aid each of them in the process and probably prevent the development of additional difficulties.

The components of good interventions for PTSD would include a psychoeducational component. This would involve a rationale for treatment and would help the individual understand how people respond to trauma. The trauma survivors would also learn how avoiding the issue creates more difficulty for them and would be taught practical ways to process what they have experienced.

Trauma based cognitive behavioral therapy has been found to be effective in reducing anxiety, depression, and sexual problems for children ages 8-15 who have been sexually abused.[164]

Howard would probably benefit from the assistance of a psychologist who could utilize some techniques to address the panic he experiences. It might become necessary to take medication as well. There are many medications that might help alleviate his situation. A health care professional could assist in identifying aspects about his life that could be exacerbating his problem. For example, many people will need to eliminate or at least limit their caffeine intake. Excessive amounts of sugar, candy, and soft drinks also contribute to the problems of individuals with anxiety disorders.[165]

Once a health care professional determines that a person suffers from panic disorder rather than some other medical condition, medication can be prescribed to alleviate the attacks. Panic disorder patients would benefit from the services of a psychologist, who could teach them relaxation-training techniques. The psychologist could also teach them a technique called systematic desensitization. This is an exercise in which the client imagines the fearful stimuli and then pairs it with relaxation techniques. By repeating this process, the client learns better ways of controlling or managing the panic attacks.

Good interventions include a symptom-monitoring component to help judge the progress of the individual. Counselors will also encourage the client to reestablish their normal daily routines, which will help prevent further lifestyle deterioration. Clients will learn coping skills that may involve relaxation training, and they may experience graded exposure to anxiety producing events. This would involve addressing some of the cues that have brought on the stress.

In almost all circumstances, you will need to find professionals to assist with problems involving eating disorders. The first step in helping people suffering with eating disorders is to encourage them to see a health care professional. Research has indicated that pharmacological treatments can be helpful, but the most effective interventions involve family therapies.[166]

Some individuals will need to be hospitalized or receive residential treatment to recover. As you look for professional treatment for these individuals, consider the components in the treatment model that follows.

Treatment Model

> *You yourselves like living stones are being built up as a spiritual house, to be a holy priesthood, to offer spiritual sacrifices acceptable to God through Jesus Christ.*
> 1 Peter 2:5

Phase I: Laying the Foundation

Since 50 percent of those who suffer with eating disorders injure themselves, it is important to put a safety plan in place. In this phase, those who've often felt hopeless need to be reminded of their identity in Christ.

> *Do not be conformed to this world, but be transformed by the renewal of your mind, that by testing you may discern what is the will of God, what is good and acceptable and perfect.*
> Romans 12:2

Phase II: Transformation

In this phase, we will need to address issues of trauma. Those suffering from illness will need to resolve issues of loss and learn to grieve.

> *And I am sure of this, that he who began a good work in you will bring it to completion at the day of Jesus Christ.*
>
> Philippians 1:6

Phase III: Integration

People suffering from eating disorders need to focus on their body image and develop a continuing care plan. The skills and truths they have learned need to be integrated.[167]

Left unchecked, trauma, fear, and anxiety can ravage lives. However, there is help. Resources are available that can alleviate these difficult conditions. As a believer, you have the most valuable resource of all, God. God can help people during their darkest hour, so be sure to point them to His Word.

> *How precious to me are your thoughts, O God!*
> *How vast is the sum of them!*
> *If I would count them, they are more than the sand.*
> *I awake, and I am still with you.*
>
> Psalm 139:17-18
>
> *And my God will supply every need of yours according to his riches in glory in Christ Jesus.*
>
> Philippians 4:19

For more information go to www.FirstAidForEmotionalHurts.com.

Resources

Anxiety

Anxiety Panic Attack Resource Site
P.O. Box 1421
Nampa, ID 83653
Toll Free: 888.584.7112
FAX: 208.468.0753
Website: www.anxietypanic.com
E-mail: help@anxietypanic.com

The International Association of Anxiety Management
www.anxman.org
The Anxiety Disorders Association of America (ADAA)
11900 Parklawn Drive, Suite 100
Rockville, MD 20852
Phone: 301.231.9350
Website: www.adaa.org

Eating Disorders

Remuda Ranch (a biblically based treatment facility for females with eating disorders)
One East Apache Street
Wickenburg, AZ 85390
Toll Free: 1.800.445.1900
Phone: 928.684.3913
E-mail: info@remudaranch.com; www.remudaranch.com

Sexual Assault

The American College of Obstetricians and Gynecologists (ACOG)
(A resource for violence against women)
409 12 Street, SW
P.O. Box 96920
Washington, DC 20090-6920
Phone: 202.638.5577
Website: www.acog.org
E-mail: violence@acog.org

RAINN (The Rape, Abuse & Incest National Network)
Toll Free: 1.800.656.HOPE
Website: www.rainn.org
E-mail: info@rainn.org

Trauma

PTSD Alliance Resource Center
Toll Free: 1.877.507.PTSD
Website: www.PTSDAlliance.org

The International Society for Traumatic Stress Studies (ISTSS)
60 Revere Drive, Suite 500
Northbrook, IL 60062
Phone: 847.480.9028
Website: www.istss.org

Chapter 7

Breaking the Deadly Cycle

For I do not understand my own actions. For I do not do what I want, but I do the very thing I hate.

Romans 7:15

Sin can be dangerous and deadly; it can lead to a vicious cycle of addiction. Consider the cases that follow of people who find themselves entangled in addictions.

Jamie

Jamie has repeatedly been stopped by the Police for driving under the influence of alcohol. The problem has become so bad that his license has been revoked and he is having trouble keeping his job. Friends have talked to him about not drinking, but he says it is no use. He has tried to stop and he cannot.

Samantha

Samantha recently finished high school and moved out from her parent's house. People describe her as being "wild." Before she moved out on her own, she often came home drunk. She has been seen in places where some people go to find cocaine. Her parents say they can do nothing with her.

John

John likes to gamble online. In fact, John likes anything that is linked to gambling. It seems crazy, but once he gambled all day by playing bridge online. At other times, he has used all of his spare money to buy lottery tickets. Once he went to a casino on a Native American reservation and lost several thousand dollars. It is not so bad until he comes across some sort of gambling outlet. He has tried to hide it from his wife, but she's aware and constantly complaining about it. She said if it happens again, she's leaving.

Howard

Howard confides that he cannot get away from pornography. When he goes to a book store he says he is drawn to "adult" magazines. When he is online, he is drawn to pornographic sites. Even as he drives down the road, he feels drawn to adult bookstores. He feels like he is out of control. He says he cannot stop.

Why Don't They Just Stop?

When someone is addicted to something they can become very anxious and agitated when they go without the substance. It is as if the substance or activity control and defines them.

So now it is no longer I who do it, but sin that dwells within me. For I know that nothing good dwells in me, that is, in my flesh. For I have the desire to do what is right, but not the ability to carry it out. For I do not do the good I want, but the evil I do not want is what I keep on doing. Now if I do what I do not want, it is no longer I who do it, but sin that dwells within me.

Romans 7:17-20

There are all kinds of sins in which a person can become entangled. When people are in these situations, they often feel like the description the Apostle Paul gave, "I do not understand my own actions. For I do not do what I want, but I do the very thing I hate." Some people fear they cannot be freed from these entanglements. They say the cycle cannot be broken.

Substance and Addictive Issues	
Problem	**Prevalence**
Alcohol use disorder	4.6 percent among 12 to 17-year-olds
	8.5 percent among adults 18 and older
Alcohol intoxication	44 percent of 12th grade students
	70 percent of college students
Cannabis use disorder	3.5 percent of 12 to 17-year-olds
	1.5 percent among adults 18 and older
Phencyclidine use disorder	0.3 percent of 12 to 17-year-olds
	1.3 percent among adults 18 to 25
	2.9 percent among adults 26 and older
Inhalant use disorder	0.4 percent of 12 to 17-year-olds
	0.1 percent among adults 18 to 29
	0.02 percent for all Americans 18 and older
Opioid use disorder	1.0 percent of 12 to 17-year-olds
	0.37 percent among adults 18 and older
Stimulant use disorder	0.2 percent of 12 to 17-year-olds
	0.2 percent among adults 18 and older
Gambling disorder	0.2-0.3 percent
APA 2013	

A Primer on Addiction

The volume of people who struggle with substances and behaviors require that we become somewhat knowledgeable of them if we are to help people.[168] The term addiction is frequently used casually in our culture, but addiction can destroy bodies, families, and ministries. It is important to know the difference between dependence and abuse. How do you know if someone is dependent upon a substance or activity? When someone is dependent on a substance or activity

> 24.6 million Americans aged 12 and over (9.4 percent of the population) have used an illicit drug in the last month

they experience tolerance and withdrawal symptoms. Tolerance is when a person requires increasing amounts of a substance or activity to experience the feeling or the "high" they felt when they began using the substance or engaging in the particular activity.

When a person is dependent to something, they experience withdrawal symptoms after a brief period without it. This is an indication that the body has become dependent upon that substance or activity. Symptoms of withdrawal continue until the body begins to learn to function again without it. The type of withdrawal depends upon the specific substance used or activity in which the person has engaged.

People who are addicted, "crave" the substance or the activity. The person spends significantly more time engaging in an activity than they had planned. This happens despite knowledge that one may experience enormous consequences for the behavior (e.g., loss of a job, driving privileges, or a relationship). For example, someone might say they intended to take one drink only to find they started drinking and couldn't stop. There is a tendency for the person to be preoccupied with the substance or activity to the point they have difficulty thinking about anything else.

Addiction has an impact upon the brain. In chapter 3, we looked at the impact of psychotropic medication upon the brain. Psychotropic medication is used to correct a problem or address a deficiency in the body. However, any substance that is introduced into the body has an impact upon the brain. It is very dangerous to use a drug without the care of a health care provider.

The brain has around 100 billion neurons. Neurons contain multiple transmitters. The table below provides a list of drugs and some of the neurotransmitters they impact.[169] Engaging in activities like pathological gambling or viewing pornography has an impact upon the brain. People who view pornography seem to engage in viewing more graphic images as they continue this behavior. Many believe that the viewing of such material has an impact upon neurotransmitters in the brain.

Drugs and the impact upon the brain

Drug	Neurotransmitter
Alcohol	GABA, Serotonin
Marijuana	Acetylcholine
Cocaine/amphetamines	Epinephrin, norepinephrine, serotonin, dopamine, acetylcholine
Crystal Meth	Dopamine, serotonin, norepinephrine
Heroin	Endorphin, dopamine
Opiates	Gamma-aminobutyric acid (GABA)
LSD	Acetylcholine
PCP	Dopamine, acetylcholine
MDMA (ecstasy)	Serotonin, endorphin, acetylcholine
Nicotine	Adrenalin, endorphin, acetylcholine
Caffeine	Dopamine, norepinephrine

Addictive Substances and Behaviors

There are many in the United States who struggle with substances. In fact, it is estimated that every month 9.4 percent of the total population engages in illicit drug use. Some commonly abused substances will be reviewed here to help the reader better anticipate the problems those they are trying to help might experience.

> *Who has woe? Who has sorrow?*
> *Who has strife? Who has complaining?*
> *Who has wounds without cause?*
> *Who has redness of eyes?*
> *Those who tarry long over wine;*
> *those who go to try mixed wine.*
> Proverbs 23:29-30

Alcohol

In the opening case, Jamie struggled with alcohol use disorder, which is believed to impact 4.6 percent of youth aged 12 to 17, and 8.5 percent of adults 18 and older. The rate among adult men is higher at 12.4 percent of the United States population. Problem drinking is prevalent in our culture with the highest prevalence being among young adults ages 18 to 25. One out of every five individuals with a substance abuse disorder also develop a mood or anxiety disorder. Americans spend 99 billion dollars a year on alcohol. Abuse of or dependence upon alcohol can be very detrimental. Every year there are 500,000 head injuries in the United States. Alcohol is believed to directly or indirectly be responsible for half of those injures.[170]

Alcohol can have an adverse effect upon the body. Even low concentrations of alcohol seem to have a negative impact upon a person's stomach. Some research has indicated that beverages containing as little as 5 to 10 percent of alcohol can damage the lining of the stomach.

> *Woe to those who rise early in the morning,*
> *that they may run after strong drink,*
> *who tarry late into the evening as wine inflames them!*
> *They have lyre and harp,*
> *tambourine and flute and wine at their feasts,*
> *but they do not regard the deeds of the Lord,*
> *or see the work of his hands.*
> Isaiah 5:11-21

It is believed that every year in the United States, more than 2 million people experience symptoms of alcohol withdrawal syndrome (AWS). AWS is an acute brain syndrome that is exasperated by how much a person has used alcohol and for how long. Only 10 to 20 percent of the people who develop it are hospitalized from it. However, even with the best medical care, AWS can be life threatening. It appears that AWS becomes worse every time a person experiences it. The symptoms develop 4-12 hours after the persons last drink in 90 percent of the cases.[171]

> *Do not look at wine when it is red,*
> *when it sparkles in the cup*
> *and goes down smoothly.*
> *In the end it bites like a serpent*
> *and stings like an adder.*
> *Your eyes will see strange things,*
> *and your heart utter perverse things.*
> *You will be like one who lies down in the midst of the sea,*
> *like one who lies on the top of a mast.*
> *"They struck me," you will say, "but I was not hurt;*
> *they beat me, but I did not feel it.*
> *When shall I awake?*
> *I must have another drink."*
>
> Proverbs 23:31-35

In the most severe cases of AWS, people develop delirium tremens (DTs). This happens to 1 to 10 percent of chronic drinkers. Symptoms of DTs include confusion, agitation, hallucinations, delusions, fever, and tachycardia. In the past, anywhere from 5 to 25 percent of people who experienced DTs died from heart attacks or strokes as a result of the severe neurotransmitter and electrolyte imbalance as well as extreme anxiety. However, it appears that with medical care death from DTs can be decreased to 1 to 5 percent for those who experience these symptoms.[172]

Cocaine

In the opening example, Samantha was described as using two substances. One of those substances was cocaine. Cocaine is a very dangerous drug. Around 40 to 50 percent of the people who die from substance abuse in the United States each year do so from using cocaine.[173] Death has been reported from all forms of cocaine use. Cocaine acts directly on the heart. The muscle as well as vessels around the heart can be damaged. Chronic users often experience seizures. The most common causes of death from cocaine are heart attacks, strokes, respiratory failure, paralysis, and heart rhythmic disturbances.[174] Cocaine is also linked to dangerous behavior. One study in New York City indicated that one-fifth of the suicides of people under the age of 60 were related to cocaine.[175]

Cocaine elevates the mood of the user and produces a feeling of exhilaration. Feelings of fatigue depart and a person may feel as though they have unlimited energy. People inhale the drug through the nose, inject it under their skin, as well as smoke it in the form of crack. An intense high can be felt from smoking cocaine 8 to 10 seconds after inhaling the smoke. The effects only last 5 to 10 minutes. Cocaine impacts the neurotransmitter dopamine. Normally the brain replenishes dopamine from protein in food, but in people addicted to cocaine, dopamine is quickly depleted because of poor diet. The lack of dopamine in the brain leads to depression.[176]

People who smoke cocaine often cough frequently and experience chest pain as well as damage to their lungs. One-third of chronic crack users develop a wheezing sound when they breathe. In addition to damaging the heart, cocaine abuse has been associated with liver damage and damage to the central nervous system. Cocaine impacts a person's emotional state and perceptions. It's estimated that most people experience depression a few hours after snorting the drug or within 15 minutes of ingesting it.[177]

Marijuana

Marijuana is the most frequently abused illicit substance in the United States. Famously marijuana users have "bloodshot eyes," that is caused after the small blood vessels in the eyes dilate. Around 40 to 60 percent of marijuana users experience one or more adverse drug-induced side effects. About 15 percent experience anxiety or panic attacks.[178] Marijuana use results in relaxation feelings of euphoria, increased appetite, impaired memory, and loss of concentration. Strong doses can result in fluctuation of emotions, disoriented behavior, and even psychosis.

Marijuana can be very harmful to the body. A marijuana cigarette is believed to contain 421 chemicals before ignition. When ignited, this can convert into 2,000 chemicals. It's believed that marijuana burns 16 times hotter than tobacco cigarettes resulting in greater damage to the lungs. People using marijuana are more likely to experience depression and anxiety.[179]

Many people believe incorrectly that there are no side effects from withdrawing from marijuana. However, marijuana abusers experience withdrawal symptoms that include irritability, aggressive behavior, anxiety, insomnia, nausea, loss of appetite, sweating, and vomiting. The withdrawal symptoms begin one to three days after the last use of the substance and peak between the second and tenth day. These symptoms can last 28 days or more.[180]

Amphetamines

Other widely abused drugs are amphetamines. These are stimulants that characterize drugs like "speed" and some diet pills. Amphetamines can be taken orally, injected, snorted, or smoked.

Amphetamines and other central nervous system stimulants like ephedrine and Ritalin can have adverse effects upon the body when they are abused. Their properties mimic cocaine and act on the neurotransmitters dopamine and norepinephrine. Large doses of amphetamines can produce rapid heartbeat, profuse sweating, and severe chest pain. Severe intoxication can also produce delirium, panic, paranoia, and hallucinations.

Up to 50 percent of the dopamine-producing cells in the brain might be damaged from prolonged exposure to low-level amphetamine usage. In fact, amphetamine abuse may result in temporary and even permanent changes in cerebral blood-flow patterns. Amphetamines affect the emotions of those who abuse them. In one study, 75 percent of those who abused amphetamines reported significant levels of anxiety.

Amphetamine users can also experience irritability and insomnia. They may also engage in more aggressive behavior and be more likely to assault others. Murders and violent offenses have been attributed to amphetamine intoxication. Prolonged use of amphetamines can result in formication, which is where a person experiences the urge to scratch or burn their skin because they believe unseen bugs are oppressing them.[181] Withdrawal symptoms include depression, fatigue, increased appetite, and prolonged sleep.[182]

> 91 Americans die every day from opioid-related overdose
> (includes heroin & prescription opioids)

Opiates

Opioid abuse has spread and become very deadly. We tend to think of opiates like heroin as being most dangerous but so many today struggle with prescription opiates like Percocet, oxycodone, and Norco-hydrocodone. In 2015, more than 33,000 people died from opioid-related overdoses in the United States, which set a new record. Drug overdose deaths have tripled since 1999, and more that 60 percent of these deaths involve an opioid. The trend can be traced in large part to easy access to opiods.[183]

At least 30 percent of Americans experience chronic pain or chronic recurrent pain.[184] This has resulted in 1 out of every 5 patients (with non-cancerous related pain or pain related diagnosis) being prescribed an opioid in office-based settings.[185]

> See *First Aid for Your Emotional Hurts: Addiction* for more information about dealing with these problems.

These painkillers are derived from opiates like OxyContin, vicodin, morphine, codeine, and heroin and can lead to addiction if not carefully monitored. Opiate use results in euphoria, drowsiness, constricted pupils, and nausea; overdose can produce coma, respiratory distress, and death. The predominate drug used in this category is heroin, which is usually injected. The result is a feeling of euphoria within 7 to 8 seconds. Chronic use of opiates results in changes in dopamine and brain changes that are observed after prolonged use.

Tolerance from opiates can result quickly in which someone might go from using 60 milligrams of morphine a day to 500 milligrams per day in as little as 10 days. Finally, the user reaches a "threshold effect" where they no longer get high, but use the drug to maintain normal functioning.

During withdrawal from opiates, a person can experience nausea, repeated yawning, sweating, tearing, and a runny nose. People report intense craving for the drug.[186]

Ecstasy

There are some people, mostly young people, who will use only one substance that may be part of a larger area of problematic behavior. Ecstasy is one of those substances. For some adolescents, it is the only drug they have experienced. Use of MDMA can result in a greater sense of introspection and intimacy.[187] MDMA use results in drowsiness, disinhibition, and agitation.

Ecstasy disables the body's ability to regulate temperature that can result in dehydration, coma, and death. Studies of ecstasy use indicate that prolonged use can lead to confusion, depression, sleep problems, anxiety, aggressiveness, and memory impairment.[188]

There can be a depletion of serotonin and dopamine can be impacted as well. There is some evidence that even using MDMA a few times can risk permanent problems with learning and memory. Chronic abusers experience weight loss and inattentiveness. Prolonged use can result in damage to the brain and nervous system by depriving the body of oxygen, which forces the heart to beat more rapidly and erratically.[189]

Nicotine

Almost everyone knows someone who is trying to stop smoking cigarettes or using some other tobacco product. Why is it so difficult to stop using substances that contain nicotine? Nicotine accumulates in the body and remains in body tissues for about 24 hours. This results in a high potential for dependence. Chronic cigarette smokers can experience numerous withdrawal symptoms when deprived of cigarettes for 24 hours. These include, increased anger, hostility, and difficulty regaining emotional equilibrium after a stressor.[190] The best action is to prevent smoking from ever beginning. It is rare for a person to begin smoking after the age of 21. About 20 percent of adolescents in the United States smoke at least monthly by the time they are 18 years of age. More than 80 percent of individuals who use tobacco products attempt to quit at some point in their lives, but 60 percent begin using again within one week. Only 5 percent of those who stop using tobacco products remain abstinent for the rest of their lives.[191]

Nonsubstance Addictions

There are also addictions that do not involve substances. The American Psychiatric Association refers to these as behavioral addictions and places them in the same chapter as substance related disorders because of the impact they have upon the reward system of the brain.[192]

> *A man with an evil eye hastens after wealth*
> *And does not know that want will come upon him.*
> Proverbs 28:22 NASB

Gambling Disorder

In one of our opening cases, John struggled with gambling. Gambling is one of our fastest growing industries in the United States and Pathological Gambling is one of the fastest growing addictions in the United States. Gambling disorder interferes with the person's family, job, and overall ability to function in life. One poll has suggested that of those who engage in problematic gambling behaviors, 70 percent do so at least three times a week. Why do people gamble? People with gambling problems indicate they do it to forget about their troubles and to have fun.[193]

Gambling disorder is marked by a desire for excitement and action where one takes greater and greater risks. Gambling may continue in spite of efforts to control it. A pattern of "chasing" losses can develop with greater risks taken to undo the losses incurred from gambling. If an individual is no longer able to borrow resources, they might resort to forgery, fraud, or theft.

> *Whoever is greedy for unjust gain troubles his own household,*
> *but he who hates bribes will live.*
> Proverbs 15:27

There seems to be an overriding distortion in thinking where money is seen as the cause and the solution to the person's problems. The incidence of pathological gambling is often tied to one's culture and the availability of gambling outlets. However, people with this problem resort to gambling over far-ranging areas from horse racing to the stock market.[194]

Internet Gaming

In the new DSM-5, a category that is being explored for a future diagnosis is internet gaming disorder. The proposed criteria involve a preoccupation with internet games to the point that it becomes the dominant activity in daily life. There are feelings of irritability, anxiety, or sadness when internet gaming is taken away. As with other issues like this, there is tolerance, where one feels the need to engage in increasing amounts of gaming as well as unsuccessful attempts to control one's participation in the activity. Further, there is a loss of interest in previous hobbies and continued excessive usage even though the individual has experienced many psychosocial problems because of the excessive usage. An individual may lie about the amount of gaming in which they engage, and use games to escape or relieve a negative mood. Further, significant relationships, jobs, and career opportunities have been jeopardized because of excessive usage. These individuals often devote 8-10 hours a day and as many as 30 hours a week to gaming. They tend to become agitated and angry when prevented from gaming and may go long periods without food or sleep to continue. They often talk about "avoiding boredom" as a reason for their behavior.[195]

> You have heard that it was said, "You shall not commit adultery." But I say to you that everyone who looks at a woman with lustful intent has already committed adultery with her in his heart.
> Matthew 5:27-28

Pornography

In the opening case, Howard struggled with pornography. Pornography is a bigger problem than most people realize. Some think pornography is harmless, but Jesus viewed lust as adultery. The Internet has resulted in this problem being more prevalent. Even pastors are vulnerable to the lure of Internet pornography. A study conducted upon Protestant clergy in the United States indicated that 40 percent reported struggling with pornography largely obtained through the Internet. In addition, one third indicated they had viewed pornography via the Internet within the last 30 days.

How does one know if someone with whom they are working is entangled in pornography? Some of the criteria that was used for substance addiction can be used here as well. First, one looks

> For more on helping those who struggle with pornography and other sexual issues see *First Aid for Your Emotional Hurts: Sexual Issues and Ministering in a Changing Sexual Landscape.*

for unmanageability. This is similar to substance abuse where one wishes to stop or plans to engage in a behavior for a short period of time, only to engage in that activity for a longer than intended period. It appears that viewing pornography creates neuro-chemical tolerance as well. What used to satisfy and excite no longer does, so there is a period of escalation to achieve the same elevated mood.[196]

Biblical Examples

You will not find examples of people struggling with gaming, online gambling, or online pornography in the Bible, but you will find those ensnared in entangling behaviors just as damaging. David and Sampson are clear examples (they will be discussed later), as was Rahab.

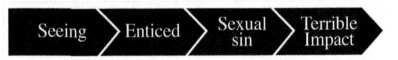

Seeing → Enticed → Sexual sin → Terrible Impact

They see something (Sampson sees a woman from Timnah, David sees Bathsheba), they are enticed by it (Sampson demands the Philistine woman, David demands Bathsheba), they commit the sin, and a terrible impact follows.[197]

> *But each person is tempted when he is <u>lured</u> and enticed by his own desire. Then desire when it has <u>conceived</u> gives birth to sin, and sin when it is fully grown brings forth <u>death</u>.*
>
> James 1:14-15

In the New Testament, we see Mary Magdalene, the Samaritan woman, tax collectors, and others that were entangled in this same chain. Jesus freed many of them from that bondage, and He has given us the tools we need to help people in these deadly cycles.

> *And call upon me in the day of trouble;*
> *I will deliver you, and you shall glorify me.*
> Psalm 50:15

Use Your Tools

Prayer

We must pray for those who struggle with different entanglements. We can also teach them to pray, but they must begin with repentance. Often people will say they are sorry when they get into trouble because of an addiction. They get arrested for drug use or for driving while intoxicated, or they incur great debt because of the behavior. Remember, that it is of no benefit to them unless they are truly repentant. In other words, those you are trying to help will not get better unless they have a sorrow that leads to repentance.

> *For the sorrow that is according to the will of God*
> *produces a repentance without regret, leading to salvation,*
> *but the sorrow of the world produces death.*
> 2 Corinthians 7:10 NASB

Paul wrote about this and indicated there is a sorrow that leads to repentance and a sorrow that produces death. Just being sorry about getting caught will not have a good outcome. There are many examples in Scripture of those that were sorry essentially because of the impact their behavior had upon them.

Sorry, Just Not Sorry

Then Pharaoh sent and called Moses and Aaron and said to them, "This time I have sinned; the L<small>ORD</small> is in the right, and I and my people are in the wrong.

Pharaoh, Exodus 9:27

Then Balaam said to the angel of the L<small>ORD</small>, "I have sinned, for I did not know that you stood in the road against me. Now therefore, if it is evil in your sight, I will turn back."

Balaam, Numbers 22:34

Saul said to Samuel, "I have sinned, for I have transgressed the commandment of the L<small>ORD</small> and your words, because I feared the people and obeyed their voice.

Saul, 1 Samuel 15:24

"I have sinned by betraying innocent blood."

Judas, Matthew 27:4a

Pharaoh, Balaam, Saul, and Judas admitted they had sinned, but they did not repent. Unfortunately, many of the people we try to help will admit to their sin and even say they are sorry, but only sorrow that leads to repentance is beneficial.

David said to Nathan, "I have sinned against the L<small>ORD</small>."

David, 2 Samuel 12:13a

Fortunately, David was truly sorry and repented of his behavior when Nathan confronted him regarding Bathsheba. This led him to pray a model prayer of repentance in Psalm 51. This can be a good model for those you try to help.

> *Have mercy on me, O God,*
> *according to your steadfast love;*
> *according to your abundant mercy*
> *blot out my transgressions.*
> *Wash me thoroughly from my iniquity,*
> *and cleanse me from my sin!*
> *For I know my transgressions,*
> *and my sin is ever before me.*

David began by seeking God's mercy. He freely acknowledged his sin, and asked God to wash his sin away. There was no blame of others, but an acceptance of his responsibility.

> *Against you, you only, have I sinned*
> *and done what is evil in your sight,*
> *so that you may be justified in your words*
> *and blameless in your judgment.*
> *Behold, I was brought forth in iniquity,*
> *and in sin did my mother conceive me.*
> *Behold, you delight in truth in the inward being,*
> *and you teach me wisdom in the secret heart.*
> *Purge me with hyssop, and I shall be clean;*
> *wash me, and I shall be whiter than snow.*

David acknowledged that he had sinned against God. This is a key element that must be recognized. David acknowledged his sinful nature and asked God to cleanse him again.

> *Let me hear joy and gladness;*
> *let the bones that you have broken rejoice.*
> *Hide your face from my sins,*
> *and blot out all my iniquities.*
> *Create in me a clean heart, O God,*
> *and renew a right spirit within me.*
> *Cast me not away from your presence,*
> *and take not your Holy Spirit from me.*
> *Restore to me the joy of your salvation,*
> *and uphold me with a willing spirit.*

It is not until after David repented that he asked God to allow him to experience joy again. Even in that request, he speaks of his relationship with God, and asks God to help him start again by creating a new heart and spirit within him.

> *Then I will teach transgressors your ways,*
> *and sinners will return to you.*
> *Deliver me from bloodguiltiness, O God,*
> *O God of my salvation,*
> *and my tongue will sing aloud of your righteousness.*
> *O Lord, open my lips,*
> *and my mouth will declare your praise.*

David asks that he might be able to teach others the way they should go. It is interesting to see how many people who were once addicted to a substance or activity begin to work as an addiction counselor. It sounds like David prays for this kind of outcome.

> *For you will not delight in sacrifice, or I would give it;*
> *you will not be pleased with a burnt offering.*
> *The sacrifices of God are a broken spirit;*
> *a broken and contrite heart, O God, you will not despise.*
> *Do good to Zion in your good pleasure;*
> *build up the walls of Jerusalem;*
> *then will you delight in right sacrifices,*
> *in burnt offerings and whole burnt offerings;*
> *then bulls will be offered on your altar.*
> Psalm 51:1-19

David recognizes that God is concerned more about his heart than anything else. In essence, he asked God to help him delight in Him as he moved forward. It is helpful to study this Psalm and make it one's own.

There are also prayer problems associated with addiction. Some do not understand why their craving for a substance or activity does not go away when they pray and ask God to remove it. Sometimes one wonders, "Why am I having all of this trouble after I have decided to do what is right?" We address this more thoroughly in *First Aid for Your Emotional Hurts: Sexual Issues.*

Sometimes it helps when a helper shares how they have struggled over time with a particular issue (e.g., anger, overeating) to demonstrate that we all are going to struggle with something in life, and will continue to do so until we reach heaven or the LORD returns. Though our struggle does not end, it gets easier as the LORD walks beside us and helps carry our cross daily.

The Word and Your Words

You can use the Word to help with some of these prayer difficulties. Initially, it may be very difficult when one stops using a substance or engaging in a sinful activity. Often people experience withdrawal symptoms, strong cravings, and even problems with peers and others who used to be supportive of them. Sometimes it seems harder after one has stopped, or you might say, "I have experienced more trouble after trying to do right." This can be very confusing.

Did Joseph Suffer for Doing Right?

He is not greater in this house than I am, nor has he kept back anything from me except you, because you are his wife. How then can I do this great wickedness and sin against God?"

Genesis 39:9

What Did Potiphar's Wife Try to Get Joseph to Do?

And Joseph's master took him and put him into the prison, the place where the king's prisoners were confined, and he was there in prison.

Genesis 39:20

What Happened to Joseph After He Refused to Go Along?

Consider Joseph in the aftermath of his refusal to have an affair with Potiphar's wife. He went to prison as a result of his decision. In the short run, there was great pain. In the long run, his life went much better. We do not want people to assume their life will always be perfect, immediately better, after a decision and action that results in stopping an entangling activity. In the immediate aftermath, some can become very ill and feel very down. In the long run though, they will be much better off as was Joseph for the hard decision he made. Jesus taught us about this.

> *And calling the crowd to him with his disciples,*
> *he said to them, "If anyone would come after me,*
> *let him deny himself and take up his cross and follow me.*
> Mark 8:34

Deciding to follow Jesus and refusing to continue in these types of sins is a way of denying our own will. In other places, Jesus taught that following Him was like taking the narrow road (Matthew 7:13-14). Most will not choose to follow Him because doing so can bring immediate difficulty.

Another area of confusion is whether one must stop engaging in these behaviors. Some will say, "God has forgiven me, why must I quit?"

> *Let not sin therefore reign in your mortal body, to make you obey*
> *its passions. Do not present your members to sin as instruments*
> *for unrighteousness, but present yourselves to God as those who*
> *have been brought from death to life, and your members to God as*
> *instruments for righteousness. For sin will have no dominion over*
> *you, since you are not under law but under grace.*
> Romans 6:12-14

This Scripture teaches us that we ought not to let sin reign or rule our lives. Further, we are not to let our passions rule us. So instead of using our hands, feet, and eyes to do that which we ought not, we are to use them for good for God.

> *Whoever is slow to anger is better than the mighty,*
> *and he who rules his spirit than he who takes a city.*
> Proverbs 16:32

As the Proverb indicates, we are called to rule our own spirit. We cannot be effective if we are ruled by our passions. In another

Proverb, a king's mother told her son that kings should not be ruled by strong drink.

> It is not for kings, O Lemuel,
> it is not for kings to drink wine,
> or for rulers to take strong drink.
>
> Proverbs 31:4

Similarly, it is not for those who are followers of Christ to be ruled by their own passions. Often individuals who struggle with these types of behaviors have errors in thinking about the particular behavior (e.g., gambling and money). Real change will require a change in thinking. The Word can be used to help them with their thinking by flooding their mind with Scripture. For example, someone who was having a problem with gambling would benefit from studying 1 Timothy 6.

> But godliness with contentment is great gain, for we brought nothing into the world, and we cannot take anything out of the world. But if we have food and clothing, with these we will be content.
>
> 1 Timothy 6:6-8

A healthy attitude about gain and a spirit of contentment can go a long way in combatting faulty thinking.

> But those who desire to be rich fall into temptation, into a snare, into many senseless and harmful desires that plunge people into ruin and destruction. For the love of money is a root of all kinds of evils. It is through this craving that some have wandered away from the faith and pierced themselves with many pangs. But as for you, O man of God, flee these things. Pursue righteousness, godliness, faith, love, steadfastness, gentleness.
>
> 1 Timothy 6:9-11

Though this passage is not directly about gambling, it describes the nature of this problem, as the person who falls into temptation is caught in a snare that leads to ruin and destruction. This aptly describes what can happen when one continues in this entanglement without intervention. Any entangling behavior must be replaced with something healthy. The passage ends by focusing on a proper use of resources, which is our goal as we work with those who struggle with these kinds of difficulties.

> *They are to do good, to be rich in good works, to be generous and ready to share, thus storing up treasure for themselves as a good foundation for the future, so that they may take hold of that which is truly life.*
>
> 1 Timothy 6:18-19

For example, consider Zacchaeus who was entangled in greed, that led him to steal from others. In addition to paying back fourfold those he had stolen from, he gave to the poor. Perhaps, this was the antidote for his greed.

> *Behold Lord, the half of my goods I give to the poor. And if I have defrauded anyone of anything, I restore it fourfold.*
>
> Luke 19:8b

The Church and Relationships

The church must be the hospital for those who are entangled in these behaviors and the refuge for those who are fleeing them. Paul recorded a long list of these behaviors and then noted of the Corinthians, "Such were some of you." The early church was extremely effective in breaking these chains.

> *And such were some of you. But you were washed, you were sanctified, you were justified in the name of the Lord Jesus Christ and by the Spirit of our God.*
>
> 1 Corinthians 6:11

> *A truthful witness saves lives, but one who breathes out lies is deceitful.*
>
> Proverbs 14:25

Each of the individuals in our opening cases need someone who will partner with them to help them out of their situation. People need good, trustworthy friends who will tell them the truth and confront them when they slip up Relationships are needed to keep people from feeling isolated and to protect them—at times from themselves.[198]

> Therefore, confess your sins to one another and pray for one another, that you may be healed. The prayer of a righteous person has great power as it is working.
> James 5:16

Research indicates the relationships that work with those fighting addictions consist of at least two people working together for mutual growth in partnership. The key ingredients for success are availability, affinity, intensity, maturity, and accountability. The meetings should have an agenda where Scriptural passages, as well as relational and personal progress, are discussed.[199]

Use Your Techniques

Observe

As you observe others, you are looking for cognitive, behavioral, and physiological symptoms. Some errors in the cognitive domain will revolve around myths they have engaged. For example, some minimize their behavior by thinking, "Well at least I don't do . . ." Others do what they do out of a sense of entitlement, and some are quick to quip that, "It only hurts me" when confronted about their behavior. You will also see behavioral impact that may present as depression, mood swings, or an inability to care for themselves. Further, there are physiological responses like shaking when a person has been without a substance.[200] As you observe, you are trying to determine how bad the situation may be.

The Continuum of Chemical Use	
Total abstinence from drug use	Level 0
Rare social use of drugs	Level 1
Heavy social use/early problem use of drugs	Level 2
Heavy problem use/early addiction to drugs	Level 3
Clear addiction to drugs	Level 4

For example, there is a continuum of different levels of chemical use.[201] The type of treatment or intervention needed for a person is determined by their substance use upon the continuum. It is probable that one could intervene with a friend or loved one at level 1. Someone at level 2 of the continuum could probably be treated on an outpatient basis whereas those at level 3 and 4 would likely require inpatient intervention.

It is also important to look at the stage of change which a person is currently. In their work with addictive individuals, Prochaska, DiClemente, and Norcross noted five stages of change experienced by their clients who struggled with substances. The first stage was the precontemplation stage. At this stage, the person does not seek help for the behavior and does not see the behavior as a problem. If anything, the person blames others for the problems he or she experiences. In this situation, people usually refuse any type of treatment unless they are forced to receive it, as someone addicted to alcohol is required to receive treatment in a correctional facility after incurring a substance related offense. At this stage, the person tends to refuse treatment unless circumstances force them to participate.

Then there is the contemplation stage. At this stage, an individual is aware he has a problem, but has not made a serious commitment to do anything about it. This person may consider making changes within six months.

The next stage is the preparation stage. At this stage, an individual has begun to make small changes about their problematic behavior and plans to make more complete changes within a month. Someone at this stage might be able to be treated as an outpatient. This is followed by the action stage when a person is actively involved in treatment and has changed their behavior for a short time. This stage is followed by the maintenance stage when a person is actively involved in maintaining the attitude and behavioral changes that have occurred.[202]

Attend

Once we observe there is a problem, we must attend to the person. That requires us to intervene. As mentioned earlier, the Old Testament describes the sexual sin of David and Sampson. Consider the case of Sampson. One never sees Sampson really confronted for his behavior.

A Weak Intervention

Samson went down to Timnah, and at Timnah he saw one of the daughters of the Philistines. Then he came up and told his father and mother, "I saw one of the daughters of the Philistines at Timnah. Now get her for me as my wife." But his father and mother said to him, "Is there not a woman among the daughters of your relatives, or among all our people, that you must go to take a wife from the uncircumcised Philistines?" But Samson said to his father, "Get her for me, for she is right in my eyes."

Judges 14:1-3

Sampson did something he was not supposed to do by going to the Philistines. He saw someone he was not supposed to be with and demanded her, someone forbidden by God. This is his entitled thinking on display. In fact, he seems to demand and push his way around.

His parents pointed out to him how the Philistine woman was not right for him (Judges 14:3). He insisted that he receive her and does not appear to have really been confronted.

Later, the Israelites came to Sampson and complained to him (Judges 15:11), but they did not appear to confront him about his inappropriate behavior either. His behavior deteriorated with Delilah, and we see him engage in more risk taking. He goes into the stronghold of the Philistines (Judges 16:1) and eventually met his demise (Judges 16:20-21). Though he was a very powerful man, he was destroyed because he remained entangled in sexual sin.

On the other hand, consider the intervention that Nathan engaged with David. David had engaged in very bad behavior. He had an affair (2 Samuel 11:4), conspired to take the life of an innocent man (2 Samuel 11:15), and then took that man's wife for himself upon the man's death (2 Samuel 11:27). The prophet Nathan confronted David and pointed out his sin to him.

A Real Intervention

Nathan said to David, "<u>You are the man</u>! Thus says the LORD, the God of Israel, 'I anointed you king over Israel, and I delivered you out of the hand of Saul. And I gave you your master's house and your master's wives into your arms and gave you the house of Israel and of Judah. And if this were too little, I would add to you as much more. Why have you despised the word of the LORD, to do what is evil in his sight? You have struck down Uriah the Hittite with the sword and have taken his wife to be your wife and have killed him with the sword of the Ammonites.

2 Samuel 12:7-9

The confrontation was specific and direct. What might have happened to David had Nathan failed to confront him? The lesson for us is to intervene when those for whom we care are doing things to themselves that will ruin their lives. In much of the substance abuse counseling field, this is referred to as an "intervention." In situations like this today, we would do well to follow the model found in Matthew 18. As we see a person deteriorate, we must confront them. If they refuse to hear us, we involve others. With many entangling sin, one will need to engage in serious treatment after being confronted about their behavior.

An Intervention Model

"If your brother sins against you, go and tell him his fault, between you and him alone. If he listens to you, you have gained your brother. But if he does not listen, take one or two others along with you, that every charge may be established by the evidence of two or three witnesses. If he refuses to listen to them, tell it to the church. And if he refuses to listen even to the church, let him be to you as a Gentile and a tax collector.

Matthew 18:15-17

Jesus described the process. It can be difficult and messy, but it is necessary to help another person get out of the dangerous cycle. Often, when people are confronted, they experience remorse. That was the reaction of David when he was confronted by Nathan.

> David said to Nathan, "I have sinned against the LORD."
> And Nathan said to David, "The LORD also has
> put away your sin; you shall not die."
> 2 Samuel 12:13

Listen

After we attend and confront, it is critical that we listen and observe. David said the right thing. But as we mentioned earlier, the same words were uttered by Pharaoh, Saul, Balaam, and Judas to no avail. Another example of a prayer of repentance prayed by David is found in Psalm 31.

> In you, O LORD, do I take refuge;
> let me never be put to shame;
> in your righteousness deliver me!
> Incline your ear to me;
> rescue me speedily!
> Be a rock of refuge for me,
> a strong fortress to save me!
> For you are my rock and my fortress;
> and for your name's sake you lead me and guide me;
> you take me out of the net they have hidden for me,
> for you are my refuge.
> Into your hand I commit my spirit;
> you have redeemed me, O LORD, faithful God.
> Psalm 31:1-5

Notice the relief David felt after he repented. Many people experience that sensation after "coming clean" about their behavior. However, this will just be the beginning of their restoration. There will still be hard work ahead for those who are truly repentant.

Care and Respond

True repentance will result in relief, a change in behavior, and a willingness to be held accountable. Though Job did not experience his difficulties because of sin, he indicated in his discourse with his friends that he had made a covenant with God about what he would and would not look at. You too are listening for people to make a commitment or covenant about what they will or will not do.

> *I have made a covenant with my eyes;*
> *Why then should I look upon a young woman?*
> Job 31:1 (NKJV)

Depending on the behavior or activity, most people will go through a period when they must get the substance or the impact of the behavior, out of their system. They must learn to live without the substance or activity. The individual who is addicted to a substance will often need to go to a hospital or a treatment facility for detoxification. In that treatment facility, they will receive medical help so they can safely withdraw from the substance to which they are addicted. In addition, they will learn how to live without the substance or activity, address the seemingly unimportant decisions (SUDs) they make, and learn the cues that make them vulnerable to engage in the behavior.[203]

You are listening for this process. What are the seemingly unimportant decisions in which they engage? In the case of David, it was sleeping in and not going to work (2 Samuel 11:1). For those with whom you work, it might be deciding to avoid certain places or certain people. What are the cues that trigger them to crave a substance or engage in a behavior? For David, it was seeing Bathsheba (2 Samuel 11:2). There are many visual cues that make someone susceptible to a behavior. Listen for the cues the person you are trying to help and you will be better prepared to respond to them.

> *So flee youthful passions and pursue righteousness, faith, love, and peace, along with those who call on the Lord from a pure heart.*
>
> 2 Timothy 2:22

In a treatment setting, those who are recovering from an addiction will develop a relapse prevention plan whereby to avoid succumbing to these temptations in the future. This plan will involve fleeing from the cues and triggers that make one more susceptible to relapse. Rather than seeing how close one can get without crossing a line or relapsing, one will need to plan for ways to get away from the substance or activity.

> *Be not among drunkards*
> *or among gluttonous eaters of meat,*
> *for the drunkard and the glutton will come to poverty,*
> *and slumber will clothe them with rags.*
>
> Proverbs 23:20-21

A major part of the plan often involves the kinds of relationships one will have going forward. Avoiding the wrong relationships and nourishing positive relationships is key to success. Be ready to respond when someone says, "I have been freed from . . ." or "I have this licked." This statement may be true but unless one is on guard, they can be involved in the entangling sin again.

> *Be on guard, keep awake. For you do*
> *not know when the time will come.*
>
> Mark 13:33

In fact, one of the most dangerous positions in which to be is not to be on guard to a potential threat. Consider the example of David.

> *Now King David was old and advanced in years. And although they covered him with clothes, he could not get warm. Therefore his servants said to him, "Let a young woman be sought for my lord the king, and let her wait on the king and be in his service. Let her lie in your arms, that my lord the king may be warm." So they sought for a beautiful young woman throughout all the territory of Israel, and found Abishag the Shunammite, and brought her to the king. The young woman was very beautiful, and she was of service to the king and attended to him, but the king knew her not.*
>
> 1 Kings 1:1-4

This is one of the saddest passages of the Bible. On his death-bed, the problem of sexual sin seems to rear its ugly head again. Many are quick to point out that David and Abishag (the woman who laid with him) did not have a sexual relationship. Try to explain that to Bathsheba or Solomon. When Adonijah, the brother of Solomon, asked if he could marry Abishag (1 Kings 2:13), Solomon had him killed (1 Kings 2:22-23). Help those with whom you work remain vigilant to avoid entanglement with these sins.

> *But I say, walk by the Spirit, and you will not gratify the desires of the flesh.*
>
> Galatians 5:16

You may also need to help people understand the process that transpires as they try to remain away from an entangling sin. Fighting back against an addiction is more of a journey rather than a one-step process. But as one continues to walk by the Spirit or concentrate upon prayer, Scripture reading, and their relationships with other people, it will get easier. Feeding the Spirit leads to life.[204]

Feed the Spirit > **Life**

Every day, they will make a choice. It will get easier as they "feed the Spirit." On the other hand, when one "feeds the flesh," they are putting themselves in places where they are more likely to be tempted. In a practical sense, we choose to put water or gasoline on our fiery desires by what we do and where we go.[205]

Feed the Spirit

Feed the Flesh

Act

By our actions, we can help people through this process. One area where we may need to help is sanitizing the environment one is in. Real change often is not easy; the environment of a person is very critical. Consider the case of someone addicted to cigarettes. Research has indicated that some of the best ways to avoid smoking is to stay away from the places where they face strong urges to smoke. Smokers who find themselves in environments where they used to smoke experience greater cravings than in the standard context. Specifics of one study indicated that the actual couch in a person's home could be a terribly strong cue that creates a craving to smoke. It was observed that a key to quitting smoking was breaking the association between smoking and familiar environment.[206] So to help someone who struggles with smoking, we would help them identify the things that hamper them and find ways to avoid it.

For example, someone addicted to pornography might avoid certain situations where they are alone and temped to go online to look at images. There are some who are struggling with alcohol who battle with cues when they are in pizza parlors where they are tempted to consume again. In many ways, this is what Jesus was referring to in Matthew 5:29.

> *If your right eye causes you to sin, tear it out and throw it away.*
> *For it is better that you lose one of your members than*
> *that your whole body be thrown into hell.*
>
> Matthew 5:29

Sometimes the person with whom we are working will have to make some hard choices to stay on track and away from an entangling sin. At times, you will struggle to know when you need to continue to try to help someone and when you have reached a point where you can no longer help them (Matthew 10:14). It will help if you can determine if the person has slipped or relapsed. When someone slips, they tend to acknowledge the "slip" quickly within a day or two. They are willing to accept more accountability and they seek help quickly. On the other hand, when one has relapsed, they withdraw from others, refuse their help, lie, and are no longer willing to seek treatment. There is nothing you can do in that situation.

Find the Inn

Help them find the inn. Look for groups like Alcoholics Anonymous (AA) and Narcotics Anonymous (NA), that have proven to be very helpful for avoiding relapse. These groups tend to ask the hard questions and see through the lies a person might tell. They also are quick to notice a shift in attitude that is the first indication something has gone awry. In short, a person needs an accountability partner.

It appears that while people are in treatment, they strongly believe that they can refrain from using substances after they return to their community. However, some facts have emerged that place people at a higher risk for relapsing. These factors include situations where the person is with friends and places where they previously used the substances or engaged in the activity. In reality, it seems that 75 percent of all relapses involve a failure to deal successfully with these kinds of situations. Interpersonal problems and social conflict also increase the risk for relapse. The emotional state of a person also places them at risk such as feelings of anger, frustration, anxiety, depression, and boredom.

It is important for the individual to learn alternate ways of coping with these situations. Dealing with life problems requires a person to deal appropriately with seemingly unimportant situations. It is also crucial that they work on their thinking. Thinking that expects relapse is referred to as "stinking thinking" by those in AA and NA. Many twelve-step programs also address negative emotions with the acronym HALT (hungry, angry, lonely, tired). The idea is that when someone begins to have these feelings, they are at greater risk for relapse. When people fail to get relational support, they are also at greater risk for relapse.[207] When we provide them with the support they need, chances increase that they will go on to live a more productive and enjoyable life. For many, their lives are transformed and Paul's words long ago about Philemon become true of them.

> For more on helping people with addictions see *First Aid for Addictions.*

(Formerly he was useless to you, but now he is indeed useful to you and to me.) I am sending him back to you, sending my very heart.

Philemon 1:11-12

For more information go to www.FirstAidForEmotionalHurts.com.

Resources

ALCOHOL AND DRUG ABUSE

Al-Anon Family Groups
1600 Corporate Landing Parkway
Virginia Beach, VA 23454
Voice: 757.563-.600
Fax: 757.563.1655
Website: www.al-anon.alateen.org

Alcoholics Anonymous
A.A. World Services, Inc.
P.O. Box 459
New York, NY 10163
Voice: 212.870.3400
Fax: 212.870.3003
Website: www.aa.org

American Society of Addiction Medicine
4601 North Park Ave. Suite 101, Upper Arcade
Chevy Chase, MD 20815
Voice: 301.656.3920
Fax: 301.656.3815
Website: www.asam.org
E-mail: email@asam.org

National Clearinghouse for Alcohol & Drug Information
P.O. Box 2345
Rockville, MD 20847-2345
Voice: 800.729.6686
Fax: 301.468.6433
Website: www.samhsa.gov

National Council on Alcoholism and Drug Dependence (NCADD)
22 Cortland St., Suite 801
New York, NY 10007-3128
Voice: 212.269.7797
Fax: 212.269.7510
Website: www.ncadd.org
E-mail: national@ncadd.org

Reformer's Unanimous
333 E State Street, # 201
Rockford, IL 61104
Voice: 866-733-6788
Website: www.rurecovery.com
E-mail: weneedu@reformu.com

DRUG ABUSE

Do It Now Foundation
P.O. Box 27568
Tempe, AZ 85285
Voice: 408.736.0599
Fax: 408.736.0771
Website: www.doitnow.org
E-mail: doitnow@cbazillion.com

Resources for Dealing with Pornography

Arterburn, S., Stoeker, F., & Yorkey, M. (2000). *Every Man's Battle*. Colorado Springs, CO: Random House, Inc.

Hall, L. (1996). *An Affair of the Mind: One Woman's Courageous Battle to Salvage Her Family From the Devastation of Pornography*. Carol Stream, IL: Tyndale House.

Perkins, B. (1997). *When Good Men are Tempted*. Grand Rapids, MI: Zondervan Publishing House.

Chapter 8

Helping People With Problems We Don't Understand

Behold, I am with you always, to the end of the age.

Matthew 28:20b

Some of the problems people have can frighten us. Some are confusing to us. How can we help someone who sees or hears things that are not present? How can we help someone who has trouble tracking time or becomes confused not knowing where they are? What can we do to help someone who awakes one morning and is unable to move? In this chapter, we will look at helping people with problems we do not understand.

Jim

Jim confides to you that he hears things and sees things that are evidently not present. For example, one evening he was in bed and he thought he heard two people arguing in his kitchen. He ran into the kitchen and no one was there. He has begun to have a general sense that people are out to get him. Sometimes he is very suspicious of others. He tells you that his father had problems like this and went to stay in a psychiatric hospital when Jim was a teen.

Jim seems to be experiencing a psychotic episode and to be struggling with a disease called schizophrenia.

What Is Schizophrenia?

The most debilitating of all mental illnesses is schizophrenia. Only 0.5 percent to 1.5 percent of the United States population suffers from schizophrenia. However, individuals with a biological relative with schizophrenia are 10 times more likely than the general population to have schizophrenia. Schizophrenia consists of hallucinations, delusions, and disorganized thinking. The symptoms of schizophrenia have been divided into positive and negative categories and they last for at least six months to meet the diagnostic criteria. Those who have the disease will likely have a lifelong struggle. Positive symptoms are active symptoms that include delusions (distortions in thought content), hallucinations (disturbances in perception), disorganized speech (distortion of language and thought processes), and disorganized or catatonic behavior (distortion of the body).[208] Negative symptoms involve restrictions in behavior where one may withdraw from others.

People that suffer from schizophrenia often believe things that are not true. These delusions are incorrect beliefs that involve a misinterpretation of perceptions or experiences. For example, one may see a utility worker and believe they are a CIA agent spying on them.

They also suffer from hallucinations. Hallucinations involve seeing, hearing, smelling, or feeling something that doesn't exist. Auditory hallucinations are the most common. A person may think they hear arguing in another room but when they enter the room no one is present.

Disorganized speech is characterized by a person easily "slipping off track" and moving from one topic to another. The individual may provide answers to questions that are completely unrelated to the question asked. Sometimes this is seen when a person talks but their words do not make up a coherent thought, more like a word salad.

In the DSM5, catatonia is a separate disorder. Catatonic behavior includes a very rigid posture or an extreme resistance to being moved. One is quick to recognize this behavior when it is seen because it is so unusual.

Disorganized behavior can be characterized by a markedly disheveled appearance. For example, a person might wear an overcoat or scarves on an extremely hot day. Other symptoms include un-triggered agitation when a person might begin shouting and swearing suddenly. This can result in talking in a manner that doesn't make much sense. Schizophrenia can also impact memory, and it seems that certain memory deficits can be observed prior to the onset of psychosis.[209]

Schizophrenia also consists of negative symptoms. Negative symptoms include restrictions in the range and intensity of emotional expression, difficulty with social interaction, and limited goal-directed activity. Many negative symptoms are tied to positive symptoms. For example, if someone has a delusion and paranoia that everyone is out to get them, they might avoid others and become socially withdrawn. Medication has limited impact on negative symptoms. Schizophrenia is far more prevalent than people think. According to the National Institute of Mental Health (NIMH), there are 2.2 million people in the United States who suffer from schizophrenia every year. Consider the chart below.[210]

No One You Know Has Schizophrenia, Right?

Do you know someone with alzheimer's disease? The prevalence rate for schizophrenia is two times that of alzheimer's disease. Do you know someone with multiple sclerosis? The prevalence rate for schizophrenia is five times that for multiple sclerosis.

Do you know someone with insulin-dependent diabetes? The prevalence rate for schizophrenia is six times that for insulin-dependent diabetes.

Do you know someone with muscular dystrophy? The prevalence rate for schizophrenia is sixty times that for muscular dystrophy. Chances are you know someone with schizophrenia.

For men, schizophrenia usually occurs in their teens or twenties. For women, schizophrenia first appears in their twenties and early thirties. What seems most surprising for many is its sudden onset. However, schizophrenia will frequently occur after a stressor like going off to college, starting a new business, or immediately after getting married.

Some studies have indicated that as many as 65 percent of patients with schizophrenia also suffer from depression.[211] This can exacerbate the illness. Ten percent of individuals with schizophrenia will commit suicide and between 20 and 40 percent will attempt suicide.[212]

Dissociative Identity Disorder

Another disorder that can frighten and confuse us is dissociative identity disorder. If you have ever watched a soap opera, you have seen a character portray dissociative identity disorder. It is the mental illness that sounds most similar to that of demon possession and it used to be called multiple personality disorder. The key feature of this problem is the presence of two or more personality states. It reflects a failure of a person to integrate aspects of their identity, memory, and consciousness. Each personality state may be experienced as if it had a distinct history, personality, self-image, and identity. People who have this disorder experience frequent gaps in memory. The number of identities have been reported as from 2 to 100.

How would one know the difference between this disorder and demon possession? One can look to the etiology of a problem for answers and the lack of other symptoms of demon possession. People who are diagnosed with dissociate identity disorder have typically experienced severe physical or sexual abuse, usually in childhood, and the disorder seems to be rare. For example, the disorder has been observed in some who survived the holocaust. Imagine experiencing that terror day after day and seeing the lives of those one loved taken. Some people seem to "zone out" to cope with such trauma. They might imagine being another personality and perhaps it is this kind of situation that such a disorder develops. If one did have a friend or family member who suffered with this problem, they would need to seek the assistance of a psychologist to help them integrate their different personalities.

Conversion Disorder

Conversion disorder impacts voluntary motor or sensory functioning. Initially, it often appears that a person has a neurological or some other medical condition. However, conversion disorder is often referred to as pseudoneurological since as it is psychological in nature. Conversion disorder with motor symptoms or deficit may impact a person's balance, result in paralysis, or some other physical problem. Conversion disorder with sensory symptom deficit involves problems like loss of touch, double vision, blindness, or deafness. There is also a conversion disorder with seizures or convulsions. The key aspect of these problems is there is not a physical reason for the difficulty. However, these problems are often associated with stress and there tends to be some secondary gain derived from the problem. For example, a student who is worried about taking the SAT might wake up one morning unable to move their legs. The apparent paralysis would result in them being unable to make the exam. The individual is not faking a disorder, but they are experiencing a high degree of psychological stress.

A Biblical Example

A good example of these types of problems is what Nebuchadnezzar experienced. Imagine what it would be like to begin to lose the ability to reason. That is what can happen to someone who suffers from some of these difficulties. The Bible describes the plight of Nebuchadnezzar, the powerful king of Babylon.

> *All this came upon King Nebuchadnezzar. At the end of twelve months he was walking on the roof of the royal palace of Babylon, and the king answered and said, "Is not this great Babylon, which I have built by my mighty power as a royal residence and for the glory of my majesty?"*
> Daniel 4:28-30

The Bible describes Nebuchadnezzar as a man who was full of pride. Because of his behavior, he appeared to have been struck by the disease of schizophrenia. He began to eat grass like an ox and he went outside and lived on the street. Anyone who saw

King Nebuchadnezzar must have been afraid of him and his disheveled appearance.

> *Immediately the word was fulfilled against Nebuchadnezzar. He was driven from among men and ate grass like an ox, and his body was wet with the dew of heaven till his hair grew as long as eagles' feathers, and his nails were like birds' claws.*
>
> Daniel 4:33

Apparently, after seven years, his reasoning returned. Nebuchadnezzar's reaction demonstrates the relief he received when his illness was removed and he recovered.

> *At the end of the days I, Nebuchadnezzar, lifted my eyes to heaven, and my reason returned to me, and I blessed the Most High, and praised and honored him who lives forever.*
>
> *Now I, Nebuchadnezzar, praise and extol and honor the King of heaven, for all his works are right and his ways are just; and those who walk in pride he is able to humble.*
>
> Daniel 4:34, 37

The picture of Nebuchadnezzar demonstrates the awful nature of psychosis. The disease comes with stigma and fear from those who are around. However, people who suffer from psychosis desperately need their friends and family in order to survive and thrive.

> *When you pass through the waters, I will be with you; and through the rivers, they shall not overwhelm you; when you walk through fire you shall not be burned, and the flame shall not consume you.*
>
> Isaiah 43:2

Use Your Tools

Our God offers real hope. He promised to bring Israel through fires and floods. He can help those who are even in danger of losing their ability to reason. As a friend who is trying to help others, it helps to remember and remind them of the hope they have in God. There is always hope. In fact, 70 percent of patients who suffer from schizophrenia will partially or fully respond to treatment.[213]

Prayer

We must be faithful to pray for those who struggle with these kinds of illnesses. Psalm 23 and 46 are good psalms to memorize and pray for those who struggle with these issues. If ever there were a time when the mountain fell into the middle of the sea, it is with a bout with schizophrenia.

For we do not wrestle against flesh and blood,
but against the rulers, against the authorities,
against the cosmic powers over this present darkness,
against the spiritual forces of evil in the heavenly places.
Ephesians 6:12

The Word and Your Words

You must know the Word well to help people with these problems. Sometimes those who suffer from psychosis may begin to fear they are being oppressed by demons or devils. You might even be fearful of the source of the symptoms caused by schizophrenia or these other disorders. The Bible describes the behavior of demons. Could someone you know be influenced by this kind of evil? How would you know the difference between mental illness and a spiritual illness?

The gospels record several cases of demon possession to demonstrate the power of Christ over demons. Almost every New Testament book mentions demons or evil angels. Hebrews is the exception with a focus on good angels.

> *When Jesus had stepped out on land, there met him a man from the city who had demons. For a long time <u>he had worn no clothes</u>, and <u>he had not lived in a house</u> but among the tombs. When he saw Jesus, he cried out and fell down before him and said with a loud voice, "What have you to do with me, Jesus, Son of the Most High God? I beg you, do not torment me." For he had commanded the unclean spirit to come out of the man. (For many a time it had seized him. He was kept under guard and <u>bound with chains and shackles</u>, but he would break the bonds and be driven by the demon into the desert.) Jesus then asked him, "What is your name?" And he said, "Legion," for many demons had entered him. And they begged him not to command them to depart into the abyss. Now a large herd of pigs was feeding there on the hillside, and they begged him to let them enter these. So he gave them permission. Then the demons came out of the man and entered the pigs, and the herd rushed down the steep bank into the lake and drowned.*
>
> Luke 8:27-33

Notice that the symptoms reported of this spiritually sick man sound similar to the mental illnesses many face. He went around naked and appeared to have nowhere to live. He had a demon that spoke to Jesus. He had unnatural power. He spoke in a different voice. In fact, the chart below demonstrates that many of the symptoms of mental illness are shared by those who are spiritually ill.[214]

Spiritual Illness Versus Physical Illness	
Characteristics of Demonic Influence	*Parallels among mental illness*
Supernatural knowledge	Schizophrenia Some people claim to have supernatural knowledge during psychotic episodes
Supernatural strength	Bipolar Disorder, Schizophrenia Observed in some manic and psychotic episodes

Going around naked	Schizophrenia Observed in some psychotic episodes
Unable to speak, hear, or visual impairment	Conversion Disorder People suffering from conversion disorder have deficits that effect motor or sensory functioning
Seizures	Conversion Disorder with seizures or convulsions
Use of a different voice or the presence of a distinct personality	Dissociative Identity Disorder (formerly Multiple Personality Disorder)
Bizarre behavior	Schizophrenia
Violent Behavior	At times Paranoid Schizophrenia Antisocial Personality Disorder

At first appearance, it might seem like spiritual and mental illness are very similar. However, there is a big difference between spiritual and mental illness. Notice in Scripture that one person who is under the influence of a demon can have all of the symptoms listed for demon possession. Although a mental illness might have one or two of the symptoms of possession, none of them have all.

> *You believe that God is one; you do well.*
> *Even the demons believe—and shudder!*
> James 2:19

So, what are some indicators of demonic influence? Look for involvement in and the practice of magic or mysticism as well as involvement in occultic practices. There seems to be a conscious invitation to Satan and demons to become involved in the person's life. Note in Luke 8 that the man is living among the dead (Luke 8:27). Often there is a history of Satanic worship in the family and a personal use of Tarot cards, Ouija boards, horoscopes, or fortune tellers. It appears that demonic influence is much greater in areas without a strong Judeo-Christian cultural influence.

Other clues include disinterest in spiritual growth and extreme negative reaction to the mention of God or Jesus. There tends to be evidence of unforgiveness, bitterness, and vengeance. There is also resistance to the benefits from medication and psychotherapy.[215]

There seems to be a lot of fear about the concept of demon possession. However, it is important to get some perspective on the situation. God is the Creator of all things—including demons. He has power over them as well, as Jesus demonstrated upon this earth (Luke 8:32).

> *For by him all things were created, in heaven and on earth, visible and invisible, whether thrones or dominions or rulers or authorities—all things were created through him and for him.*
>
> Colossians 1:16

Those who are oppressed by demons have usually sought to be involved with them. Those who repent and make Jesus the Lord of their lives will be freed. The Bible teaches us to draw close to God and His Word, which is our protection from demons.

> *Finally, be strong in the Lord and in the strength of his might. Put on the whole armor of God, that you may be able to stand against the schemes of the devil. For we do not wrestle against flesh and blood, but against the rulers, against the authorities, against the cosmic powers over this present darkness, against the spiritual forces of evil in the heavenly places. Therefore take up the whole armor of God, that you may be able to withstand in the evil day, and having done all, to stand firm.*
>
> Ephesians 6:10-13

The Bible also teaches us that these evil forces can be defeated by the power of Jesus Christ. We also have the promise of God's protection. For those that follow Him, God has His own angels who are there to serve and protect.

> *Let them be put to shame and dishonor*
> *who seek after my life!*
> *Let them be turned back and disappointed*
> *who devise evil against me!*
>
> Psalm 35:4

The Church and Relationships

When considering those who struggle with psychosis, the actions of their family and friends most often determines the quality of life of that individual. This is defined in the research literature as social support, which involves meeting the unmet needs of these individuals.[216] Our goal is to stay as involved as we can with those who struggle with these illnesses. Doing what we can to keep them active and involved with people in the church, and keeping track of them and their living conditions can improve outcomes.

Use Your Techniques

Observe

Often we are aware of individuals who struggle with these kinds of illnesses because they have experienced previous difficulties in adolescence or early adulthood. As we interact with them, we observe them closely as they experience stressors (e.g., going away to school, getting married, starting a business). When we spot difficulties, we need to be prepared to respond. Consider the case below.

The United States Capital Shooting

On July 24, 1998, Russell Eugene Weston, Jr. entered the United States Capitol. After being instructed to walk through the metal detector by the Police, he shot Capitol Police Officer Jacob Chestnut in the head, killing him. Weston then entered some of the congressional offices and shot Capitol Police Detective John Gibson. Gibson would later die at George Washington University Hospital.

Soon after the incident, it was learned that Weston had a history of bizarre behavior. He had returned a class reunion invitation with obscenities written across it and believed that Navy SEALS were hiding in a nearby cornfield. He suspected the government and his neighbors were spying on him. He had shot 14 cats with a shotgun and separated himself from others. Six years earlier he had been diagnosed with schizophrenia, but he had stopped taking his medication.

When people think of schizophrenia they often think Russell Eugene Weston, Jr. or John Hinkley, Jr. who have harmed others while suffering from schizophrenia. Despite appearances, this kind of behavior is very rare for people who suffer from schizophrenia or any other disorder. However, these examples do point to the need to attend to those who struggle with these types of illnesses. Nevertheless, it is important that you be able to identify when someone is a danger.

When Is Someone a Danger?

1. People can become dangerous when they refuse to take their medications. This is especially pronounced when one sees medication as part of their delusions (e.g., they want me to take medication so they can control my mind).
2. Are they having legal problems? Look for incidents where the person has incurred charges, like disturbing the peace or assault. This demonstrates a lack of control and agitation.
3. Do they have access to weapons? Individuals who are experiencing delusions or hallucinations can become extremely dangerous when they have access to weapons.
4. Are they isolated? If they do not have anyone to talk to or confide in they become more desperate.

Therefore, O king, let my counsel be acceptable to you: break off your sins by practicing righteousness, and your iniquities by showing mercy to the oppressed, that there may perhaps be a lengthening of your prosperity.

Daniel 4:27

Attend

Just as Daniel attended to Nebuchadnezzar, we too should attend by providing social support. Those who suffer the most from schizophrenia are socially isolated. If they do not have others who are following their progress, their problems will deteriorate. At the extreme, this can result in violence or a situation where the individual becomes homeless. It is easy to become frightened by someone who is actively psychotic or by the term schizophrenia. People with this disease do not need to be feared. The only time people are particularly dangerous is when they are actively paranoid and experiencing thoughts of harming themselves or others.

Listen

We can help others by being there for them and listening to them. As you do, be careful about your body language. Talking to someone who is actively psychotic can be unnerving, but it is important to convey hope and to be aware of your appearance. Try to be relaxed. Don't get too close. Most Americans want people no closer than three feet. Be careful that the person does not feel crowded. Stay pleasant, but don't laugh—keep a concerned look and convey interest. Avoid pointing or gesturing and constant eye contact.

As you talk to them, do not argue with them about the "voices" or their beliefs. Realize they have an altered reality and there is nothing that can be done about that without medication. Stay calm and it might be necessary to lower your voice. Take care of the environment. Remove anything that could become a weapon and decrease the noise level and remove bright lights. Flashing lights, loud noises, and distractions like the television and a dishwasher can be problematic.

Care

As someone shares with you that they hear things others do not hear, you may at first think they are joking. As you realize they are not joking, take the time to listen to them and pay attention to their fears.

Try to empathize with the person. Do not be patronizing or authoritative toward them. Instead, say things like, "You seem really afraid/upset. Please tell me what is bothering you." Don't argue with or challenge them. Encourage them to discuss what they are experiencing with a healthcare provider.[217]

Respond

The danger with psychosis is that a person can lose their ability to reason and in some cases, become a danger to themselves or others. In these cases, one must intervene. The ideal way to intervene is through a person's healthcare provider. If the person suffering from these symptoms will report them to their provider, the provider can take the appropriate action. It might be possible for the individual to be treated on an outpatient basis. However, if more restrictive intervention is required, the provider should be able to assist in that process.

Act

It seems that people who suffer from serious mental illnesses are much less active than the general population. In fact, as many as 60 percent of those who have a serious mental illness also have a physical illness like heart disease, diabetes, hypertension, or respiratory disease. Exercise for those who suffer from psychotic illnesses helps to address the depression, low self-esteem, and social withdrawal that are often experienced. Low intensity exercises like walking are more beneficial than high intensity exercises.[218]

When an individual is in a state of great crisis, one might take them to the hospital emergency department. In that setting, the patient can be assessed and placed in a setting where they can be appropriately treated. Unfortunately, some people can suffer from such debilitating symptoms that they are unwilling to go to a provider or hospital for treatment. In those cases, it may become necessary to involve local law enforcement. One might have to go before a magistrate and describe the situation. If the magistrate finds sufficient cause, they can issue an involuntary commitment order for the person and law enforcement officials will then attempt to find the individual and take them to be evaluated. If the person is deemed to be a danger to themselves or others, they will be involuntarily committed until their mental status improves.

Find the Inn

Encouraging them to get help is your way of helping them find the inn. When people participate in treatment, they can have some very good outcomes. You may also need to work with them to encourage them to take their medications. Family members can have a negative influence on patient's treatment compliance. If family and friends are not supportive of the client taking medication, they are unlikely to persist. Examine the well-publicized tragedies dealing with schizophrenia. You will notice that in those cases, the people had stopped using their medication and in many cases, had become very isolated. Since there is such a stigma associated with taking medication, helpers will need to encourage those with whom they work to take their medication by doing what they can to remove the stigma. For example, many take medication for heart problems or diabetes every day. A helpful helper would do well to point that out to the person struggling with psychosis. The best and safest prognosis for someone with psychosis is to carefully follow their treatment regimen. However, noncompliance with taking medication can run as high as 70 to 80 percent.[219]

Why are people so resistant to taking medication? Even though medication is extremely helpful, it does not completely alleviate the problems of schizophrenia. At best, psychopharmacological treatment is no more than 80 percent effective. Additionally, psychosis impacts a person's ability to understand the medication regimen.[220]

Fear of the effects of medication are also a major reason people give for not taking their medication. If fact, medication can be incorporated into their delusions, especially when people have paranoid symptoms. Antipsychotic medication can lead to sedation, restlessness, and abnormal muscle movements called extrapyramidal symptoms (EPS). If untreated, EPS can progress to tardive dyskinesia. Tardive dyskinesia includes involuntary tremors and is permanent. However, tardive dyskinesia can be alleviated with anticonvulsive medications.

Encourage them to talk to their healthcare provider about the side effects of their medications. If they have dry mouth, they can chew sugarless gum or candy. Perhaps a change in dosage or type of medication can help. The more they talk to their provider about their concerns with side effects, the better the prognosis will be.

Although positive symptoms like delusions and hallucinations can be greatly reduced by medications, negative symptoms like disorganized thought and motivational deficits persist. These symptoms will need to be addressed through professional counseling and therapy. These symptoms do not respond well to medication. Often people with psychotic symptoms do not notice the benefit of the medication they are taking; however, they are quick to notice the side effects of their medications.

A Diagnosis of Schizophrenia Means Life Is Over, Right?

Elyn R. Saks was first officially diagnosed with schizophrenia during her first year of law school at Yale University. She was told she would never finish school, would probably never have a job, and would not be able to get married. Although Saks began battling schizophrenia in college, she was able to graduate at the top of her class at Vanderbilt University. She went on to earn a master's degree in philosophy at Oxford University and got married. After being hospitalized, she completed her law degree at Yale University. She went on to become an associate dean and professor of law at the Gould School of Law at the University of Southern California. Who says life is over after developing schizophrenia? Elyn Saks certainly does not.

See her Ted Talk at https://www.ted.com/talks/elyn_saks_seeing_mental_illness.

There are many frightening problems people can have. We have a promise from the Lord that He will protect us and always be with us. He has also given us tools to help us assist those who have these problems. Study and prepare to be the kind of helper who can help those in great need.

For more information go to www.FirstAidForEmotionalHurts.com.

Atypical Antipsychotic Medications

Trade Name	Generic Name	Level of Sedation
Clozaril	clozapine	Significant
Risperdal	risperidone	Minimum
Seroquel	quietapine	Significant
Abilify	aripiprazole	Minimum
Symbyak	fluoxetine and olanzapine	Moderate

Sinacola, R. S., & Peters-Strickland, T. (2012). *Basic Psychopharmacology for Counselors and Psychotherapists*—Second Edition. Boston, MA: Pearson.

Typically Used Antipsychotic Medications

Trade Name	Generic Name	Level of Sedation
Thorazine	chlorpromazine	Significant
Mellaril	thioridazine	Significant
Serentil	mezoridazine	Significant
Loxitane	loxapine	Moderate
Trilafon	perphenazine	Moderate
Navane	thiothixene	Minimal
Haldol	haloperidol	Minimal
Orap	pimozide	Minimal

American Academy of Neurology
1080 Montreal Ave.
St. Paul, MN 55116
Voice: 800.879.1960
Fax: 651.695.2791
Website: www.aan.com
E-mail: aan@aan.com

American Association of Suicidology
5221 Wisconsin Avenue, NW
Washington, DC 20015
Phone: 202.237.2280
Fax: 202.237.2282
Website: www.suicidology.org
E-mail: ajkulp0124@ix.netcom.com

American Society for Adolescent Psychiatry
P.O. Box 570218
Dallas, TX 75357-0218
Voice: 972.686.6166
Fax: 972.613.5532
Website: www.adolpsych.org
E-mail: adspsych@aol.com

Federation of Families for Children's Mental Health
9605 Medical Center Drive, Suite 280
Rockville, MD 20850
Phone: 240.403.1901
Fax: 240.403.1909
Website: www.ffcmh.org
E-mail: ffcmh@ffcmh.org

Harvard Brain Tissue Resource Center
McLean Hospital
115 Mill St.
Belmont, MA 02478
Voice: 800.272.4622; 617.855.2400
Fax: 617.855.3199
Website: www.brainbank.mclean.org
E-mail: btrc@mclean.org

National Alliance for the Mentally Ill (NAMI)
Colonial Place Three
2107 Wilson Blvd., Suite 300
Arlington, VA 22201
Phones: 800.950.6264; 703.524.7600
Fax: 703.524.9094
Website: www.nami.org

Mental Health America
2000 N. Beauregard St., 6th Floor
Alexandria, VA 22311
Voice: 800.969.6642
TTY: 800.433.5959
Fax: 703.684.5968
Website: www.nmha.org
E-mail: infoctr@nmha.org

National Institute of Mental Health
Public Inquiries
6001 Executive Blvd., Rm. 8184, MSC 9663
Bethesda, MD 20892-9663
Voice: 301.443.4513
Website: www.nimh.nih.gov
E-mail: nimhinfo@nih.gov

SCHIZOPHRENIA

National Alliance on Mental Illness (NAMI)
Colonial Place Three
2107 Wilson Blvd., Suite 300
Arlington, VA 22201-3042
Voice: 800.950.6264
Fax: 703.524.9094
Website: www.nami.org

National Alliance for Research on Schizophrenia and Depression
60 Cutter Mill Rd., Suite 404
Great Neck, NY 11021
Voice: 800.829.8289
Fax: 516.487.6930
Website: www.narsad.org
E-mail: info@narsad.org

Chapter 9

Helping Families Survive and Thrive

Therefore a man shall leave his father and his mother and hold fast to his wife, and they shall become one flesh.

Genesis 2:24

In this chapter, we will look at what we can do to help families survive and thrive. We will use just one case and infuse ways we might use our tools and techniques to assist families as they journey through life.

Jeremy and Stephanie

Two babies are born, Jeremy and Stephanie. What will happen to them? What will they become? What kind of life will they have? What will they become in twenty, forty, or even eighty years, assuming they live that long? That depends largely on what happens in their family over the course of the next few years.

What Kind of People Will Jeremy and Stephanie Become?

By far, the most influential people in the lives of Jeremy and Stephanie will be their parents. However, they will also be influenced by grandparents, uncles, aunts, pastors, Sunday School teachers (assuming they are taken to church), neighbors, and even the friends of their parents. But, it is the parents to whom God has entrusted with their well-being as is clear in Deuteronomy 6. That is where we will find a development plan for families.

Hear, O Israel: The LORD our God, the LORD is one.

Deuteronomy 6:4

Make God the Top Priority

God does not allow for any middle ground; "the LORD is one" the Scripture says. In other words, get it settled; there is only one God. It is not Buddha, Mohammed, materialism, or fame. God is the God. God demands our full devotion, "Love the LORD with all your heart, soul, and might," He said. There is no room for half-heartedness. Why is it so critical for parents to be spiritually sound?

Parents who make God their top priority make a difference in the lives of their children. For example, a study of 810 fathers indicated that the more involved fathers were with religion, the better relationships they had with their children. The study examined six areas that included the importance of faith, guidance provided by faith, religious attendance, religious identity, denominational affiliation, and belief in the importance of religion for their children.[221]

What will happen to Jeremy and Stephanie if they have a good relationship with their fathers? Stephanie is less likely to engage in premarital sex if she has a close relationship with her dad, and she is less likely to be depressed. One study involving a sample of adolescent virgins from intact, two parent families indicated that teenage girls who reported having a close relationship with their father during the initial interview were less likely to report having engaged in sexual intercourse during a follow-up interview one year later, when compared to teenage girls who did not report having a close relationship with their fathers.[222] Another study indicated that the higher teenage girls rated the relationship with their fathers, the less likely they were to experience depression.[223]

Jeremy's relationship with his father is important as well. One study of teenage boys indicated that compared with peers who did not feel close to their biological fathers, teenage boys who did feel close to their fathers were less likely to expect that they would themselves divorce in the future, whether or not they lived with their fathers.[224]

The relationships that Jeremy and Stephanie have with their parents can also reduce their susceptibility to the use of drugs. One study of teenagers and drug use indicated that teenagers that had friends who used drugs were more likely to use marijuana. However, this association was weakened if the teenagers felt close to their fathers or if they felt their parents would catch them using marijuana.[225] Step one to building a strong family is for the parents to know and fervently follow God and develop close relationships with their children.

> *You shall teach them diligently to your children, and shall talk of them when you sit in your house, and when you walk by the way, and when you lie down, and when you rise.*
>
> Deuteronomy 6:7

Step two is teaching God's commands to our children. Again, we are not talking about half-hearted teaching. God's Word says we should teach them diligently, when we sit, when we walk, when we lie down, and when we rise up. Basically, parents are to model applying the Scriptures before their children. Parenting is a 24/7, 365 days a year responsibility.

Using Your Tools and Techniques

Working with families in situations like this you might advocate for parents embracing the D6 Model. As part of the process, you could use your words to encourage them not to subcontract their role to schools, little league, the media, or even the church and church ministries. Use your tools and techniques to be a voice for vibrant families.

Jeremy and Stephanie need to see the application of Scripture applied in their parents own marriage. What they see will greatly influence the kind of families they have. For example, a study examined the personality and characteristics of the family environment and quality of family interactions of high school seniors. After seven years, the participants were interviewed again about their personal lives. Results indicated that the parenting and personality traits measured seven years earlier predicted the qualities of the relationships the seniors had seven years later. Another study compared boys who were reared in a home with married parents to boys whose parents were never married. They found that the boys whose parents never married were significantly less likely to marry and were more likely to be unfaithful to their romantic partners.[226]

Grandchildren are the crown of the aged,
and the glory of children is their fathers.
Proverbs 17:6

The Bible teaches that even grandparents are influential in the lives of their grandchildren. One study indicated that having grandparents who divorced has been associated with having a lower level of educational attainment, a greater likelihood of marital discord, and a poorer quality of parent-child relationship.

This association held even if the grandparents' divorce occurred before the grandchild was born.[227]

Counteracting the Culture

The culture in which Jeremy and Stephanie grow up will probably not be very family friendly or supportive of a biblical worldview. Data from the National Survey of Family Groups indicated that almost all Americans have sex before they get married. The data showed that 75 percent of the respondents had had premarital sex by age 20, and 95 percent of respondents had premarital sex by age 44.[228]

> *Let marriage be held in honor among all, and let the marriage bed be undefiled, for God will judge the sexually immoral and adulterous.*
>
> Hebrews 13:4

Apparently, very few in America are following God's command to be pure. Most will conclude from this study that people are not capable of sexual purity. However-

> For more on rearing children to counteract the culture see E. Moody. *Surviving Culture: Parent Edition.* (2014). Nashville, TN: Randall House.

er, premarital sex has many unintended consequences, even for those who take "precautions."

Premarital sex appears to impact the quality of a marriage. One study compared women who did not engage in premarital sex to those who had their first sexual encounter before marrying. Those who had premarital sex before marriage were approximately 34 percent more likely to divorce. For every year they delayed sex, the risk of marital disruption was reduced by about 8 percent.[229]

A good marriage can counteract the cultural trend toward sexual promiscuity. One study showed that women who had experienced their parents' separation during childhood were more likely to have an early pregnancy. The effects of parental separation were dependent on the child's age at the time at which the separation occurred. Relative to women that lived with both parents from birth to age 18, those whose parents separated when the girls were new born to 5 years old were 2.46 times more likely to have a pregnancy during adolescence. Those whose parents separated when the girls were 6-11 years old were 1.78 times more likely to have a pregnancy during adolescence. Those whose parents separated when the girls were 12 to 17 years old were 1.52 times as likely to have a pregnancy during adolescence.[230]

Using Your Tools and Techniques

Suppose you were in a church setting and observed Stephanie, who is in her senior year of high school. You have known Stephanie since she was two-weeks old as she and her parents attended church with you. Her parents have been good role models for her. Lately, she has begun to date a young man who is two years older. He is a bit rebellious and has had many girlfriends in his young life. He does not appear to treat Stephanie well either. What should you do?

What you can do for Stephanie depends upon who you are. However, the tools of prayer, the Word, your words, and your relationship with her will certainly pave the way. The closer you are and the better your relationship with her, the more direct you can be. She needs someone to speak the truth in love and help her identify positive characteristics she should expect in a potential husband.

Rather, speaking the truth in love, we are to grow up in every way into him who is the head, into Christ.

Ephesians 4:15

What to Look for in a Date (and Mate)

Either teach (if you are Stephanie's parent or someone in authority) or ask her questions to ask about the young man she is dating to help her think clearly about her situation. Help her critique her dating prospects.

Do not be unequally yoked with unbelievers. For what partnership has righteousness with lawlessness? Or what fellowship has light with darkness?

2 Corinthians 6:14

Is the Prospective Date a Believer?

The Bible is clear that believers are not to date non-believers. Every person we date is a potential mate, so Stephanie needs to clarify with the young man whether he knows the Lord. You can help her understand the importance of making this a priority in the dating relationship, rather than an afterthought.

Does the Prospective Date Value Spiritual Growth?

We have all seen young men (and women) who attend church until they get married. Once they are married, however, they no longer want to have anything to do with the church. We are not asking Stephanie to find someone who is perfect, but she does need to consider whether the young man she is dating is genuinely concerned about following God. You can encourage her to consider how he spends his free time. What does this young man like to do?

Is the Prospective Date Relationally-Based or Anti-Relationship?

In other words, you want Stephanie to consider whether this young man cares more about himself than he cares about her. A selfish man can be an unsafe man, who is a predator women need to avoid. At best, the selfish man will put his plans and desires before Stephanie. At worst, this could degenerate into great difficulty.

Is the Prospective Date Truth-Oriented or Dishonest?

You want Stephanie to consider whether this young man lovingly confronts in truth or focuses upon flattery or charm? Can he be trusted not to cheat on her? Stephanie will want someone who has a high regard for the truth.[231] The best predictor of future behavior is past behavior, so Stephanie wants to examine that information as she moves forward.

There are key questions we can ask someone to get them to think about whether someone is right for them. In the church and in our families, we need to teach people how to date and what to look for in a potential mate.

The Dangers of Cohabitation

According to the data released by the Census Bureau from the American Community Survey, married couples are now actually in the minority in the United States. They found that 49.7 percent, or 55.2 million, of the nation's 111.1 million households in 2005 were made up of married couples. This was down from 52 percent five years earlier.[232]

Many people who cohabitate say it is easier and cheaper. Are they correct? Compared with peers who are not married, married men earn a 20 percent higher wage, even when controlling for such factors as educational attainment.[233] In another study, married mothers showed greater psychological well-being, and reported less ambivalence and conflict. On the positive side, they reported greater love and intimacy in their relationships with their partners than cohabiting or single mothers.[234]

Many people choose to cohabit to test the marital waters. Today, at around age 22 for women and 22.5 for men cohabitation, instead of marriage takes place. Seventy-five percent of women's first unions in the late 2000s were cohabiting. This was a 58 percent increase over the past 20 years.[235] Dr. Pamela Smock, an associate professor of sociology at the University of Michigan, put it this way: "In some sense, cohabitation is replacing dating."[236] However, the research indicates that those who cohabit do not fair that well. For example, one study indicated that, the longer couples cohabited before marrying, the more likely they were to resort to heated arguments, hitting, and throwing objects when conflicts arose in their subsequent marriage. A longer length of cohabitation was linked to a greater frequency of heated argu-

monto.[237] You could use your techniques to try to provide this kind of information to Jeremy and Stephanie.

Before They Say, "I do"

> ### Jeremy and Stephanie Get Engaged
>
> Jeremy and Stephanie are in love. After 14 months of serious dating, they have decided to get married on the anniversary of their first date. The date is just three months away. When asked about premarital counseling they say, "Oh, we're Christians. We don't need that."

George Barna has actually found that people who say they are Christians have a higher incidence of divorce than non-Christians.[238] Jeremy and Stephanie would be in error if they think that being a Christian means they do not need to take the steps to prepare for marriage. Why do Christians divorce as frequently (or more frequently) than non-Christians? Les and Leslie Parrot have hypothesized that it may actually be the high regard Christians have for marriage that makes them more susceptible to divorce. This can result in Christians jumping into marriage too quickly without important pre-marital work. At one of their seminars, they asked a couple if they'd received pre-marital counseling to which they responded, "We got our counseling from the Holy Spirit." Sometimes Christians don't recognize the tools they need to have for a successful marriage.[239]

A study in the journal *Family Relations* indicated that couples who had completed some form of premarital counseling had a 30 percent increase in marital satisfaction when compared to those who had not received such counseling.[240] There are numerous premarital counseling materials available. One by the Parrott's includes a psychoeducational approach called *Saving our Marriage Before It Starts*. Another widely used program is PREPARE. In addition, there are numerous workbooks such as, *Before You Say "I Do"* by H. Norman Wright. In premarital counseling, couples should look at their expectations of marriage. Some approaches involve the development of a vision statement for a marriage. In addition, couples need to look at their roles and the roles of in-laws.

Some couples will need to do extensive work on their communication. For example, Dr. John Gottman, a psychologist who worked at the University of Washington, is well-known for his work with couples. Dr. Gottman studied more than 2,000 married couples over two decades and identified maladaptive patterns in how they relate with each other. He and his team said they can predict with 94 percent accuracy which marriages will end in divorce within four years by looking at their communication.[241] Some couples will need to spend a lot of time improving how they interact if their marriage is to be successful.

Other areas that premarital counseling need to address are finances, sex, and their spiritual life together. Jeremy and Stephanie should not be discussing their finances for the first time after they get married. These issues are critical to their survival and need to be thoroughly and carefully thought through and discussed.

Sometimes, couples claim they do not have the financial resources for premarital counseling. However, many spend large

> People who reported being happily married were 61 percent less likely to report using Internet pornography

amounts of money on the wedding and reception. It is important to see premarital counseling as an investment in the couple's future. A happy and healthy marriage can keep a lot of problems away.[242]

Getting Off to a Good Start

> 813,862 couples divorce every year
> 40-50 percent of all first marriages end in divorce

A good start for any newly married couple is to be mentored by an older couple. That is what Paul had in mind when he told the older women to teach the younger women. In premarital work, Jeremy and Stephanie should set up marriage mentoring with an older couple. As a helper, you could assist with developing such a program in your church. Marriage mentors are especially important in our mobile

> Consider becoming a marriage mentor. See Drs. Les and Leslie Parrott's Marriage Mentoring Information www.marriagementoring.com

society when many couples are separated from parents and in-laws.

Marriage mentors can assist couples with getting off to a good start and in overcoming new hurdles, like having children and the inevitable bumps in the road that will be coming. When couples have healthy marriages, there are numerous benefits.

> *And let us consider how to stir up one another to love and good works, not neglecting to meet together, as is the habit of some, but encouraging one another, and all the more as you see the Day drawing near.*
> Hebrews 10:24-25

Go to church

Being involved in "religious" activities has consistently been identified as a factor associated with marital adjustment.[243] In fact, the odds of being divorced are related to the religious density of one's community, as measured by church attendance. After controlling for ethnic and group factors, individuals who lived in communities with high religious densities were less likely to be divorced than those who lived in communities with lower religious densities.[244]

Having a marriage mentor(s) is like having an accountability partner. One area in which mentors can really help is with the spiritual growth of a couple. Spiritual growth is tied to the health of the married couple. For example, one study indicated that both husbands and wives in families who participated in religious activities and prayed, even occasionally, were more likely to provide encouragement to one another than parents in families who were not religiously active.[245] That growth also appears to be tied to being involved in a local church congregation. Another study indicated that higher levels of marital socializing, and wives' reports of happiness with the affection and understanding of their husbands, was associated with higher religious attendance.[246]

More specifically, a husband's familistic beliefs, including belief in the value of marriage and childbearing, belief in the importance of adult children caring for elderly parents, greater concern about divorce that involves couples with children, and gender-role traditionalism are strongly and significantly associated with a wife's report of happiness with the love and affection received from her partner.[247]

Today, many condemn husbands who have a literal view of the Bible. However, wives of conservative Protestant husbands are significantly more likely to report happiness with the love and affection they receive from their husbands than wives of unaffiliated men, and more than wives of mainline Protestant men.[248]

Be a Cheerleader

Marriage mentors can teach couples to be cheerleaders for one another. Those whose mates energetically cheered after positive events, such as a raise or a promotion were more satisfied with their relationship. Active enthusiasm results in positive relationship growth.[249]

As Jeremy and Stephanie continue to grow, they should be encouraged to participate in marriage enrichment activities. Marriage enrichment may involve a marriage seminar, workshop, or retreat. The focus is upon rekindling romance, facilitating growth, and helping couples. In these settings, couples can get knowledge and skills that will enhance their marriage.

> *Did he not make them one, with a portion of the Spirit in their union? And what was the one God seeking? Godly offspring. So guard yourselves in your spirit, and let none of you be faithless to the wife of your youth.*
>
> Malachi 2:15

Adjusting to Children

Marriage mentors can also help with the arrival of children. The arrival of children represents the most significant milestone in the life of a family. Unsurprisingly, one study indicated that the more infants cry during the night, the more dissatisfied parents—particularly mothers—become with their marriage. Parent's marital satisfaction significantly diminished in relation to how much their children cried. Parents who were already hav-

ing sleep problems before the baby was born had even more pronounced difficulties. When fathers were capable of handling their
infant's needs, the wives were happier. This was especially important for first-time parents. A key for first-time parents is to
learn how to calm the crying of children.[250] Therefore, this must
be a target as we try to help these parents.

Training Children

One potentially fatal mistake parents make is a failure to discipline their children. We see this recorded in Scripture where
Amnon committed a terrible sin against his sister Tamar. Both
were David's children. Apparently, David was very angry about
the incident.

> *When King David heard of all these things, he was very angry.*
> 2 Samuel 13:21

However, he did not do anything about it. Perhaps he failed to
do so because of his past affair with Bathsheba. Failure to discipline Amnon was a terrible mistake that irreparably damaged
Tamar and probably resulted in Amnon later losing his life. When
it comes to disciplining children, a parent's past is irrelevant. As
a parent, one has the authority and responsibility to put their
child on the right path. Often parents need to be reminded of this.
We want to learn from our mistakes rather than see our children
repeat them.

Common Children Problems

Problem	Prevalence
Intellectual disability	1 percent
Severe intellectual disability	6 per 1,000
Autism spectrum disorder	1 percent
Attention-deficit/hyperactivity disorder	5 percent of children
	2.5 percent of adults
Specific learning disorder	5-15 percent of school-age children
	4 percent of adults

There are many children who will struggle with a disability or other problems. Time and space do not permit us to deal with this here. I encourage you to take a look at *First Aid for Your Emotional Hurts: Helping Children With Learning Problems* for difficulties related to attention-deficit hyperactivity disorder and specific learning difficulties. Look at *First Aid for Your Emotional Hurts: Helping Children With Emotional Problems* for assistance dealing with depression, anxiety, and eating difficulty.

Jeremy and Stephanie Are at Each Other's Throats

Jeremy and Stephanie have been married for about three years now. Initially, their marriage grew stronger and more stable as time passed. But the last few months, they have experienced problems in their relationship. Before they got married, they had a tendency to argue a lot and would sometimes call each other names. They thought this tension would improve after they got married, but it has gotten progressively worse.

Jeremy and Stephanie have some of the attitudes that Dr. John Gottman and his team have identified as toxic to the survivability of a marriage. In this section, we will examine those ways of communicating as well as remedies for them.

> See *First Aid for Your Emotional Hurts: Marriage.*

Criticism

Couples whose marriages fail, engage in criticism. They attack one another's personality and character with the intention of hurting each other. They might say things like, "You can't do anything right!" There are a lot of generalizations about the shortcomings of each other.

But now you must put them all away: anger, wrath, malice, slander, and obscene talk from your mouth.

Colossians 3:8

Contempt

Contempt for one another is a poison to the relationship. This is an attack with the intention of insulting or hurting one another. This is when people call one another hurtful names like "wimp, slob, and lazy." There is hostile humor and sarcasm. The body language displays the attitude and can involve sneering and rolling of the eyes.

Defensiveness

Some couples choose to interact in a defensive manner. They prefer to see themselves as the victim of a perceived attack. They often look and make excuses, trying to pretend as if they have no control of their situation. There is a lot of "It's not my fault" in these relationships. There is no end of whining and complaining.

Stonewalling

Stonewalling involves withdrawing from the relationship as a way to avoid conflict. By their stonewalling, couples convey disapproval often by keeping their distance or acting smug. In this situation, people respond shortly or briefly to their spouse. They often simply leave the partner instead of talking to them about what is bothering them.

> *Be kind to one another, tenderhearted, forgiving one another, as God in Christ forgave you.*
> Ephesians 4:32

Remedies

Couples need to learn to make specific complaints and requests. An example of this might be a statement like, "when you didn't pick up after yourself, I felt like you didn't value my work." They need to engage in conscious communication by speaking the truth and listening generously.

As much as possible, spouses need to shift to appreciation. A good rule is to say five times as many positive things for one negative statement. When things go badly, they need to ask, "What can I learn from this?" and "What can I do about it?" People can rewrite their inner thoughts by focusing on appreciation, responsibility, and validation. They can also work on getting unoffended and letting their spouse speak about them to clear the air without interruption.

This is an area where you could help Jeremy and Stephanie by "finding the inn" and getting them to a place where they would benefit from more intensive work with a marriage counselor. The average number of marriage therapy sessions a client attends is one. Anywhere from 75 to 80 percent of clients refuse to attend fewer than five marriage counseling sessions.[251] So this is a difficult task. As a rule, it is better to seek assistance for a marriage earlier rather than later.

Some couples would benefit from a marriage intensive. A marriage intensive is like a marriage ER. The target is couples in crisis, who are stuck, discouraged, and feeling hopeless. They might say, "We've tried everything else." A marriage intensive is not a cookie-cutter approach nor is it a replacement for marriage therapy. Intensives involve between one and four days of intense work and can consist of 8 to 30 hours of therapy. It's a way to "jump start" the healing process. The advantages of the intensives are they provide safety where people can share the secrets plaguing them. Couples who engage in marriage intensives are making an investment since this treatment tends to be expensive. However, it shows the priority the couple has for one another and allows them to work together in hospitable, sequestered environments away from distractions.[252]

Jeremy Has an Affair

Stephanie learns that Jeremy has had an affair. She cannot imagine forgiving him and at this point, she does not want to have anything to do with him.

Use your tools and techniques to try to salvage this marriage. As bad as an affair is, a divorce is far worse. Divorce spreads through a family and

Check out
www.FaithfulandTrue.com

has a negative influence for generations. However, one would be mistaken to minimize the trauma and impact that is associated with an affair. There are various stages a married couple can go through as they deal with an affair, according to Dr. Mark Laaser and his spouse Debbie.

Recovering From Infidelity

The first stage involves discovery that can take several months to a year. In this phase, the infidelity must end. The offended spouse will need plenty of support, and the safety of the couple should be negotiated. Truth must be told and the couple will need to plan to take at least a year to process the event.

Stage 2 is often called chaos. The offending spouse will need to continue to stay free from all sexual sin. The time is spent with counselors and others to help with the relationship.

Stage 3 involves a new intimacy. Here, both husband and wife find a deepening sense of the true worth of Christ. They've accepted their own weaknesses and trust has been restored. The couple becomes allies rather than enemies on the healing journey. They often find it good to serve one another and finally they receive a sense of meaning in their journey.[253]

What If They Divorce?

In the USA, nearly 90 percent of people will marry at least once. When people cohabit, 70 percent permanently separate. How is one to deal with all of this animosity? There are two types of forgiveness. One is emotional forgiveness, which involves replacing negative emotions with positive ones. The positive emotion that helps the fastest is the rekindling of romantic love. Decisional forgiveness is a decision not to exact revenge on the partner or to avoid them, but to separate them from the act. Jesus commands it in Matthew 6:14-15. It doesn't necessarily remove the partner's feelings of bitterness or anger. Feelings of unforgiveness take a longer time to heal.[254]

> For if you forgive others their trespasses, your heavenly Father will also forgive you, but if you do not forgive others their trespasses, neither will your Father forgive your trespasses.
>
> Matthew 6:14-15

The lives of people go better when they forgive. One study examined the relationship between forgiveness of an ex-spouse and post-divorce adjustment. Forgiveness was correlated with religious well-being and the majority of the participants believed that forgiveness of one's ex-spouse was important to healing.[255]

When dealing with divorce, infidelity, and many other problems in a marriage, a couple will find it necessary to forgive. Dr. Everette Worthington has designed the REACH model to forgiveness as a guide. Even if the relationship cannot be salvaged, the model is helpful. We can try to guide others through Dr. Worthington's steps.

Step one is to recall the hurt. Sometimes we try to deny our hurt or waste time waiting for an apology. Instead, it is best to admit that a wrong was done to you. Try to empathize or see the situation from the offender's point of view. Try to feel the transgressor's feelings. It is difficult, but try to think of how they might explain their actions. Think about the gift of forgiveness as you work with people. Ask "Have you ever harmed or offended someone who forgave you?" Think about your own guilt and how it felt when they forgave you. They may be willing to give a selfless gift of forgiveness to the one who harmed them. Encourage them to commit publicly to forgive. If they make their decision public, they are less likely to doubt it later. Encourage them to hold on to forgiveness. When they have doubt, encourage them to reflect on why they forgave and work on becoming a more forgiving person.[256]

Divorce recovery groups can be very beneficial to assisting couples with the trauma and adjustment that takes place as a result of a divorce. It would be wise to encourage people to seek out this resource if they have been through a divorce.[257]

Marriage Later in Life

Even as Jeremy and Stephanie head later into life, they will need to nurture their relationship. There is a spike in the number of people who divorce after the age of 60, and it appears that the negative impact is greater for this age group.[259]

There are various hypothesis for this phenomenon. However, one aspect that is becoming clearer of this generation is the large number of people taking care of aging parents. This responsibility can add greater strain to a marriage. Among the 8.9 million family caregivers of older adults, 59 to 75 percent are women.[260] These women need a safe outlet to discuss their feelings, frustrations, and fears. Be alert for signs of depression or anxiety. Encourage her to take time with her husband and children, and tell her that she is not neglecting her care-giving role when she does so. Find ways to keep her connected to her church family.

Domestic Violence

Perhaps the greatest problem that a family can encounter is that of domestic abuse. Unfortunately, domestic violence is far too prevalent. It can also be deadly. Approximately half of the women who experience domestic violence will be subjected to rape and stalking. At least 1,500 women are killed every year by a current or former spouse or boyfriend.[261] Over their lifetime, around 8 percent of women will be stalked, around 18 percent will be raped, and 52 percent will be physically assaulted.[262] It is believed that as many as 90 percent of battered women never report their abuse. Many women stay in these violent relationships because of fear of retaliation by the perpetrator.[263]

It has been estimated that 50 to 60 percent of marriages have involved battering. When children see violence in their homes, they are at a greater risk for becoming perpetrators of that violence in adulthood or the victim of that violence.[264]

We need to be prepared for those caught in the web of domestic violence because they will come to the church for help. One study indicated that 43 percent of the victims of domestic violence and 20 percent of the perpetrators sought help from clergy. All of the clergy surveyed in the study indicated they'd dealt with domestic violence, and 80 percent indicated they had violence-related contact in the last year.[265]

When someone who is being abused presents themselves, do all within your power to help them find safety. Be careful not to disbelieve a claim of abuse or to judge the person making the claim. Don't minimize the person's experience or incorrectly assess their safety. Don't concentrate on who provoked whom, but rather focus on safety and spiritual help. Hold the abuser responsible, but do not meet with the abuser alone. Use the Matthew 18 model in confronting. Don't assume that the abusing behavior will change if the person becomes a Christian or repents. Real repentance will result in one doing whatever is necessary to help the victim be safe and feel safe. Abusers must participate in a treatment program. At a minimum, these programs will last 24-26 weeks.[266]

Real repentance will involve an honest admission of the sin, as we saw of David when Nathan confronted him. There will not be an effort to manage their image as there was with Saul (1

Samuel 15:14). There will be sacrificial efforts to make repairs as Zacchaeus made after his repentance (Matthew 13:44-46). The abuser will flourish under discipline, but remember Jesus' story of the house swept clean of soils (Matthew 12-13). Be careful because time will tell if it is true repentance.[267]

So, what will become of Jeremy and Stephanie? That is largely dependent upon people like you and me. Look around at a way you can help to make a difference in the development of a family today.

For more information go to www.FirstAidForEmotionalHurts.com.

Resources

Premarital and Marriage Enrichment Resources

PREPARE/ENRICH Programs
Website: www.prepare-enrich.com

Saving Your Marriage Before It Starts
Phone: 206.281.2543.

National Healthy Marriage Institute
Website: http://healthymarriage.org

Workbooks

Parrott, L. & Parrott, L. (2006). *Saving Your Marriage Before It Starts*. Grand Rapids, MI: Zondervan.

Parrott, L. & Parrott, L. (2006). The Complete Resource Kit for Marriage Mentoring: Everything you need to know to launch a marriage mentoring program. Grand Rapids, MI: Zondervan.

Wright, H. N., & Roberts, W. (1997). *Before You Say "I Do."* Eugene, OR: Harvest House Publishers.

Marriage Intensive Programs

Center for Relational Care
Phone: 877.567.5656, ext. 201
Website: www.relationalcare.org

Haven of Safety
Website: www.havenofsafety.com

Lifetime Marriage
Website: www.lifetimemarriage.net

National Institute of Marriage
Phone: 866.875.2915
Website: www.nationalmarriage.com

Winshape Marriage
Phone: 877.977.3873
Website: www.winshape.org

Domestic Violence National Hotline
Phone: 1.800.799.SAFE

Resources for Caregivers

National Family Caregivers Association
Website: www.thefamilycaregiver.org

Family Caregiver Support Programs
Toll Free: 800.677.1116
Website: www.eldercare.gov

Conclusion

*Do not neglect to show hospitality to strangers, for thereby some
have entertained angels unawares.*

Hebrews 13:2

What will happen to many of the people with whom we interact who struggle with grief, depression, anxiety, entangling sin,
and any number of difficulties? That is determined by whether we
utilize the emotional first aid tools and techniques that God has
given us. On November 19, 2016, Jeng Yoong Tan ran the Apex
Turkey Trot 5K in 23 minutes and 16 seconds. Though he won
his age category, he felt like his time was a little slower than he
would have liked. As he passed me early in the race I thought,
"What a difference first aid makes!" Someone responding was the
first step in his recovery. Often, we do not see the results of our
emotional first aid efforts, but they are very important. There are

people who have lives of much greater quality because they have been helped to cope with a loss. Some would not be here if they had not been aided in their bout with depression or an entangling sin. Still others know the relief of not having to face their fear or psychosis alone. Then there are families that have been saved because someone took the time to render aid. It is my prayer that you will take the time to respond with the tools God has graciously given to us.

> *Everyone to whom much was given, of him much will be required, and from him to whom they entrusted much, they will demand the more.*
>
> Luke 12:48b

End Notes

[1] American Heart Association, CPR Facts. Accessed at http://cpr.heart.org/AHAECC/CPRAndECC/AboutCPRFirstAid/CPRFactsAndStats/UCM_475748_CPR-Facts-and-Stats.jsp. Accessed on November 30, 2016.

[2] National Academies of Sciences, Engineering, and Medicine. *Ending Discrimination Against People With Mental and Substance Use Disorders: The Evidence for Stigma Change.* Washington, DC: National Academies Press. (2016).

[3] Centers for Disease Control and Prevention. Accessed at https://www.cdc.gov/nchs/nvss/marriage_divorce_tables.htm. Accessed on December 1, 2016.

American Psychological Association. Marriage and Divorce. Accessed at http://www.apa.org/topics/divorce/. Accessed on December 1, 2016.

National Institute on Drug Abuse. Accessed at https://www.drugabuse.gov/publications/drugfacts/nationwide-trends. Accessed on December 1, 2016.

USA Today (February 4, 2014). Accessed at http://www.usatoday.com/story/news/nation/2014/02/04/cdc-too-many-kids-die-unbuckled/5204127/. Accessed on December 1, 2016.

[4] American College Health Association's National College Health Assessment (2012). Accessed at http://www.acha-ncha.org/docs/ACHA-NCHA-II_ReferenceGroup_ExecutiveSummary_Spring2012.pdf. Accessed on December 1, 2016.

[5] National Institute of Mental Health. Accessed at https://www.nimh.nih.gov/health/statistics/prevalence/any-anxiety-disorder-among-adults.shtml. Accessed on December 1, 2016.

[6] American Foundation for Suicide Prevention. Accessed at https://afsp.org/about-suicide/suicide-statistics/.

[7] J. R. Carkhuff. Different functioning of lay and professional helpers. *Journal of Counseling Psychology, 15,* (1968):117-128.

[8] E. E. Moody. Pair Counseling: An intervention for disturbed children when nothing else works. *Elementary School Guidance and Counseling, 31*(3), (1997):171-179.

E. E. Moody. Lessons from pair counseling with incarcerated juvenile delinquents. *Journal of Addictions & Offender Counseling, 18*(1), (1997):10-25.

[9] National Academies of Sciences. (2016).

[10] WHO (2013). Accessed at http://www.who.int/mental_health/media/investing_mnh.pdf. Accessed on December 28, 2016.

[11] V. Patel. (2003). *Where There Is No Psychiatrist: A Mental Health Care Manual.* London: The Royal College of Psychiatrists.

[12] Mayo Clinic. First aid. Cardiopulmonary resuscitation (CPR): First aid. Accessed at http://www.mayoclinic.org/first-aid/first-aid-cpr/basics/art-20056600. Accessed on January 1, 2017.

[13] M. D. Glicken. (2006). *Learning from Resilient People*. Thousand Oaks, CA: Sage, p. 16-17.

[14] A. Ellis. The advantages and disadvantages of self-help therapy materials. *Professional Psychology: Research and Practice, 24*(3), (1993):335-339.

[15] L. K. George, D. B. Larson, H. G. Koenig, & M. E. McCullough. Spirituality and health: What we know, what we need to know. *Journal of Social and Clinical Psychology, 19*(1), (2000):102-116.

[16] K. Dervic, M. A. Oquendo, M. F. Grunebaum, S. Ellis, A. K. Burke, & J. J. Mann. Religious affiliation and suicide attempt. *American Journal of Psychiatry, 161*, (2004):2303-2308.

[17] G. G. Ano, & E. B. Vasconcelles. Religious coping and psychological adjustment to stress: A metaanalysis. *Journal of Clinical Psychology, 61*, (2005):461-480.

[18] L. K. George. Social factors and the onset and outcome of depression. In K. W. Schaie, J. S. House, & D. G. Blazer (Eds.), *Aging, Health Behaviors, and Health Outcomes* (pp. 137-159). Hillsdale, NJ: Lawrence Erlbaum. (1992).

[19] G. P. Koocher. Psychological science is not politically correct (President's Column). *Monitor on Psychology, 37*(9), (2006):5.

[20] F. Walsh. Family Resilience: Framework for clinical practice—theory and practice. *Family Processes, 42*, (2003):1-18.

[21] R. Gist & G. J. Devilly. Post-trauma debriefing: The road too frequently traveled. *Lancet, 360*, (2002):741-743.

[22] G. Barna. *The Emotional and Spiritual Aftermath of 9/11 and Boston* (September 5, 2013). Assessed at https://www.barna.com/research/the-emotional-and-spiritual-aftermath-of-911-and-boston/ on June 2, 2017.

[23] J. Glass & P. Levchak. Red States, Blue States, and Divorce: Understanding the Impact of Conservative Protestantism on Regional Variation in Divorce Rates. *American Journal of Sociology, 119*(4), (2014):1002-1046

[24] American Counseling Association. Code of Ethics. Accessed at https://www.counseling.org/resources/aca-code-of-ethics.pdf. Accessed on January 1, 2017.

[25] American Association of Christian Counselors. Accessed at http://aacc.net/files/AACC%20Code%20of%20Ethics%20-%20Master%20Document.pdf. Accessed on January 19, 2017.

[26] W. I. Johnson, C. G. Pearce, & T. L. Tuten. Self-imposed silence and perceived listening effectiveness. *Business Communication Quarterly, 66*(2), (2003):23-45.

[27] R. C. Kessler, P. Berglund, O. Demler, R. Jin, & E. E. Walters, Lifetime prevalence and age of onset distributions of DSM-IV Disorders in the National Comorbidity Survey Replication. *Archives of General Psychiatry, 62*(6), (2005):593-602.

[28] U. S. Department of Labor: Bureau of Statistics (2015). *Occupational Outlook Handbook* (OOH), *2015 Edition*. Accessed at www.bls.gov/ooh. Accessed on January 19, 2017.

[29] Ibid.

[30] Ibid.

[31] American Psychiatric Nurses Association. Accessed at https://www.apna.org/i4a/pages/index.cfm?pageid=3292#1. Accessed on June 14, 2017.

[32] U. S. Department of Labor. (2015).

[33] U. S. Department of Labor. (2015).

[34] E. Moody. (2010). *First Aid for Your Emotional Hurts: Finding Help.* Nashville, TN: Randall House.

[35] American Counseling Association (2005). *ACA Code of Ethics.* www.counseling.org. Ethics Committee, ACA Headquarters, 5999 Stevenson Avenue, VA 22304.

American Psychiatric Association (2006). *The Principles of Medical Ethics With Annotations Especially Applicable to Psychiatry.* Arlington, VA: American Psychiatric Association. American Psychiatric Association, 100 Wilson Boulevard # 1825, Arlington, VA 22209.

[36] E. Moody. (2010).

[37] R. S. Sinacola & T. Peters-Strickland. (2012). *Basic Psychopharmacology for Counselors and Psychotherapists—Second Edition.* Boston, MA: Pearson.

[38] Ibid.

[39] Ibid.

[40] Ibid.

[41] N. Abi-Hashem. Grief, loss, and bereavement: An Overview. *Journal of Psychology and Christianity, 18*(4), (1999):309-329.

[42] A. Lang & L. Gottlieb. Parental grief reactions and marital intimacy following infant death. *Death Studies, 17,* (1993):233-255.

[43] P. C. Smith, L. M. Range, & A. Ulmer. Belief in afterlife as a buffer in suicidal and other bereavement. *Omega, 24,* (1991-1992):217-225.

[44] T. A. Rando. An investigation of grief and adaptation in parents whose children have died from cancer. *Journal of Pediatric Psychology, 8,* (1983):3-20.

[45] J. M. Strength. Grieving the loss of a child. *Journal of Psychology and Christianity, 18*(4), (1999):338-353.

[46] I. Wheeler. Parental Bereavement: The crisis of meaning. *Death Studies, 25*(1), (2001):51-67.

[47] J. M. Strength (1999).

[48] P. S. Fry. Grandparents' reactions to the death of a grandchild: An exploratory factor analytic study. *Omega, 35*, (1997):119-140.

[49] A. V. Nikcevic, R. Snijders, K. H. Nicolaides, & E. Kupek. Some psychometric properties of the Texas Grief Inventory adjusted for miscarriage. *British Journal of Medical Psychology, 72*, (1999):171-178.

[50] K. Doka. *Disenfranchised Grief: New Directions, Challenges, and Strategies for Practice*. Champaign, IL: Research Press (2002).

[51] J. M. Strength (1999).

[52] J. M. Strength (1999).

[53] L. Parrott. Grieving the death of a spouse. *Journal of Psychology & Christianity, 18*(4), (1990):354-366.

[54] N. Abi-Hashem. (1999).

[55] H. Norman Wright. (2006). *Recovering From the Losses of Life*. Grand Rapids, MI: Fleming H. Revell.

[56] B. C. Trolley. Kaleidoscope of aid for parents whose child died by suicidal and sudden, non-suicidal means. *Omega, 27*(3), (1993):239-250.

[57] T. A. Rando. (1993). *Treatment of Complicated Mourning*. Champaign, IL: Research Press.

[58] L. M. Range. When a loss is due to a suicide: Unique aspects of bereavement. *Journal of Interpersonal Loss, 1*(1), (1996).

[59] H. V. Kemp. Grieving the death of a sibling or the death of a friend. *Journal of Psychology & Christianity, 18*(4), (1999):354-366.

[60] Ibid.

[61] T. Rando. (1984). *Death and Dying: Clinical Interventions for Caregivers*. Champaign, IL: Research Press.

[62] American Counseling Association Online Grief Counseling Course Materials.

[63] N. Abi-Hashem. (1999).

[64] N. Abi-Hashem. (1999).

[65] S. A. Murphy, L.C. Johnson, J. Lohan, & V. J. Tapper. *Family & Community Health, 25*(1), (2002):71-82.

[66] D. L. Allumbaugh & W. T. Hoyt. Effectiveness of grief therapy: A meta-analysis. *Journal of Counseling Psychology, 46*(3), (1999):370-380.

[67] American Psychiatric Association (APA), (2013). *Diagnostic and Statistical Manual of Mental Disorders: Fifth Edition* (DSM-5). Washington, DC: American Psychiatric Association.

[68] Ibid.

[69] E. Moody. (2010). *First Aid for Your Emotional Hurts: Grief.* Nashville, TN: Randall House.

[70] J. L. Hillman. (2002). *Crisis intervention and trauma: New approaches to evidence-based practice.* New York, NY: Kluwer Academic/Plenum Publishers.

[71] APA. (2013).

[72] APA. (2013).

[73] APA. (2013).

[74] N. Abi-Hashem. (1999).

[75] D. Smith & T. Chapin. (2000). *Spiritual Healing.* Madison, WI: Psycho-Spiritual Publications.

[76] D. L. Allumbaugh & W. T. Hoyt. (1999).

[77] H. N. Wright. (2006).

[78] D. L. Allumbnaugh & W. T. Hoyt. (1999).

[79] APA. (2013).

[80] APA. (2013).

[81] APA. (2013).

[82] M. L. Perlis, L. Smith, J. M. Lyness, S. R. Matteson, W. R. Pigeon, C. R. Jungquist, & X. Tu. Insomnia as a risk factor for onset of depression in the elderly. *Behavioral Sleep Medicine, 4*(2), (2006):104-111.

[83] APA. (2013).

[84] APA. (2013).

[85] APA. (2013).

[86] APA. (2013).

[87] APA. (2013).

[88] APA. (2000).

[89] APA. (2013).

[90] R. C. Kessler, P. Berglund, D. Demler, et al. The epidemiology of major depressive disorder: Results from the National Comorbidity Survey Replication (NCS-R). *JAMA, 289*(23), (2003):3095-3105.

[91] J. I. Hudson, E. Hiripi, H. G. Pope, & R. C. Kessler. The prevalence and correlates of eating disorders in the National Comorbidity Survey Replication. *Biological Psychiatry, 61*(3), (2009):687-705.

[92] A. C. Swann, B. Lafer, G. Perugi, et al. Bipolar Mixed States: An International Society for Bipolar Disorders Task Force Report of Symptom Structure, Course of Illness, and Diagnosis. *American Journal of Psychiatry, 170*(1), (2013):31-42.

[93] C. Faravelli, S. Gorini Amedei, M. A. Scarpato, & L. Faravelli. Bipolar disorder: An impossible diagnosis. *Clinical Practice and Epidemiology Mental Health, 5,* (2002):13.

[94] APA (2000).

[95] J. W. Barnhill (Ed.). *DSM-5 Clinical Cases.* Washington, DC: American Psychiatric Association.

[96] C. Faravelli, et al. (2002).

[97] M. R. Lyles. Bipolar Blues. *Christian Counseling Today, 12*(3) (2004):54-56.

[98] APA. (2013).

[99] APA. (2000).

[100] APA. (2013).

[101] M. B. First & A. Tasman. (2004). *DSM-IV-TR Mental Disorders: Diagnosis, Etiology, and Treatment.* West Sussex, England: Wiley.

[102] R. H. Gracely, M. Ceko, & M. C. Bushnell. Fibromyalgia and Depression. *Pain Research and Treatment,* 2012.

[103] E. Alderete, C. P. Kaplan, R. Pasick, & E. J. Pérez-Stable. Depressive symptoms among women with an abnormal mammogram. *Psycho-Oncology, 15,* (2006):66-78.

[104] E. Moody. (2010). *First Aid for Emotional Hurts: Depression.* Nashville, TN: Randall House.

[105] Psychiatry Research. http://www.psy-journal.com/article/S0165-1781(15)30368-1/abstract.

E. Fuller-Thomson, et al. Flourishing after depression: Factors associated with achieving complete mental health among those with a history of depression. *Psychiatry Research, 242,* (2016):111–120.

[106] W. J. Strawbridge, R. D. Cohen, & S. J. Shema. Comparative strength of association between religious attendance and survival. *International Journal of Psychiatry in Medicine, 30* (4), (2000):299-308.

[107] H. G. Koenig. (2013). *Spirituality in Patient Care, Third Edition.* Philadelphia, PA: Templeton Foundation Press.

[108] P. A. Nisbet, P. R. Duberstein, Y. Conwell, & L. Seidlitz. The effect of participation in religious activities on suicide versus natural death in adults 50 and older. *Journal of Nervous and Mental Disease, 188*(8), (2000):543-546.

[109] CNN. Accessed at http://www.cnn.com/2015/02/04/politics/22-veterans-kill-themselves-every-day/index.html. Accessed on March 15, 2017.

[110] K. D. Kochanek, J. Xu, S. L. Murphy, et al. Deaths: Final Data for 2009. *National Vital Statistics Reports, 60*(3). Hyattsville, MD: National Center for Health Statistics, 2012.

[111] B. Gilland & R. James. (1997). *Crisis Intervention Strategies*. Bolmont, CA: Brooks/Cole.

D. H. Granello & P. F. Granello. (2007). *Suicide: An essential guide for helping professionals and educators*. Boston, MA: Pearson Education, Inc.

[112] E. M. Forman, M. S. Berk, G. R. Henriques, & A. T. Beck. History of multiple suicide attempters as a behavioral marker of severe pathology. *American Journal of Psychiatry, 161,* (2004):437-443.

[113] G. Henriques, A. Wenzel, G. K. Brown, & A. T. Beck. Suicide attempters' reaction to survival as a risk for eventual suicide. *American Journal of Psychiatry, 162,* (2005):2180-2182.

[114] E. Moody. (2011). *First Aid for Your Emotional Hurts: Helping Children with Emotional Problems*. Nashville, TN: Randall House.

[115] S. Nolen-Hoeksema & C. Davis. "Thanks for sharing that": Ruminators and their social support networks. *Journal of Personal and Social Psychology, 77*(4) (1999):801-814.

[116] D. Burns. (1980). *Feeling Good: The New Mood Therapy*. New York, NY: Avon Books.

[117] E. Moody. (2010). *First Aid for Emotional Hurts: Depression*.

[118] E. Packard. Reminder: Exercise helps with therapist self-care. *Monitor on Psychology, 114,* (2005):421-431.

[119] F. Peters, J. Berkhof, P. Delespaul, J. Rottenberg, & N. A. Nicolson. Diurnal mood variation in major depressive disorder. *Emotion, 6* (2006):383-391.

[120] J. Sutherland, S. Sutherland, & J. Hoehns. Achieving the best outcome in treatment of depression. *The Journal of Family Medicine, 52*(3), (2003):201-209.

[121] C. L. H. Bockting, A. H. Schene, P. Spinhoven, M. W. J. Koeter, L. F. Wouters, L. F. Huyser, & J. H. Kamphuis. Preventing relapse/recurrence in recurrent depression with cognitive therapy: A randomized controlled trial. *Journal of Consulting and Clinical Psychology, 73,* (2005):647-657.

[122] R. S. Sinacola & T. Peters-Strickland. (2006). *Basic Psychopharmacology*. Boston, MA: Pearson.

[123] Ibid.

[124] Ibid.

[125] Ibid.

[126] K. Kelly & M. Zisselman. Update on electroconvulsive therapy (ECT) in older adults. *Journal of the American Geriatrics Society, 48*(5), (2000):550-566.

[127] F. Colom & E. Vieta. (2006). *Psychoeducational Manual for Bipolar Disorder*. Cambridge: Cambridge University Press.

[128] R. S. Sinacola & T. Peters-Strickland. (2006).

[129] F. Colom & E. Vieta. (2006).

[130] N. Williams, J. Reardon, K. Murray, & T. Cole. (2005). Anxiety disorders: A developmental vulnerability-stress perspective. In B. L. Hankin & J. R. Abela (Eds.) *Development of Psychopathology: A Vulnerability-Stress Perspective* (pp. 289-327). Thousand Oaks, CA: Sage Publication.

[131] B. J. Shen, Y. E. Avivi, J. F. Todaro, et al. Anxiety characteristics independently and prospectively predict myocardial infarction in men. The unique contribution of anxiety among psychological factors. *Journal of the American College of Cardiology, 51,* (2008):113-119.

[132] J. Denollet, K. Mass, A. Knottnerus, J. J. Keyzer, & V. J. Pop. Anxiety predicted premature all-cause and cardiovascular death in a 10-year follow-up of middle-aged women. *Journal of Clinical Epidemiology, 62,* (2009):452-456.

[133] W. M. Welch (February 28, 2005). Trauma of Iraq war haunting thousands returning home. *USA Today.*

[134] E. Foa, T. Keane, & M. Freidman. (2000). *Effective treatments for PTSD: Practice guidelines for the International Society for Traumatic Stress Studies.* New York, NY: Guilford Press.

[135] J. S. Shelby & M. G. Tredinnick. Crisis intervention with survivors of natural disaster: Lessons from Hurricane Andrew. *Journal of Counseling and Development, 73,* (1995):491-497.

[136] APA. (2013).

[137] J. W. Barnhill. (2014).

[138] E. Moody, & D. Trogdon. (2016). *First Aid for Your Emotional Hurts: Veterans.* Nashville, TN: Randall House.

[139] https://www.rainn.org/statistics/victims-sexual-violence.

[140] D. DiLillo, A. E. Jaffe, L. E. Watkins, J. Peugh, A. Kras, & C. Campbell. The occurrence and traumatic impact of sexual revictimization in newlywed couples. *Couple and Family Psychology: Research and Practice, 5,* (2016):212-225.

[141] L. M. Orange & M. G. Brodwin. Childhood sexual abuse: What rehabilitation counselors need to know. *Journal of Rehabilitation, 71*(4), (2005):5-11.

[142] APA. (2013).

[143] APA. (2013).

[144] R. T. LeBeau, D. Glenn, B. Liao, et al: Specific phobia: A review of DSM-IV specific phobia and preliminary recommendations for DSM-V. *Depress Anxiety, 27*(2), (2010):148-167.

[145] E. Moody. (2011). *Helping Children with Emotional Problems.*

[146] H. W. Hoek & D. van Hoeken. (2003). Review of the prevalence and incidence of eating disorders. *Wiley InterScience* (www.interscience.wiley.com).

[147] APA. (2013).

[148] APA. (2013).

[149] APA. (2013).

[150] K. J. Steffen, J. E. Mitchell, J. L. Roerig, & K. L. Lancaster. The eating disorders medicine cabinet revisited: A clinician's guide to ipecac and laxatives. *International Journal of Eating Disorders, 40* (2007):360-368.

[151] APA. (2013).

[152] J. L. Roerig, A. S. Fargo, J. E. Mitchell, M. de Zwaan, S. A. Wonderlich, S. Karman, & S. Engbloom. The eating disorders cabinet revisited: A clinician's guide to appetite suppressants and diuretics. *International Journal of Eating Disorders, 33* (2003):443-457.

[153] M. Eberly. Trauma and eating disorders: Exploring the connection. *Christian Counseling Today, 14*(2), (2006):34-37.

[154] E. Moody. (2013). *First Aid for Your Health. 10 Therapeutic Life Changes.* Nashville, TN: Randall House.

[155] M. D. Glicken. (2006). *Learning from Resilient People.* Thousand Oaks, CA: Sage. p. 16-17.

[156] D. Zehnder, A Prchal, M. Vollrath, & M. A. Landolt. Prospective study of the effectiveness of coping in pediatric patients. *Child Psychiatry and Human Development, 36*(3), (2006):351-368.

[157] L. Collier (November, 2016). Growth after Trauma: Why are some people more resilient than others—and can it be taught? *Monitor on Psychology, 47(10)*, 48-52.

[158] E. Moody. (2011). *Helping Children with Emotional Problems.*

[159] E. Moody & D. Trogdon. (2016).

[160] E. Moody. (2011). *Helping Children with Emotional Problems.*

[161] L. Collier (November, 2016).

[162] E. Moody. (2011). *Helping Children with Emotional Problems.*

[163] J. I. Ruze, M. J. Brymer, A. K. Jacobs, C. M. Lyne, E. M. Vernberg, & P. J. Watson. Psychological First Aid. *Journal of Mental Health Counseling, 29*(1), (2007):17-49.

[164] J. A. Cohen, A. P. Mannarino, & K. Knudsen. Treating sexually abused children: 1 year follow-up of a randomized controlled trial. *Child Abuse & Neglect, 29,* (2005):135-145.

[165] R. S. Sinacola & T. Peters-Strickland. (2006).

[166] M. Eberly. (2006).

[167] M. Chavez & T. R. Insel. *American Psychologist, 62*(3), (2007):159-166.

[168] National Institute of Drug Abuse. Accessed at https://www.drugabuse.gov/publications/drugfacts/nationwide-trends. Accessed on June 1, 2017.

[169] P. Stevens, & R. L. Smith. *Substance Use Counseling: Theory and Practice (Sixth Edition)*. Columbus, Ohio: Merrill Prentice Hall. (2018).

[170] APA. (2013).

[171] H. E. Doweiko. (2012). *Concepts of Chemical Dependency (Eighth Edition)*. Belmont, CA: Thompson Brooks/Cole.

[172] Ibid.

[173] S. B. Karch. (2002). *The Pathology of Drug Abuse (Third Edition)*. New York, NY: CRC Press.

[174] H. E. Doweiko. (2012).

[175] A. Roy. Characteristics of cocaine-dependent patients who attempt suicide. *American Journal of Psychiatry, 158,* (2001):1215-1219.

[176] P. Stevens, & R. L. Smith (2004).

[177] H. E. Doweiko. (2012).

[178] A. J. Budney, S. C. Sigmon, & S. T. Higgins. (2003). Contingency management in the substance abuse treatment clinic. *In Treating Substance Abuse: Theory and Technique (Second Edition)*. F. Rotgers, J. Morgenstern, & S. T. Walters Eds). New York, NY: Guilford.

[179] P. Stevens, & R. L. Smith (2004).

[180] N. Sussman & L. Westreich. Chronic marijuana use and the treatment of mentally ill patients. *Primary Psychiatry, 19*(9), (2003):73-76.

[181] H. E. Doweiko. (2012).

[182] P. Stevens & R. L. Smith (2004).

[183] K. Weir (April, 2017). Psychologists' Roles in Helping to Treat Opioid-Use Disorders and Prevent Overdoses. *Monitor on Psychology, 48*(4), 29-32.

[184] H. Orfgen & A. Dijkstra. (2016). A cross-sectional study of psychological Comparison process that may underlie the acceptance of chronic pain. *Clinical Psychotherapy, 23,* 487-495.

[185] K. Weir (April, 2017).

[186] P. Stevens & R. L. Smith (2004).

[187] S. S. Martins, G. Mazzotti, & H. D. Chilcoat. Trends in ecstasy use in USA from 1995 to 2001; comparison with marijuana users and association with other drug use. *Experimental and Clinical Psychopharmacology, 13*(3), (2005):244-252.

[188] D. W. Smith Ecstasy—Club Drugs. *Christian Counseling Today*, 10(2), (2002):34-36.

[189] P. Stevens & R. L. Smith (2004).

[190] P. Stevens & R. L. Smith (2004).

[191] APA. (2013).

[192] APA. (2013).

[193] T. D. Burger, D. Dahlgren, & C. D. MacDonald. College students and gambling: An examination of gender differences in motivation for participation. *College Student Journal, 40*(3), (2006):704-714.

[194] APA. (2013).

[195] APA. (2013).

[196] M. R. Laaser & L. J. Gregoire. Pastors and cybersex addiction. *Sexual and Relationship Therapy, 18*(3), (2003):395-404.

[197] E. Moody. (2015). *First Aid for Your Emotional Hurts: Sexual Issues.* Nashville, TN: Randall House.

[198] E. Moody. (2011). *Helping Children With Emotional Problems.*

[190] G. D. Talbott & L. R. Crosby. (2001). Recovery Contracts: Seven key elements. In Addiction Recovery Tools: A Practical Handbook. R. H. Coombs (Ed.). Thousand Oaks, CA: Sage.

[200] E. Moody. (2010). *First Aid Your Emotional Hurts: Addictions.* Nashville, TN: Randall House.

[201] H. Doweiko. (2012).

[202] A. B. Hood & R. W. Johnson. (2007). *Assessment in Counseling (Fourth Edition).* Alexandria, VA: American Counseling Association.

[203] E. Moody. (2010). *Addictions.*

[204] E. Moody. (2010). *Addictions.*

[205] E. Moody. (2010). *Addictions.*

[206] C. Conklin. Environments as cues to smoke: Implications for extinction-based research and treatment. *Experimental and Clinical Psychopharmacology, 14*(1), (2006):12-19.

[207] Stevens & Smith. (2014).

[208] APA. (2013).

[209] W. J. Brewer, S. M. Francey, S. J. Wood, H. J. Jackson, & L. J. Pantelis. Memory impairments identified in people at ultrahigh risk for psychosis who later develop first episode psychosis. *American Journal of Psychiatry, 162,* (2005):71-81.

[210] J. A. Liberman. Relative Prevalence of Schizophrenia. http://www.schizophrenia.com/szfacts.htm#. Assessed June 1, 2017.

[211] A. Hausmann & W. W. Fleischhacker. Depression in patients with schizophrenia: Prevalence, and diagnostic and treatment considerations. *CNS Drugs, 14*(4), (2000):288-289.

[212] APA. (2000).

[213] A. L. Hoff & W. S. Kremen. Neuropsychology in schizophrenia: An update. *Current Opinion Psychiatry, 16,* (2003):149-155.

[214] D. Akin. (n.d.). *Christian Theology Book V: Angelology, Satanology, Demonology.* Wake Forest, NC: The Southeastern Baptist Theological Seminary.

[215] Ibid.

[216] S. M. Eack, C. M. Newhill, C. M. Anderson, & A. Rotondi. Quality of life for persons living with schizophrenia: More than just symptoms. *Psychiatric Rehabilitation Journal, 30*(3), (2007):219-222.

[217] S. Nance. (2001). *Handling people in psychological crisis.* Eau Claire, WI: PESI Healthcare.

[218] C. H. Richardson, G. Faulkner, J. McDevitt, G. S. Skrinar, D. S. Hutchinson, & J. Piette. Integrating physical activity into mental health services for persons with serious mental illness. *Psychiatric Services, 56,* (2005):324-331.

[219] R. Breen & J. T. Thornhill. Noncompliance with medication for psychiatric disorders. *CNS Drugs, 9*(6), (1998):457-471.

[220] Ibid.

[221] V. King. The influence of religion on fathers' relationship with their children. *Journal of Marriage and Family, 65*(2), (2003):382-395.

[222] M. D. Regnerus & L. B. Luchies. The Parent-Child Relationship and Opportunities for Adolescent Well-Being. *Journal of Family Issues, 27*(2), (2006):159-183.

[223] T. M. Viedeon. The Effects of Parental-Adolescent Relationships and Parental Separation on Adolescent Well-Being. *Journal of Marriage and Family, 64,* (2002):498.

[224] S. C. Risch K. M. Jodl, & J. S. Eccles. Role of the Father-Adolescent Relationship in Shaping Adolescents' Attitudes Toward Divorce. *Journal of Marriage and Family, 66*(1), (2004):46-58.

[225] C. J. Dorius, S. J. Bahr, J. P. Hoffmann, & E. L. Harmon. Parenting practices as moderators of the relationships between peers and adolescent marijuana use. *Journal of Marriage and Family, 66*(1), (2004):163-178.

[226] A. Coleman & C. S. Widon. Childhood abuse and adult intimate relationships: A prospective study. *Child Abuse & Neglect, 28*(11), (2004):1133-1151.

[227] P. R. Amato & J. Cheadle. The long reach of divorce: Divorce and child well-being across three generations. *Journal of Marriage and Family, 67*(1), (2005):191-206.

[228] L. B. Finer. Trends in premarital sex in the United States, 1954-2003. *Public Health Reports, 122,* (2007):73-78.

[229] J. Teachman. Premarital sex, premarital cohabitation, and the risk of subsequent marital dissolution among women. *Journal of Marriage and Family, 65,* (2003):444-455.

[230] R. J. Quinlan. Father absence, parental care, and female reproductive development. *Evolution and Human Behavior, 24,* (2003):376–390.

[231] J. Townsend. How to tell a safe man from an unsafe man. *Christian Counseling Today, 13*(3), (2005):34-35.

[232] S. Roberts. (October 15, 2006). To be married means to be outnumbered. *New York Times.* www.nytimes.com.

[233] K. Antonovics & R. Town. Are all the good men married. Uncovering the sources of the marital wage premium. *American Economic Review, 94,* (2004):317-321.

[234] S. R. Aronson & A. C. Huston. The mother-infant relationship in single, cohabiting, and married families: A case for marriage? *Journal of Family Psychology, 18*(1), (2004):5-18.

[235] A. Sutherland. Delaying Marriage, But Not Cohabitation. *Institute for Family Studies,* Accessed on December 18, 2017 at https://ifstudies.org/blog/marriage-age-rises-cohabitation.

[236] J. Jayson. (July 18, 2005). Cohabitation is replacing dating. *USA TODAY,* 6D.

[237] J. R. Hill, & S. G. Evans. Effects of cohabitation length on personal and relational well being. *Alabama Policy Institute,* (August), (2006):1-13.

[238] G. Barna. (October-December, 1999). *Christians are more likely to experience divorce than non-Christians.* http://www.barna.org.

[239] L. Parrott & L. Parrott. The SYMBIS approach to marriage education. *Journal of Psychology and Theology, 31*(3), (2003):208-212.

[240] T. DeAngelis (April, 2017). Premarital counseling: A vital, untapped niche. *Monitor on Psychology, 48*(4), 58-59.

[241] J. Gottman. (1994). *Why Marriages Succeed or Fail: And how you can make yours last.* New York, NY: Fireside Rockefeller Center.

[242] S. Stack, I. Wasserman, & R. Kern. Adult social bonds and use of internet pornography. *Social Science Quarterly, 85*(1), (2004):75-88.

[243] G. L. Hansen. (1992). Religion and marital adjustment. In J. F. Schumaker (Ed.), *Religion and Mental Health.* New York, NY: Oxford University Press.

[244] J. Gruber. Religious market structure, religious participation, and outcomes: Is religion good for you? *National Bureau of Economic Research, 113,* (2005):77.

[245] C. Smith & P. Kim. Family religious involvement and the quality of parental relationships for families with early adolescents. *Research Report for the National Study of Youth and Religion, 5* (2003):1-23.

[246] W. B. Wilcox. (2004). *Soft Patriarchs, New Men: How Christianity Shapes Fathers and Husbands.* Chicago, IL: University of Chicago Press.

[247] Ibid.

[248] Ibid.

[249] L. Parrott & L. Parrot. When bad things happen to good marriages. *Christian Counseling Today, 12*(1), (2004):38-40.

[250] S. L. Gable, G. Gonzaga, & A. Strachman. Will you be there for me when things go right? Social support for positive events. *Journal of Personality and Social Psychology, 91,* (2006):904-917.

[251] G. J. Oliver, M. Hasz, & M. Richburg. (1997). *Promoting Change Through Brief Therapy in Christian Counseling.* Wheaton, IL: Tyndale House Publishing, Inc.

[252] G. Smalley. Intensive marital interventions: What are they and do they really work? *Christian Counseling Today, 12*(1), (2004):48-51.

[253] M. Laaser & D. Laaser. Recovering from infidelity. *Christian Counseling Today, 12*(1), (2004):48-51.

[254] E. Worthington. Forgiveness in marriage: Research findings and therapeutic applications. *Christian Counseling Today, 12*(1), (2004):60-61.

[255] M. S. Rye, C. D. Folck, T. A. Heim, B. T. Olszewski, & E. Traina. Forgiveness of an ex-spouse: How does it relate to mental health following a divorce? *Journal of Divorce & Remarriage, 41*(3-4), (2004):31-51.

[256] E. Worthington. (2003). *Forgiving and Reconciling: Bridges to Wholeness and Hope.* Downers Grove, IL: Intervarsity Press.

[257] D. M. Quinney & G. T. Fouts. Resilience and divorce adjustment in adults participating in divorce recovery workshops. *Journal of Divorce & Remarriage, 40*(1-2), (2003):55-68.

[258] Tech (2003) as quoted in M.D. Glicken. *Learning from Resilient People,* p. 3005. Thousand Oaks, CA: Sase (2006).

[259] S. L. Brown, & L. I-Fen. The gray divorce revolution: Rising divorce among middle aged-and older adults, 1990-2010. *Journal of Gerontology Series B: Psychological Sciences & Social Sciences, 67B*(6), (2012):731-741.

[260] K. Erwin. Parenting her aging parents. *Christian Counseling Today, 31*(4), (2005):44-45.

[261] D. B. Berry. (2000). *The Domestic Violence Sourcebook (Third Edition).* Los Angeles, CA: Lowell House.

[262] J. Fantuzzo, R. Boruch, & A. Beriama. Domestic violence and children: Prevalence and risk in five major U.S. cities. *Journal of Academy of Child and Adolescent Psychiatry, 36,* (1997):116-122.

[263] R. L. Nabi, B. Southwell, & R. Hornik. Predicting intentions versus prediction behavior: Domestic violence prevention from a theory of reasoned action perspective. *Health Communication, 14,* (2002):429-449.

[264] D. G. Hays, E. Green, J. J. Orr, & L. Flowers. Advocacy counseling for female survivors of partner abuse: Implications for counselor education. *Counselor Education & Supervision, 46* (2007):184-198.

[265] R. J. Rotunda, G. Williamson, & M. Penfold. Clergy response to domestic violence: A preliminary survey of clergy members, victims, and batterers. *Pastoral Psychology, 52*(4), (2005):353-365.

[266] B. Branson & P. Silva. Domestic violence among believers: Confronting the destructive secret. *Christian Counseling Today, 13*(3), (2005):24-27.

[267] P. G. Monroe. Abusers and true repentance. *Christian Counseling Today, 13*(3), (2005):48-49.

CPSIA information can be obtained
at www.ICGtesting.com
Printed in the USA
LVOW03s0418270218
567974LV00002B/2/P